To Mark –

a fellow traveler and
fellow writer –

warmly with affection.
Andrew

ALONG ALIEN ROADS

隨緣遇知音

宗克能備致

馬克

Praise for Along Alien Roads

Along Alien Roads elegantly traces the trajectory of a remarkable life, revealing fascinating family, cultural, and personal histories along the way. The wide-ranging, beautifully-written story spans family secrets and political intrigue in the era of Chiang Kai-shek, as well as the perils and pleasures of medical school, fatherhood, and sexual liberation in San Francisco. Dividing lines dissolve as Chen artfully leads us across fluid boundaries between present and past, East and West, gay and straight. A deeply perceptive, intimate glimpse into the quest for love and understanding that lies at the heart of a singular life.

— Genanne Walsh, author of *Twister*

A finely woven tapestry of memories that takes the shape of a man who contains multitudes. Born to a family from Canton and Shanghai, a father in the Nationalist government, a mother who rode bareback in Siberia, her father a Chinese diplomat under the Czar and after the revolution. Exile in Taiwan, schooled in Japan . . . educated as an engineer at MIT, then as a physician, he shapeshifts from engineer to doctor, married man with children to gay man in Northern California to gay man in love with a woman. He is at once deeply Chinese and completely American; straight, gay, and bisexual he's lived each category without being defined by a category. Comfortable in his own skin, yet uneasy in the ways he is different and forever in exile. Chen's memoir is a wonder. Exquisitely written. Rich in detail. Deeply moving.

— Michael Alenyikov, author of the award-winning novel *Ivan and Misha*

ALONG ALIEN ROADS

The I Jing of A Life

Tsun Yuan Chen

Wordrunner Press
Petaluma, California

In love and languor, I dedicate this book to my seven grandchildren, from the Ox, 牛, to the Pig, 豬. In them, I see my future and my past.

And to the memory of my mother, born the year of the Lamb, 羊, like the Last Dowager Empress Cixi, who was told she'd have a hard life, to be slaughtered, and because my father told me on one of the last occasions I saw him, "I owe your mother a lot."

This is an autobiographical novel based on the author's family and life. Certain names and details have been changed and some events have been altered or combined for the sake of narrative continuity.

Memory is a tricky thing: subjective, malleable to the needs of narrative or the fog of time. Some linguists believe that preliterate societies used myths to preserve their collective memories, and it seems possible, or at least poetic, that the style of memory is toward constructive story making, not simple retention. We remember the stories we tell about our lives; we invent our lives in the remembering.

— John Leland, *New York Times*, 8 Sept. 2013

Our deepest thoughts and feelings pass to us (through) compound experiences (that dissolve the gap between one end of the time line and the other).

— Thomas De Quincey, as quoted by Dan Chiasson,
New Yorker, 17 October 2016

Contents

Foreword.. 1

Prologue.. 7

PART I 19

    Chapter One.. 21

    Chapter Two.. 24

    Chapter Three... 31

    Chapter Four 39

    Chapter Five 44

    Chapter Six... 52

    Chapter Seven.. 61

    Chapter Eight 78

    Chapter Nine.. 85

    Chapter Ten... 93

    Chapter Eleven 102

    Chapter Twelve 112

    Chapter Thirteen 121

Intermezzo 131

PART II 137

    Chapter Fourteen... 139

    Chapter Fifteen.. 144

    Chapter Sixteen 156

    Chapter Seventeen 168

    Chapter Eighteen... 175

    Chapter Nineteen 185

    Chapter Twenty 195

Dream of Constantine (detail)................................. 219

Photographs.. 220

Along Alien Roads 224

PART III 229

    Chapter Twenty-One 231

    Chapter Twenty-Two 237

    Chapter Twenty-Three 243

    Chapter Twenty-Four 263

    Chapter Twenty-Five 277

    Chapter Twenty-Six 286

    Chapter Twenty-Seven 304

    Chapter Twenty-Eight 317

    Chapter Twenty-Nine 342

    Chapter Thirty 351

    Chapter Thirty-One 357

The Bardo 373

PART IV 377

    Chapter Thirty-Two 379

    Chapter Thirty-Three 387

    Chapter Thirty-Four 392

    Chapter Thirty-Five 407

Coda 427

Historical and Personal Time Lines 435

Map of Chinese Places in Text 437

Acknowledgements 439

Foreword

As I look out the window into my garden below, I can see the weeping cherry has shed its blossoms, the magnolia's green leaves have overtaken its lotus-like petals, and the rhododendrons are in full bloom. Each tree has its turn to show color; those that have gone will circle back again. I think of the mist hovering over the hills in the painting, Hermitage in Mountain Mist, by the Yuan Dynasty poet and Daoist painter, Fang Fanghu. When the fog clears, there again is a clear day, and so it cycles from day to day.

This cycle of nature is also the basis of the ancient Chinese text, I-Jing, the Book of Change, compiled between the eleventh to the seventh century BCE. The Chinese ideogram for I, 易 meaning change, is believed by some scholars to be derived from an early symbol for the chameleon.

(±700 BC)	Great seal script (±300 BC)	Regular (1700)

The two ideograms for I Jing 易經 in Chinese are homonymous with the two ideograms 異徑 for alien paths, landscapes or even circumstances. In my life, change has coincided with a sense of not belonging, of being placed in an alien landscape, so these parallel ideograms have had a particularly vivid ring of truth.

As a boy, I remember hearing my mother say to a close friend, on her way home to Paris after the World War, *tout ça change tout c'est la même chose.* It is like the cycle of Chinese zodiac animals, from the clever Rat who rushes to be the first in line on the back of the benevolent Ox, to the wise Pig who refuses to be hurried and comes in last at its own leisurely pace. Wise because it realizes the Rat must follow it in the next cycle, and thus every twelve years the cycle repeats. I was born as the Ox, letting the Rat get ahead, oblivious of malice. Even close to her end, my mother was concerned about my incorrigible naiveté.

More deeply imprinted into my eyes, close to seven decades later, is my grandmother counting the sandalwood beads between her gnarled fingers. Every morning, bead after bead, she recited the teachings of the Buddha's *Heart Sutra*, cycle after seemingly endless cycle. Things can change, things can go, yet things can come back to the same place where I started.

My mother was the one who should have told many of the stories in this book. It was her good fortune to have been plucked by her father to live as the daughter of a Chinese diplomat in Czarist Russia, thus escaping the old custom of having her feet bound into lotus blossoms. Then she lived through four revolutions, one in Russia and three in China, if you count the Cultural Revolution. From the time she returned from Russia, as a young woman when she encountered the Last Emperor at the Peking Hotel, to the time when she was past eighty, people turned their heads when she entered a ballroom.

Stories she told me about the people whose lives she crisscrossed, I have only read in history books. I wanted her to write them down, both for myself and her grandchildren. She loved them and wanted them to learn about our roots, our culture. I even bought a tape recorder. But she did not want to talk to a machine. She was an impassioned raconteur in person only. The machine sat on the bookshelf, and she never touched it.

I tried to step into her silk pumps and embroidered slippers, wrote a number of chapters and read them to friends in my writers' group. "Write them in your own voice!" was the feedback. That was over two decades ago, and before she died of lung cancer. I have found with the retelling of my mother's stories that my voice mushroomed and soon ushered in stories about my own life. Some details in the stories, particularly my mother's, I can no longer remember. I thought I should record them before my own time is up. I am now close to her age when she came to her end. My children and grandchildren would have even less access if I waited any longer.

There was also the question of whether I should have told my mother's story in Chinese. It was the way she always spoke to me. The turns of her words in perfectly inflected Peking dialect would be hard to capture adequately in English. In addition, my mother and I used other languages to express certain thoughts or occasions that could not be easily translated, such as the way she asked if a Russian dish she put on the table was *fkoos-na*, or when she wanted to confide something was extremely bothersome, she used the Japanese word *urusai*. Both of those descriptions in English could not really convey the nuance and emotion beyond their original language.

I had seriously considered writing in Chinese in the beginning. But I could not find a Chinese writer's group close to me for feedback, and more painfully, I realized I have been away from my native tongue for too long. There were things about myself that I learned after I came here at sixteen and evolved which I would not be able to express in Chinese. Even though I felt very much a Chinese in my heart, for many reasons, I felt estranged from my first language. I thought about writers like Nabokov and Conrad, Ha Jin, and Li Yiyun, who wrote in their adopted language instead of their native tongue. Had they abandoned their past in so doing?

It was not an easy decision to write in English. I am distancing and uprooting myself from the past, yet have not really found a way to be at home in my adopted country either. I ask myself, how much have I become estranged from my roots and yet still not rooted in a strange land?

In the writing of these stories from the past, I felt I was flipping pages in my old family album, seeing snapshots along the way. From days when my mother was in Russia, and my father in the Japan of his youth, to my roots in an old China which are no longer—across the Formosan Straits to Taiwan, the East China Sea to Japan, and then by a slow boat across the Pacific to this New World. Parts of my parents' past I am still discovering as I edit the manuscript, new stories about their lives I had never heard. Here I have found relief in the words of Li Yiyun's extraordinarily insightful memoir. "To say we know a person is to write that person off. This is at times life's necessity." In not knowing all of the mysteries of my parents' lives, I am hoping to keep them all the more alive in my mind and memory.

In the process of trying to make sense of my parents' history, I have also made discoveries about myself, as a husband and then a father, as a lover to the men in my life, and about my choice of committing to my partner Adele for the last quarter of a century.

It has been a path as unpredictable as it has been tortuous. A path that led to the edge of my own mortality and then back again. It is a state of being akin to the bardo, as described by Tibetan Buddhists. The continual changes have gone through so many cycles of the zodiac, taken me along so many byways. It is something that may even surprise a student of the I-Jing.

Prologue

"We said we'd try it out for a week," Adele continued, "maybe a month?" There was a studied chill to
her voice, unrelenting as the late-afternoon mist rolling in from the coast. Others call it the fog for which
our city is known. I moved over to the counter to get
myself a cup of tea and saw the Golden Gateway outside the kitchen window was already blanketed. Adele
had stopped me when I first walked in and said she
wanted to talk. I was holding my breath.

We sat at the kitchen table in my house on the
small hill, hidden by Twin Peaks from downtown San
Francisco, and I could see the little homes nestled in
the valley below. It's an area with neither the feeling
of the Manhattanization of our downtown, nor the
typical postcard picture of Victorians. An area which
often made me feel as if we had not left the Italian
hillside villages of our summer haven.

"A full circle!" she continued. A full circle from
the first time we stayed together at the El Tovar
Lodge on the rim of the Grand Canyon, she meant.

For me, this would be my sixth go around the
Chinese zodiac cycle. Twelve years each. One for each
animal, real and mythical, from the resourceful Rat
to the smart and easy-going Pig.

I arrived as an Ox. According to legend, I allowed the quick-witted rat who rode on my back to jump ahead of me to the Jade Emperor, while I plodded along from one rice field to the next.

Year of the Ox again. Last week was another new beginning, the inauguration of our first black president. Under the freezing weather, when Yo-Yo Ma had to strum a stand-in cello rather than his famous *Guarneri*, the new president alluded to the country's very first president when he mentioned the winter of the birth of our nation. His inaugural speech was the shot in the arm I needed.

A renewed springtime in the autumn of my life. I should look forward to rather than go mellow into the remaining light of my years. It was time to gather up those chapters of a life I could still remember before they faded more into the mists of memory.

The last fifteen years of my life with Adele rolled across my bifocals. Even in the beginning, we had no illusions of walking onto sunset beaches with only warm sand between our toes. We had both tasted the bitter melons of earlier marriage dissolutions.

A good friend of mine had warned her in earnest, "You should never get involved with a gay man!"

At the time, I had to find a new therapist to untangle my confusion and surprise at being with a woman again. I thought I had laid those feelings to rest in the chair of my therapist's office years ago.

I had not forgotten when all those years before, I tried to dodge the emerging demon, to paraphrase Isherwood in *Christopher and His Kind*.

"You probably paid for the cornerstones of the

house your therapist was building," a good friend told me, when he found out the number of years I spent wailing in my therapist's room.

He gave me a list of books to read, and I latched onto the stories of famous men in the past, ones who loved other men. Book by book, year by year, I began to feel less of a freak.

I wished I had lived in a world of the old samurais, where men bonding with men was not only honorable but celebrated, and intimacy was not forbidden fruit. I could not understate the relief I felt when I read about the tender love showed by a Han Dynasty emperor to his male consorts and favorites over two millennia ago. It was a world where men had children with their wives, but also enjoyed male company, including male lovers, a world before Christianity came to China and male love could no longer be given a name.

The world I found myself in now was only a few years after the Stonewall riots, the beginning of public gay awareness. The therapist I found was the first openly gay therapist of the Bay Area. Like me, he was still married and had two children. Finally, I could hope, there was going to be a path toward finding acceptance.

I thought I could finally be myself, live my life the way I wanted to be. The author Primo Levi, who survived the Holocaust, wrote that to be oneself was worth more than life and happiness.

But once again, twenty years ago, I had surprised myself. This time because I was in love with a woman. My feelings for Adele were as palpable and profound as those I had discovered for men three decades earlier, while still married to Joyce.

The panic and confusion returned, even though there was none of the shame and public censure when I faced my feelings for men. This time it was the self-doubting that I had to face. I asked myself how many times could I face yet another change in myself. I knocked on the doors of my closest friends and swallowed hard when asking for their advice.

They put on a sympathetic face, but I could not blame them if, behind my back, they thought I was pathetic—going through another change at my late stage in life.

Although they were patient with me, several said they had been through the stage of trying to make it with a woman when they were young, but now they were happy to be themselves, to be what they were always meant to be. One said he could not even imagine being physically touched by those of the opposite sex.

My first therapist never warned me that my attraction to men could change to include a woman again. All those sessions with him turned into a house crumbling, one I helped build.

In the new therapist's office now, I fretted. Should I or should I not let myself go with Adele? A woman was different; she could be seriously hurt if I were to change my mind again someday. She'd probably never heard of one-night stands. My mind kept churning, and self-doubt surged, again and again, not letting me rest.

After several more weeks of my anguish and fretting, my therapist lowered his voice and faced me sympathetically. "Look at what is," he said, "Not what if."

I looked at *what is* and knew I was in love with Adele.

"It's been a good fifteen years together," her voice across the kitchen table sounded like it came from a courtroom judge delivering the verdict. "Maybe it's time for you to go back to your earlier life."

I had told her earlier what my doctor said at my latest check-up. Antidepressant pills or a therapist, he suggested.

Antidepressants have become as common as M&M's in our world of Apples, Blackberries, and Facebook. Some of my closest friends can't do without them. Adele's doctor had started her on combinations of these modern-day cocktails several years ago.

Heretofore I had always thought of myself as immune. If anything, I saw myself as somewhat of an eternal optimist, close to the Ah Q character in the short story by the celebrated Chinese writer, Lu Xun, unaware of the pains and pitfalls of a merciless and mercenary world, even when facing his executioner.

A close friend of mine once even pointed out, in spite of my attempts to hold his hand throughout several of his severe depressions, my irrepressible, upbeat personality made him feel I could not truly put myself into his world of darkness. Yet I liked films and plays with wrenching dialogue and fraught endings. I preferred them to sugar-coated comedies where I could hardly remember anything when I walked out of the door of the theater.

When I first heard the diagnosis of depression come out of my doctor's mouth, sitting on the examining table with my shirt still off after he listened to my heart and lungs, I could not quite believe he was talking about me. I saw him mouthing the words, but I thought they didn't really apply to me, until I put myself back into a doctor's coat and looked at what was in front of him.

The warning signs were clear—retirement from a job where my work was praised, a near fatal brush with mortality from a heart procedure, a bleeding ulcer which dropped my blood count to half what it should be, and not least, being a gay man in a committed relationship with a woman, these were what I could count, not even considering my past.

In my mind, I no longer had any conflict with being gay, although I was in love with a woman again, and most of the time, my head was still turned by men.

When I complained to my doctor that I no longer had the energy I used to have, I expected him to adjust the dose of medications I was taking for my heart condition or tell me it was from my advancing years. I had ignored all the other warnings of feeling tired, and even occasionally wondering where my life was going.

But Adele probably saw the same things that my doctor was seeing. "Don't think I haven't noticed that you have been very irritable with me lately!"

I thought I was just being firm about where I stood. Adele liked to say I was stubborn as my Chinese zodiac sign, the Ox. Maybe I was just getting better in pushing back at her. Being more assertive, in words from old therapy sessions.

I pushed her to answer the phone, so I didn't have to be the only one running to pick it up, even when I was sweeping leaves in the garden.

From across the kitchen table, Adele slid into English as she held on to what was left of her daily cup of decaf Pete's coffee. The coastal mist outside the kitchen window had drifted past us.

When it came to resolving our conflicts, we had a habit of drifting into English, instead of speaking in our native Mandarin. I often wondered whether it was because we belonged to that first-generation of Chinese immigrants where arguments between couples were silent, feelings foam covered, failures not faced, pains not bared at all costs.

In order to talk about them, we had to resort to the language of our adopted culture. There was not enough vocabulary in our mother tongue.

"I thought I would look at the cup half full, this time," she said finally, referring to her decision of thirty years ago, asking her husband to leave when she found out he was seeing another woman.

She was unable to move for six months after he moved out. Betrayed by a man who was considered the authority on modern Confucian thought, to whom she had devoted over twenty years of the springtime of her life. Confucius laid the backbones of moral behavior practiced in China for over two millennia.

"You can have Mondays, Tuesdays, and Wednesdays." I looked at her tightly drawn features in the waning afternoon light. She was trying hard to let go of me for three days of the week. Her long hair pulled firmly back. Her brows furrowed and arched high, accentuating the tiny wrinkles creeping onto her face, still beautiful against the oncoming sunset.

We were on the bus ride back from San Miguel de Allende, and the sun was hovering on the horizon when she first put her face against my shoulder. She wore her hair short and frizzled then, as if it were born free.

My son was the first to make me notice, "Auntie Adele has such a beautiful smile!" And my daughter said, "You can tell she's from Berkeley." I knew what my daughter meant. The tie-dyed T-shirts and no-iron dresses.

I kidded her about her aversion to ironing. My mother had a saying about wrinkled clothes, looking like they've been pulled out of a tight chicken's bottom.

It was that seemingly carefree spirit that drew me in. Her enthusiasm for the things she loved was infectious, hopping from rock to rock like a female deer on our first trip to the Canadian Rockies or showing me the things she loved in Florence, her favorite place in the world: from the special hue of its roof tiles, brought out by an afternoon shower, to the eighty-year-old artist who still hand-carved miniature musicians, and her not even being bothered by having to pick our way through the dog poop on uneven cobbled streets.

She made me feel I could be myself, just the way I was. She knew about my divorce and my affinity for men.

I waited now for more of her words from across the table, across the different piles and various places in the world of our lives, "You don't have to tell me whom you saw or what you did."

Could I really take her word for it? I thought about my friends, Bob and Ed, Pete and Jake, in committed relationships. Business trips out of town were exempt. They could play and no questions asked. For myself, I would not want the details, as long as I knew nothing would change the commitment.

Adele and I had walked around this minefield a year ago. She could not understand why I needed physical contact with men, no matter how casual it was, even though or because she knew my affinity. It could lead to something more, was the question that always hung in the dark corners of her mind. Could she really forget the warning of my friend about gay men?

She gave me the feeling that her life was complete just having me, even though I realized Bob Dole's ads for Viagra were pointing fingers at me. She could not bear to seek help from an outsider to discuss things happening behind our bedroom curtains. I was still too timid and proud to put the Kama Sutra on our bedside table.

The two of us came of age in a China when such things were not discussed between couples. A proper lady learned what happened between a man and a woman on the night before her wedding. She would be given a book of colored woodcuts of what to expect. It was a more delicate and sedate version of the Kama Sutra behind bamboo curtains.

For me, it took years, from contacts with those of my own kind, to find out about the nuances and sensations my own body was capable of feeling. If I was a slow and shy learner, Adele was many times more so.

"It's your problem. If you think you need to, you go see the therapist." Was her response when I suggested seeing a couples' counselor.

"I am not going!" she added in finality.

Tightly, I held onto my cup of tea across the kitchen table. But I could feel the remaining warmth behind Adele's decision through the raku ware now. The lights on the curved drive on the back side of Twin Peaks were showing up outside the window, twinkling like a big question mark in the darkening light.

Adele figured out my life with her was taking its toll on me. She could not change me, although I had told her from the beginning that I could not change myself from being what I was. I would always be that way. She was the exception.

As I sipped the green tea in my cup, I thought of its difference from the strong aroma of the roasted coffee beans Adele preferred. The delicately flavored nuances in the tea leaves, an initial mild amaro gradually turning into a lingering sweetness made me think of sitting in a garden in Hangzhou where Song Dynasty poets got their inspiration, or of a Tang Dynasty scholar practicing his calligraphy in a pavilion by a tranquil pond.

Yet stronger aromas from a cup of coffee seemed to be more part of this modern world of ours. In the town where we spend our summers, I had often seen Italian men waiting by counters ready to down their shot of double espresso, needed to face the rest of their day. I also thought of those Wall Street men dashing into the stock exchange with their cup of Starbuck's in hand, ready for the next killing.

I pondered Adele's preference for a dish of juicy beef with oyster sauce, while I favored a slow-braised celadon Chinese melon with chives and tofu. She thought cutting out red meat from my diet had something to do with my heart problems. Too much of a shock to my system, she said. While the thought of all that methane gas produced by cattle to get the beef on our table was enough to sour my appetite.

I wondered whether this was what the Daoist said about the Yin and the Yang. There should be a blend of the two. Complements circling our lives together. Adele's and mine.

Now she was lowering the stakes, giving me the time to do what I needed, for that life of ours together to survive.

To say the words, *I love you*, would be too facile from my lips at that time, without careful consideration.

I looked at her for a long time, then said, "We have chosen this path together. You are the most important person in my life. The person I see alongside myself growing old. The person I want to spend the rest of my days."

With those last words, my voice broke halfway because I realized I was standing at the sharp edge of our lives together. It was indeed a full circle from the edge of the Grand Canyon. The future seemed uncertain. I might be losing her.

"I will give it a try." She finally took a deep breath and said, "You leave me no other choice."

"Let's try together." I murmured, wondering how it was going to work out.

She was having difficulty even when she had all of my time. Now knowing that I will be spending time away from her, despite my repeated reassurances of devotion and commitment, how was she really going to handle it?

She was a year behind me in the zodiac cycle. A Tiger, fast to pounce. She could be stronger than the Dragon. But I was the Ox, the beast of labor, plodding slowly with its burden.

I thought of the fields I had plodded through in my life. My first Chinese name meant being able to withstand the weight of the large bronze urn in front of the temple. It was given to me in Hankow where I was born by the family recommended to my mother by the blind fortune teller. He had told her to find a family in which the man was a Rat and his wife a Chicken. Only such a family could shield me from the gods, the blind man warned.

At my retirement party a few years ago, a picture on the screen of myself as a four-month-old carried me back to the beginning of my journey. Dressed in a crocheted wool outfit and satin shoes, I was looking up at the world in front of me from my mother's embroidered silk shawl with an air of wonderment, no trace of apprehension for the many twisting pathways I would be traveling ahead.

PART I

Chapter One

鼠

Ming's in Palo Alto has a history of over half a century, close to the amount of time I have been in the Bay Area, a place I call home more than any other. In its heyday, the restaurant had the best Chinese cuisine on the Peninsula.

The building still has allusions to the grandeur of old China with its imperial yellow roof tiles curving skywards, unfurling like an old Chinese hand scroll, reminding me of the first time I was taken by my mother to the Imperial Palace in Beijing, also known as the Forbidden City. It was the crown jewel of the many splendors of the Ming Dynasty.

On this particular late autumn evening, I was on my way to my retirement party, taking place in the private dining room at the far end of this sprawling establishment. Hurrying my steps, not wanting to be late, I walked ahead of Adele. Over the years I have become accustomed to her reluctance to be in front, at least in public, as well as being innately incapable of arriving on time.

I had taken this to be an enigmatic attribute for someone who is a Tigress by the China zodiac, until I learned to appreciate the roots of her determined avoidance of the spotlight when an old friend and colleague of hers told me about the first time they met. She thought Adele to be a creature of youthful, angelic beauty, which in turn reminded me of an observation made by a friend in our college days: pretty girls liked to keep a distance, being leery that people would approach them only because of their looks.

When we walked into the room, the size of the crowd that evening was a little overwhelming, yet also reassuring. All familiar faces. Colleagues and co-workers I rubbed shoulders with at the hospital, and young doctors I trained showed up. One I had not seen for several years. As well as old personal friends and my extended family.

This family filled two tables and circled around me. My daughter and her family, my son and his daughter, flown in from the East Coast, my ex-wife, Joyce, who was part of my family circle again when she became friends with Adele.

On the other side of Adele were her own son and his family. His first-born was the first grandchild of the extended family, born exactly sixty years apart from me, a complete cycle in Chinese astrology thus sharing the same configuration in our stars and signs, something almost as rare as seeing Halley's Comet across the sky. I was even asked to choose the Chinese name of Adele's youngest grandchild, an honor usually reserved for the paternal grandfather related by blood.

Across the table was Teng, my friend who was like a brother to me, more attentive to my mother than I could ever have been. Next to him was his partner, Mark, in a gray satin shirt, who had brought chapters of his second novel to my writing group.

The youngest person at the table was Tenaya, the granddaughter who flew in with my son from D. C. She was barely a year old but endured the many course Chinese banquet without disruption. Adele snapped a picture of her standing up in her highchair, arms stretched wide as if she was ready to burst forth with an aria for the occasion.

The dessert of Eight Precious Rice Pudding arrived at our table at the same time the voice of Edith Piaf came on overhead, a singer whose embattled life and unyielding spirit I greatly admired. An endearing nurse, one who made things flow smoothly for us at the clinic, had asked me earlier for the name of my favorite song, along with some baby pictures for a slide show, photos going back to my childhood in Shanghai, Beijing, and Tokyo.

After the last strains of "*Je ne regrette riens,*" I saw myself as a four-month-old on the screen at the end of the dining room. It was the first picture of me I pulled out from an old family album. When Piaf's words, "I regret nothing" echoed in the room, I thought they captured well what I was feeling.

The path of my life slid across my eyes like quicksilver. China, Japan, and then this new Western World—over seven decades of change, an even more unrelenting path of changes and many more alien roads than *I Jing*, the *Book of Change* could have predicted.

1

鼠

Chapter Two

牛

"You should not count on him to be your son!" The blind sooth-sayer told my mother.

It was not the words my mother wanted to hear when she sought out the best fortuneteller in Hankow. I was only a few days old. According to my mother's calculations, I was supposed to come into that troubled world during the Year of the Tiger. A year after the Marco Polo Bridge Incident of 1937 near Beijing, a battle between the nascent Republic of China's Army and the Imperial Japanese.

I decided to arrive two months ahead of schedule. But one of my testicles did not arrive in its customary, designated location, a condition known as cryptorchidism.

The old French doctor arched his eyebrows and shrugged, "Mais non, Madame." He could not guarantee the survival of her first-born son in the surgical repair. Operations on a pre-mature baby were precarious and results unpredictable, at least in that little French Hospital in pre-World War II Hankow. "*Bien sûr!*" he added emphasis to the uncertain outcome of any intervention.

My mother was alarmed but determined in equal measure that her son having arrived early during the Year of the Ox was going to survive.

She asked the blind man what could she do to save my life.

His instructions were explicit. "Find the couple where the woman is a Chicken and the man a Rat. Offer incense to their ancestors and have them formally adopt your son and have him take their family name. This might hide him from the eyes of the gods and shield him from their wrath."

Then he repeated his warning, "Do not consider him your son!"

But my mother clung on to his last words. "At least until he passes his eighth birthday."

Although my mother received her formal education in Russia and Europe, she had absorbed enough folklore and traditional family influences to take the warnings seriously. The Chinese writer Lin Yutang of the modern era notably observed, in the West children believe in fairies while in China the adults also do.

She was much relieved when she found a couple matching those Chinese zodiac signs who worked for my father's railway lines in Hankow.

I was formally adopted into this Chinese family. Incense and food were offered at their ancestral temple, and I was to be given a name derived from sayings in their ancestral tablets, *Cheng Ding*. My mother liked the meaning of those two ideograms, Capable of Upholding the Temple Urn. Hopeful it would counter the burden of the gods, it was to be my Chinese name until I was past my eighth birthday.

My mother did not want to leave out any source of protection she might secure for her son. She remembered her closest friend when they were both young in Beijing, the daughter of the French doctor who took care of my mother's whole family in the old capitol. The friend used to go to the cathedral not far from the Forbidden City, to pray on important occasions and ask for help when her own mother was very ill.

The French priest at the hospital was only too happy to assist this Chinese woman who communicated in his own tongue fluently. He suggested that her son be baptized in the Catholic church and be given the name André because I had arrived at nine o'clock on the morning of Saint Andrew's Day.

André became the first name I was given because I had not yet received my Chinese name from my adopted parents' ancestral tablets.

When the nurse asked me to pick out some baby pictures for my retirement party, I had pulled out the old family album. It had seen better days.

The album followed us from Shanghai to semitropical Taipei, then to Tokyo and finally into this New World. Leaves stained, like the insides of old porcelain teacups. Its faded forest green cover with gold lettering hardly legible, and its spine had to be held together with a silk cord my mother brought over on the boat.

When I carefully turned its leaves to pick out those early photos of myself, I came across my mother in her wedding gown, a favorite aunt who looked like a young Audrey Hepburn on an Asian holiday, and at the end of the album, a last picture of my aunt with her husband a few months before they committed suicide, side by side, during the Cultural Revolution of the sixties.

There was one of me at eight, head shaven because I wanted to be like my father (who showed up in my life after the War with Japan). As I look back now, it also marked the end of the wrath of the gods the blind soothsayer had warned. At this stage of my life, over six decades later, the future is no longer so vast and foreboding.

There was also one of a young girl I was always told to be a distant relative, but my mother revealed two years before she died, was actually my half-sister.

Another one of me standing like the best little boy next to my mother when we first stepped ashore onto this land of promised hope and opportunity, a land that could still make me feel no less alien than that first hour, fresh off the boat in San Francisco Bay. I was twice the age of eight. Along with his forebodings on my early years, the blind man also told my mother, if I survived the first eight years, my future had no limits.

The earliest photograph of me was in a dark sepia tone. It could have been torn out of an album from some family during the last days of Imperial Russia, rather than China, which was soon to be ravaged by an all-out, eight-year war with Japan, destroying homes and uprooting families which would never be the same again. The old capitol Beijing and the commercial center Shanghai were already in the hands of the Japanese. They already occupied all of China's northeastern provinces and established a puppet regime calling it *Manchukoku*, the country of Manchuria.

The young woman in the picture next to mine was in a soft silk dress, its neckline trimmed with intricate, dark brown lace. Her Asian features aside, my mother's photo could have been mistaken for part of a Czarist Russian family portrait.

For my first photo session, she placed me on an embroidered Russian shawl brought back from her days as a diplomat's daughter in that northern country, stretching from Siberia to St. Petersburg. I was in a soft white shirt with short sleeves peeking out from under a crocheted vest, and I could see the bulge made by the cloth diaper under the crocheted shorts. Dark satin shoes were swinging in the air.

It seemed like an act of determined defiance by my mother to dress me up in such fineries, in view of everything happening around us. Christopher Isherwood described it well in his book with W. H. Auden, *Journey to a War*, when they ventured into the chaos of China as journalists.

"The Sisters had to coax and almost carry me down the stairs of the French Hospital to the bomb shelter when there was an air raid the day after I delivered you," she said. When it came to a choice between life, or death from Japanese bombs, the Sisters forced her to endure the pain from the torn birth canal sewn up not quite twenty-four hours earlier.

On the other side of the world, Hitler's Germany was just as determined in its march toward the final solution against the Jews. On my three-day visit to the Holocaust Museum in Washington, D. C., I was surprised to see photographs that could have been torn out of my old family album, scenes of serenity and luxury, when an equally devastating adversary was on their front door step. I wondered whether those Jewish families had any premonition of what was waiting for them and their world, around the corner.

There was no sign of distress in the exuberant smile and starry-eyed expectation in that cherub of my photographic debut, with his full crown of dense dark hair. No hint of the dark forebodings from the blind fortune teller.

My mother was fond of repeating an old Chinese saying, *san sui kan dao lao*. You can see the old man in the three-year-old. Ignoring the bags under my eyes and the gray cap on my head now, I would like to believe I have somehow managed to keep a corner of the worldview of that four-month-old infant.

On her deathbed, my mother pleaded with my good friend Larry from childhood days to please take care of her only son.

"He is still so *tian zhen*," she said. The words literally meant the truth from heaven. I knew what she really meant—I was still so naïve, childlike. I was already past my half-century mark when she made that remark.

Not more than a year later, when I helped scatter my friend's ashes into San Francisco Bay with Adele, who was his partner for ten years, I wondered what my mother would have been thinking if she were watching from somewhere above.

Now a quarter of a century after he succumbed to cancer, would she be even more surprised that Adele and I have been together for twenty of those twenty-five years? If I were to ask myself that question back then, I would have been equally surprised. After my divorce from Joyce and coming out, I thought my days of being with a woman were long over.

At the time of that first photo, I did not know I was going to be hustled away from my birthplace within a few months.

The fourth floor of the old French Hospital in Hankow, sat downstream from the Three Gorges on the Yangtze River as it sliced across the middle of China. Hankow no longer exists as a city, but it was once a major port city with its waterfront occupied and controlled by foreign mercantile interests after the Opium Wars of the mid-nineteenth century.

The old city has been swallowed up along with its counterparts Wuchang and Hanyang across the river to become the large metropolis of Wuhan, the hub of commerce in the bowels of what is industrial China today.

At the time of my birth, the area was still fresh from its pivotal role in the founding of the First Republic of China and the revolution in 1911 led by Sun Yat-sen, which brought an end to thousands of years of dynastic rule. It was the beginning of the Kuomingtang Party, or KMT founded by Sun.

Hankow was also the headquarters of two crucial rail lines in pre-World War II China connecting the ancient northern capitol of Beijing with the heartlands and to the southern port of Canton. Among the cities known as the infernos of China's summers, it ranked at the top.

When Sun Yat-sen first met my father, a fellow Cantonese just finishing his studies at the Imperial University of Tokyo, the founder of the Republic was impressed by the articulate young man's seriousness and determination to help develop the new republic. He thought my father could play a major role in Railways and Transportation, one of the most important areas of his government and managed by his son, Sun Fo.

Not long after my father's return to China, my father was chosen by Sun Fo to be the youngest director of the two major rail conduits for movement of material and goods from the North to the South.

In 1937, following the Marco Polo Bridge Incident, the Japanese Army started in earnest its steady advance from Manchuria and Beijing in the North into the Chinese heartland. My father thought it was safer for my mother, who was beginning to waddle around with me beating ever harder inside of her, to move away from the old capitol.

"Don't forget I can foxtrot a lot faster than you," my mother protested. She did not want to move away from the city she considered her home.

My father prevailed in the end, moving us first to Hankow, and when I was considered good enough to travel, farther south to the end of his railway line, Canton, the city where he was born and where his mother, the Matriarch, still lived.

Chapter Three

虎

The centerpiece of the lararium, off the side of my study and library, is my mother's wedding picture on the dais of this shrine, instead of a Roman god. Unlike the traditional ancestral temple in China with tablets of the forefathers, I have photos of the most important people in my life. Among them is one in an old silver frame of my father in a kimono next to the tokonoma when he was a student in Tokyo, another of my daughter waiting in the doorway before I walked her down the aisle on her wedding day, my son leaning against a brick wall when he was in high school, and Adele standing like a carefree priestess, hair blowing in the wind in Joshua Tree National Park.

My mother, framed in art nouveau sterling, was dressed in a shanghaied version of a Parisian original, wearing a tiara of white miniature rosebuds. The man on her right, in a formal black Chinese gown, is my father.

It was taken the year before the Japanese army invasion, just prior to the Marco Polo Bridge Incident and the start of the eight-year Sino-Japanese War. The last four are known in the West as the Second World War, beginning with the bombing of Pearl Harbor.

Life was lived in a frenzy in Nanjing, the new capitol, where my parents were married. The Japanese invasion was imminent in the air—especially in Beijing, the old capitol in the North and my mother's home, where the Japanese had already taken over the adjacent Manchurian provinces. It was as if there would be no tomorrow, akin to the Berlin of the early thirties.

If I squint carefully at that wedding photo with my bifocals today, I can tell my mother had a tiny gap between her front teeth, smooth as polished ivory, right below the upturn of the cupid's bow of her upper lip. It gave a hint of the natural insouciance she always presented to the outside world and reminded me of the un-retouched shots of the fashion model Lauren Hutton of the seventies.

On the other side of my mother in the wedding photograph was a man in morning coat and spats, hair parted handsomely, like a young Asian Robert Taylor. He looked perfect for the part of the bridegroom next to my mother in her meticulously copied Parisian gown.

My father, in his dark Chinese gown and shaven head, was as somber as a Buddhist monk, more spectator than a member at his own wedding.

For the eight years before I finally met my real father, the man dressed as a western bridegroom in that photograph was BaBa to me.

My mother made no attempts to change that impression when the three of us lived together under the Japanese Occupation. My mother, BaBa, and I.

When the War ended, and my real father appeared, I cut Baba out of the wedding picture. My eight-year-old mind only wanted my parents in the picture. My mother didn't stop me. After that, the man I called BaBa became Uncle Zhou to me.

At the time, I did not question the change. It did not seem strange to me that BaBa faded away from my life. Even when he was living with us, I hardly saw him. My mother was the only important person in my life then.

A few months before I got ready to leave my home in Tokyo to go to college in America, I was flipping through the pages of the old family album with my mother. There was a black and white photo of her holding me when I was eight months old.

"Your father was with us then." She pointed out. "But went to Chongqing shortly after this picture was taken."

The Japanese Army was steadily pushing its way South from Beijing. The KMT Government led by Chiang Kai-shek retreated up the Yangtze River to Chongqing, known then as Chungking. This was China's Dunkirk. Foreign Legations and journalists like Christopher Isherwood and W. H. Auden fled Hankow in droves. A vivid testament to those harrowing days can be found in their book, *Journey to A War*.

To avoid detection by the Japanese warplanes, which did not fly at night, my father put us on a night train from Hankow to Canton, the southern end of the railway line he managed.

He did not settle us into his ancestral home in Poon Yü, a relatively prosperous suburb of the provincial capital, Canton. Instead, I was taken to my grandmother's home and presented to her for the first time.

"Was I her first grandchild?" I asked.

"No," my mother said. She took a sip of her favorite jasmine tea and reached for her Pall Mall. It was the mildest American tobacco she could get in Tokyo. A poor substitute, she said, for the much mellower British 555 or 999 she preferred in Shanghai but not available in Japan.

"She had two by your father's older brother, but your father could not bring himself to tell her he married me. So she didn't know you were her own grandson by her favorite son."

My mother took a deep breath. A small smoke ring followed. This was often prelude to a long story. "He was extremely devoted to his mother. He didn't think she could take the news of him leaving his first wife. She was your grandmother's favorite

3
虎

niece, and your grandmother had forced him to marry her with the threat she would take her own life if he did not consent."

Hearing this as a teenager, added intrigue to my parents' marriage. I imagined the suspense surrounding their romance, having just seen the film, *Wuthering Heights*, with Lawrence Olivier and Merle Oberon. I was spellbound by what more my mother had to say.

She took a sip from her covered teacup, something she always had by her side. The fragrance of jasmine infused the air between us when she lifted the lid of her cup.

"I was so naïve then." She sighed. "I was also devoted to my own mother when she was alive, and I told your father I admired him for his devotion to his mother. So I did not push him." I could hear the compassion and regret in her voice, in equal measure.

Several decades later, a cousin on my father's side filled in the details of his first marriage. She was my first cousin from my father's elder sister. She and her mother stayed in my grandmother's home to make ends meet when her father died young.

"Our grandmother's niece followed when your father went to Japan to study. She ingratiated herself to the matriarch, who threatened to hang herself unless your father obeyed her wishes to marry this favorite niece she had chosen for him. Your father was a very filial son. He eventually consented to go through with the marriage on condition he would never have to share a bed with the woman."

Looking at photographs of him around that time, I could see that my father changed from a man with a full head of hair parted smartly on the right, to one with a shaven head like a Buddhist monk.

My cousin continued. "Your father was the object of many admirers. He moved into a monastery for six months, trying to avoid the marriage, before he finally consented to our grandmother's wishes.

"Our grandmother was not an easy person to live with. She always treated my widowed mother and me like servants and paupers that she had to feed and tolerate in her home," my cousin added bitterly.

As I look back now, there was a bittersweet recognition of what my father went through, because my mother had adamantly opposed my own marriage to the woman I loved. I think of the lines from the young poet Ocean Vuong I read recently— *a mother's love neglects pride, the way fire neglects the cries of what it burns.*

There was also an echo of many feelings I had after the series of relationships with men I had loved (that ended before I met Adele). I had thought of eventually joining a monastery after I retired. My father's actions tugged at my heart and soul.

Looking at my picture as an eight-month-old again, my mother continued. "Yes, I believed in your father's words, and I had too much compassion for his elderly mother. I did not want to cause any harm to her." I again heard the stirring of long submerged pain and regret mixed into her voice.

It was hard for me to forget the stress and suffering my mother had to endure when we finally lived with my grandmother after she joined us in Japan. She never accepted my mother's marriage to her son. Eventually, she went with my father to Taiwan when his work of signing the peace treaty with Japan ended. I never saw her again.

I had no recollection of my first meeting with the matriarch in the ancestral home when I was eight-months-old. My first memory of my grandmother, I was already twelve, the year she came to live with us in Tokyo. She looked much the same as she did when she was ninety in her oil portrait, which used to hang in my dining room. When facing her stern stare of a dowager empress, friends and visitors have commented she must have been a formidable woman.

My grandmother called me *BiBi* in her own reserved tone of voice, and rarely cracking a smile. *BiBi*, with the accent on the second syllable, was the Cantonese way of affectionately saying baby or the little kid. Her two other grandsons, both much older than I, were called *DaiBi* and *SaiBi*, meaning the big kid and smaller kid, from my father's older brother.

I tried very hard to be respectful and polite to the matriarch. It was how my mother taught me to behave. But I was not able to respond to the matriarch's reserved and distant affection when I could hear my mother smashing porcelain vases and ashtrays upstairs after getting another put down by my grandmother who lived downstairs in her own suite of rooms.

At twelve, I was given the task every morning of cleaning the altar of her private temple, a task reserved for a virgin boy before his body was touched by a woman's. The bodies of the maidservants were considered soiled and impure, thus not allowed to do the cleaning.

I can still see my grandmother seated in front of her altar and mumbling the verses of the Buddha's sutras, over and over, in Cantonese, tapered fingers moving along a strand of dark jade prayer beads. She was no longer able to kneel in front of the altar, the way she used to, because of her age.

Looking back now, I can begin to understand why this devoutly Buddhist, matriarch from Southern Canton strongly disapproved of my parents' marriage.

She had carefully coaxed her favorite son, who was able to recite Tang Dynasty poetry at five, to marry the person she had chosen. Not only was my mother not from the same southern province of Canton, but she was from the North, born near Shanghai, the city with a reputation of morality loosened by modernity compared to the rest of China, and furthest removed from the Confucian past of the rest of the country.

When my father eventually revealed to his mother (with five-inch bound feet), that my mother was educated in Russia and Paris, and often socialized at soirées in the French Embassy, as if these were qualifications deserving admiration and approval, I could imagine this iron-willed matriarch had no doubt she wanted nothing to do with this creature of a different world, if she could even honor her by such a name and not what she really thought my mother's profession might be.

After my recent house renovation, I moved her portrait to a sidewall of my study. The portrait is now half shielded by a door into the room. I could find no other appropriate space in my home. The other walls are covered by bookcases. I often tried to move the door out of her way, feeling guilty that I was obscuring the face of the matriarch of the family.

My grandmother's given name celebrated her birth the same year her father achieved the highest honors in the Imperial examinations of the Qing Emperor.

I had to fill in the three Chinese characters of her name clearly printed on her death certificate when I submitted the application to the authorities in Taiwan to bring her remains, along with my father's and his first wife's, to this country for re-interment into the same cemetery where my mother was. I thought it would be nearly impossible, once I am gone, for my children and grandchildren to find the secluded cemetery in Taipei where my father had chosen to be buried earlier.

Reimagining those auspicious characters of my grandmother's name, I wondered whether her father's achievement at the Imperial Court always gave her a sense of privilege to impose her strong will over other people.

For their first encounter at the ancestral home, my mother was presented to her future mother-in-law as the wife of my father's friend, Uncle Zhou. For many years thereafter, my grandmother would continue to refer to my mother as the wife of Mr. Zhou, even after my father finally told her the fact about his second marriage.

I could only guess whether her advanced age made it more difficult for the matriarch to change or she found it better suited to her own mind to continue denying my parents' marriage, an act against her expressed wishes that she was determined never to accept.

To me, my mother was the Madonna with angels of my early years, in her white Parisian wedding gown and wearing the white rosebud tiara. I have made copies of my mother's wedding picture in sepia tone and blown up her image five times its original size as if to reassure myself of the reality of her marriage. All with the hope of overcoming the suspicion that I was born out of wedlock, from a union that was denied by the family matriarch.

My grandmother's unrelenting denial of my parents' marriage and their unconventional wedding picture of having another person other than my father dressed as the bridegroom have continued to feed my lingering suspicion of whether I was indeed my father's son.

Chapter Four

兔

"One day you'll understand." My mother's voice continued the evening I was back from college over a long weekend, a voice, which at one time could sing the lyric soprano in Peking Opera, but now beginning to turn smoky from decades of tobacco. A faded sepia tone photo of her ready to go on stage in the familiar role of a wronged, faithful courtesan in the lyric soprano repertory is in the same album of my old family pictures. The role was her favorite to sing, and I remembered her practicing at home with friends.

She knew I had a long day hitching a ride with friends, driving down from Cambridge to Manhattan. I didn't tell her we barely avoided an accident in the blinding snowstorm on the New England Thruway. The driver had just gotten his jalopy a week earlier and had little experience driving in the snow. Luckily my mother was not yet tuned into checking for weather reports and road conditions. Otherwise, she would have been beside herself with worries that her only son had put himself at such great risks.

That evening, I could hear through the gravel of her voice, she wanted to tell me something seriously troubling her. From the deliberateness of her tone, I had come to know, she was setting the stage for a story like those in the Peking Operas she took me to see as a child after the war ended in China.

Her apartment was on the fourth floor of a twelve-story brick building off Morningside Heights. The faded façade, foot-worn entry court and corridors evoked the world of the silent film star Norma Desmond in the movie *Sunset Boulevard*. At one time, it was a fashionable place to be on New York's Upper West Side.

In the mid-fifties, the area was home to those unable to afford the move to the fancier East Side and to graduate students and junior faculty at the university nearby. The aging brick apartment buildings stood at the edge of the park bearing the same name, separating them from Harlem, but giving the impression that anytime they might fall over the precipice and join the fate of some of the tenement buildings below.

These buildings were under the city's rent control, and the superintendent was expected to pocket part or all of a month's rent before he would let you have a unit. Somehow the scruffy Irishman with some missing canine teeth was sympathetic to my mother.

Whether he was just sorry for her because of her few words of English spoken with a Franco-Russian accent, or he succumbed to the charm of a diminutive Chinese woman in a silk sheath with a high Mandarin collar, starting her life as a student at middle age, I could never be sure. The result was my mother got her apartment without paying the extra pocket money, and the superintendent got a lot of free babysitting, and what he proclaimed to be the best Chinese food he'd ever tasted in the city.

She supported herself sewing part-time in the back of a milliner's shop on Fifth Avenue. Evenings, she slipped on her Mandarin sheath and became a hostess in a Chinese restaurant catering to tourists near Times Square. When business was slow, she pulled out her textbooks to study English for foreigners in the language school, in preparation for applying to graduate school at Columbia.

Years later, when she looked back at this period of her life when her prime objective was to survive on her own, she said, "I could have gone an easier way, but I could never bow my head so low."

She went on to explain, she interviewed for a job on Fifth Avenue as a companion to one of the sisters-in-law of the Soong family.

"The woman didn't even get out of bed. She was treating me like a servant." My mother went on, "It's the old Chinese saying, a person would rather have his head roll to the ground, but he would never bow down so low. I realized the job might be easier in that extravagantly luxurious setting, but I preferred to keep my self-respect and work harder on my own."

In her own apartment later that evening, still fixing on me with her gaze, my mother pursed her lips around her cigarette and freshened her cup of hot jasmine tea. She leaned forward as if she was going to continue, then let out a ribbon of smoke from the long Pall Mall. She got used to them in Tokyo, the closest thing to the English cigarettes she favored in Shanghai, at a price she could afford. She was always careful and good with what she had.

I nodded quietly, but she could tell I was anxious to hear what she had to say.

"Don't worry! I'm not going to let your father or my own sister think I'm helpless."

Her hazelnut pupils flashed like coals in flame.

"Never!" She puffed. I could see her hand quivering as she tapped her cigarette on the edge of the ashtray.

I wanted to go over and hug her, the way I used to at our home in Tokyo when I was still in high school. My father's mother was living with us. The Cantonese matriarch had sharpened put-downs to a fine art. My mother listened with swallowed pride, like a proper Chinese daughter-in-law, then went upstairs, shaking in hurt and frustration.

When I went over to hug her, she would look at me and say, "You're the only one I've got!" I had heard these words from early childhood. They made me feel self- important, but I also understood it carried the message that I should always be a good boy and not disappoint her.

Once I asked my mother if I could have a younger brother to play with. She looked at me tenderly and said, "You had a little brother, but he died before he was born." When I asked her for the reason, she replied, "You jumped on my belly when he was still inside me, and I lost him."

I was about five when she told me and probably fortunate that I didn't understand the gravity of what I heard, except that I didn't have a little brother to play with because of something I had done.

My mother didn't tell me until two or three years before she passed away that I also had a half- sister, ten years older than I. She pointed to a picture of a little girl in the family album. I wish I had known earlier that someone I had always taken to be a distant relative was really my sister, even though she was not standing in front of me.

That evening in my mother's apartment, after several years in college far away from home where I had to fend for myself in the dorm and deal with a new world and people of an American college town, I was no longer the teenager living at home and hearing those double-edged words.

There was also the struggle with hormonal surges when I felt my college roommate in the lower bunk humping the mattress. I held my breath and pretended I was asleep when I really wanted to join in the act.

I thought of the nights when I stayed on my aunt's family farm the week before I went to college. My cousin tiptoed to my bed in the attic and did it with me. But by the time I was with my roommate in college, I was afraid to let myself go. I should have read St. Augustine's *Confessions* about signs of *inquieta adulescentia*, as something natural to young manhood. Instead, I thought

I should be growing out of doing what kids did, growing up to be a man and learning to control my own feelings and behavior I thought belonged to childhood.

As I sat across from my mother and seeing her hurt again, I held back from what I wanted to do, to hug and comfort her, because I was afraid of showing too much outward affection to her. I was afraid she was going to break down and cry in front of me. Awkward and embarrassed, I held my breath and waited, trying to behave like what I thought was appropriate for a grown man. It didn't help that there was the ingrained traditional Confucian reserve that I had absorbed while growing up and seeing how adults behaved.

4

兔

Chapter Five

龍

It was during those years when I was finishing my college studies, and wallowing between a career in engineering and deciding that I was going to medical school, while my mother was struggling with her own studies in graduate school that I visited her whenever I had a long weekend. In addition to feeding me her home cooking of a blend of Shanghai and Northern Chinese cuisine, she thought it was time to tell me more about herself and the past that she wanted me to know.

My parents were not brought together by a matchmaker in the village or by arrangements of their parents, where astrological signs and backgrounds were meticulously examined according to tradition. They were not even introduced by mutual friends, as was the custom for many of their contemporaries.

"I met your father for the first time in the Peking Hotel," my mother started from the beginning on one of my visits to her apartment. The hotel was a post-colonial edifice of the twenties and thirties for the social set, next to the five marble bridges with guardian lions leading into the Forbidden City, where for centuries courtiers kowtowed to the ground, at their audience with the Emperor, considered to be the Son of Heaven.

My mother usually had a front row table in the ballroom when she returned home to this old capitol city in the North. The New Republic chose Nanjing as its capitol and the new governmental offices, and foreign embassies relocated themselves to the city in the South, an overnight train ride west from Shanghai in those days. But Peking retained some of its cache and support from members of the *ancien régime.* Today it is called Beijing again, the Northern Capitol. It was the capitol from the time of Genghis Khan and many earlier dynasties.

Japan was increasing its hold of the provinces to the Northeast. Heretofore PuYi, the Last Manchu Emperor had not yet been enticed to become the puppet head of Manchukoku, a state the Japanese were on the verge of creating and controlling shortly afterward in their master plan for taking over the entire Chinese Mainland.

"Miss Guan, I'm so sorry I had to give your usual table away tonight," said the maître d, beside himself in apologies and repeatedly bowing at the entrance to the ballroom. Then he continued, sotto voce, "The Emperor is here."

"But I thought we have a New Republic now!" my mother's voice boomed forth, equal parts in protest and jest.

"I put you next to the table for Minister Sun," the man bowed again nervously.

"We don't care who sits next to us, do we?" she looked at the friends who accompanied her. "I just want to be up close so I can see who is playing in the band."

"A table next to the son of the Founder of the New Republic isn't all bad." One of the friends standing close to her added with his customary good humor. "*Yi chao Tien Zi, yi chao chen.*" With every change of the Son of Heaven, there is a new set of courtiers, was an old saying to a people who have seen so many dynastic changes through the ages.

Well put, my mother thought. And new sycophants. But she kept that to herself. Her friend could read it on her face, while they were being led to her table.

This friend returned after several years' study in France, as did promising young men sent abroad to learn the ways of the Western World. He now worked for the son of the warlord who ruled Manchuria. A handsome figure in his western suit and vest and conversant in current social French phraseology, he fancied himself a suitor at one time.

My mother liked this friend, who made her feel nostalgic for the time in the waning days of the Czarist court where French was used. He liked to tease her that she had spent too many years abroad and was too innocent and direct in her ways to be suitable for survival in her own motherland. To him, the Chinese saying was self-evident, she had absorbed too much of the ink from the West, and he felt protective of her.

Inside the ballroom, several couples moved formally to the strains of *Moonlight Serenade*. A young woman was being dragged ragdoll fashion across the dance floor by her flamboyant partner who was trying to make an impression. Sequined satins and silks sparkled with the latest local interpretations of Western haute couture and the traditional, Mandarin *qipao*, which was actually an influence from the Manchu Dynasty but also known as the *cheongsam* in Chinatowns across America. The men were almost uniformly dressed in dark western suits with vests.

My mother was not sure whether she liked the new ballroom. It was renovated a few years back to resemble one in the new Cathay Hotel on the Shanghai Bund, made famous by Victor Sassoon, the Baghdadi Jewish entrepreneur, at one time considered the wealthiest man in the Far East. Older carved rosewood panels were removed in favor of a lighter art deco look. Chinese silk lanterns depicting the four seasons were replaced by slick wall sconces. The only reminders of the former somewhat dowdy but dignified décor were the round tables hugging the dance floor. These were now close to full.

As my mother's party was being ushered to their table toward the front, there was a momentary hush in the buzz of background conversation at the other tables. Heads turned to this young woman wearing a Louise Brooks bob and a black velvet Mandarin gown slit along the sides, from her knee down to her black silk pumps. A black velvet peony was pinned close to the high collar. On her shoulder, a silver Siberian fox stole trailed down to her slim waist.

Even when she was close to eighty, my mother seemed to have a strong effect on people when she entered a room. I remembered taking her to a benefit dinner in San Francisco. Heads turned on this Chinese woman in black and gold brocade, hair tinted jet black, and jade on her to rival a museum display case. It was not so much what she was wearing as the way she carried herself like a dowager empress, charming and seductive all at once. In fact, she was told that she resembled the last Dowager Empress Cixi.

At the Peking Hotel that long-ago evening, she wore black as a tribute to her own mother who died while my mother was still away in Russia. Peony was her favorite flower.

She noticed the two tables up front, partially shielded by lacquered screens. The Emperor was no longer inside the Forbidden City, the old Imperial Palace, and he held no official position. He was living in neighboring Tianjin in those days but liked to drop in at the hotel when he was back in town.

In the section adjacent to the screens, and separated by two large round columns painted with French café scenes resembling the Moulin Rouge, were a series of four tables. The first was already occupied by a group dressed mostly in western attire.

A short man, whose hair was beginning to thin, with midriff bulging out of his smartly tailored, gray three-piece suit, was seated facing the dance floor. My mother recognized Sun Fo, son of the Founder of the Republic. She was surprised how much he had changed from the occasion of his father's state funeral when she was an usher.

On that occasion, it was a nation mourning its Founding Father. My mother remembered the Founder's wife, Soong Chingling, in particular. Petite, with finely chiseled features, more beautiful in mourning black than my mother had remembered from an earlier time; her family was also from Shanghai, the city where my mother's own maternal grandfather was prominent.

Soong Chingling spoke softly and kindly to all the ushers as if their loss was greater than her own. Although not much older than her stepson, Sun Fo, whose mother was Sun Yat-sen's village wife chosen by his parents, Soong spoke fervently of the revolution her husband started but was unable to complete because of his untimely death from liver cancer in 1925.

Seated sideways at the same table next to Sun Fo that night, my mother noticed a man whose shaven head stood out against the slick, western hairstyles of the other men. The traditional Chinese black cloth shoes he wore under his long dark Chinese gown were a sharp contrast to the polished leather wingtips on the others. She became aware he was staring at her from behind round, black-rimmed glasses. For a brief second, she thought him rude, but she was becoming more accustomed to people's stares, since her return from Russia. Her own countrymen did not seem to have the same reservations Westerners had in showing their curiosity in others.

She found herself intrigued by his nonconforming appearance and the boldness of his stare. She took note there were two or three women at his table, unremarkable in their appearance and probably secretaries or office workers at the ministry. Not wanting to feel intimidated by the man's boldness, she acknowledged his gaze and turned back to her friends.

The band started again. Her friend asked her to dance. She whispered that he should first ask her friend, the widow of a young poet recently killed in an airplane accident. There was no protest. That was what made her friend so dear to her. He was also one of the best dancers she knew and reminded her of the British movie actor, Leslie Howard. His easy acquiescence to her wishes made her feel he was like a brother.

She did not sit long at the table after her friend followed the poet's widow onto the dance floor. Other friends took turns keeping her busy on her feet.

When the band filed out at the break, the maître d brought over a large covered dish in imperial yellow with medallions of blue dragons. On the same tray was an envelope with the Emperor's insignia. PuYi had sent over some sweets made by his personal chef and requested the honor of the next dance with the lady wearing the black peony.

The band returned with a fox trot. PuYi's attaché came over to escort my mother to the Last Emperor's table, and my mother's friend accompanied her to the front. His acting protectively, like a real brother, made her appreciate his friendship even more.

When PuYi stood up to greet her, she was surprised he was not much taller than she was in her heels. He lifted her hand and said, "Mademoiselle..."

"*Guan*," her friend helped with the introduction.

"*Enchanté.*" The Last Emperor finished his sentence.

She found him a very good dancer and told him her father had been in the diplomatic corps during the reign of the Emperor's great aunt, the Dowager Empress Cixi, and that she had returned recently after living abroad for nearly twenty years.

"You have an elegant Parisian accent," she said.

"I owe that to my excellent tutor."

He learned she was her father's third child and about her preference for peonies.

"Black peonies were the Dowager Empress's favorite in her garden." He offered to send her some, but she politely declined, saying she had no talent for gardening.

"In that case, I will have the old Palace gardener plant them for you," he insisted.

5
龍

By the time PuYi's attaché escorted her back to her table, she could feel everyone's eyes following her movements. She noticed the man next to Sun Fo who stared at her was no longer at the Minister's table.

"Yes. That first brief encounter with the man who would become your father was a very brief one." My mother emphasized the short glimpse they had of one another, but went on to tell me more about what followed with her encounter with Pu Yi.

The next morning the gardener arrived with three large pots of black peonies. He chose a sunny spot in her family garden and planted them with the soil he said he was still able to sneak out of the Forbidden City.

My mother's friends started to call her the Black Peony after they heard about PuYi's peonies in her garden. It didn't take long for the nickname to catch on. But soon afterward, news spread the Last Emperor of China became the First Emperor of Manchukoku. The Japanese picked him up from Tianjin to head the puppet regime they set up in Manchuria.

"Your father was not one who followed conventions." My mother stood up to empty her ashtray, by now half filled with tips of her Pall Malls. The black cloisonné ashtray with peonies was one of few mementos from Shanghai she managed to salvage and bring to her new life in New York. She sat down again after telling me the beginning of her story with my father and took another sip of the jasmine.

"I was not to see him again for two years. By then he had found out almost everything about me." She had lost the harshness in her voice when she began. Memories of the distant past mellowed it into a soft mezzo.

How different she sounded that evening from the times I visited when she spoke about the problems she was having with him, living in different countries, an ocean and a continent apart. I could see she was still in love with him from the way she remembered those early days. Her eyes brightened up with the mellowing of her voice, her admiration of the way he stood out from the other men that evening. Seeing the evidence of that early bud of love between them, I couldn't help feeling deeply comforted and fulfilled. And that I was the product of this romantic beginning.

"His first invitation was on the formal stationery of the Ministry of Railways." She remembered it announced the celebration of the anticipated new train connection from Beijing to Hankow and from Hankow to Canton, thus connecting the North to the South of the country. "And your father was named the new head of those two railways."

"This showed your father's attention to details and his patience in pursuing me. He found out that I was acquainted with Sun Fo and thus would not refuse the invitation. The announcement of a new rail connection was a sufficiently public affair that I would not think it too intimate for our first formal meeting." She paused for a second and looked at me with an equal measure of remembered pleasure and resignation, then sighed, "I was never a match for his skills in meticulous planning."

I was intrigued to hear more about my parents' next encounter, but my mother said it was time for dinner.

Chapter Six

蛇

My mother brought out two dishes. My favorites, prepared earlier, anticipating my visit.

A julienned daikon salad drizzled with crisped spring onions in peanut oil and cucumbers marinated in sweet vinegar with slivered young ginger roots. I have learned how to make them and now like to serve them when friends come for dinner.

I helped set up the table in her kitchen and sat down watching my mother prepare the warm dishes. She turned to face me, "How about some wine?"

Her cabinet was always well-stocked, although she did not touch a drop herself. Secretly I was heartened, even wondering if somehow it might be nostalgia for her life with my father, who was a wine aficionado.

His favorite was Courvoisier Napoleon Cognac. She always kept a bottle in her cabinet even after he was no longer with her. I continued to harbor the hidden wish that my parents could live harmoniously, even though they were now separated, particularly when I sensed she has been more upset with him over the past year or two.

When my mother said wine in Chinese, I understood it meant brandy. Good grape wines were not readily available in the shops of Shanghai, even after the War was over and the city was the most modern and westernized part of China before Mao's takeover in 1949. For guests invited to our table, my father always offered his cognac.

I remembered being taken on an expedition with my parents to a French monastery when we stayed in Beijing for several months after my father's return from the War. He found out the monks made good wines from their own grapes, but only for their own consumption. He brought us along hoping my mother could convince them to sell a few bottles using her French. She didn't have to. The monks spoke very good Mandarin and didn't need much persuasion. They were proud of the wine they made.

6

蛇

I got out the bottle of Courvoisier from my mother's cabinet and poured some into the brandy snifter. Its bouquet brought back my father's enthusiasm for his cognac. He liked warming the dome glass between his palms and holding it under my nose. The snifter cupped half of my face when I was nine.

As the flavor of my mother's next dish wafted over from the stove, I felt the warmth of the sweet cognac spread over me. Crucian carp slow braised in soy, ginger, and scallions is a famous dish from my mother's ancestral Suzhou. I have not tasted one better than hers.

"Don't wait for me!" she urged, a familiar phrase she often had to say when she invited her new American friends over for dinner, who were not used to starting the meal without the hostess at the table.

My mother believed Chinese food was best enjoyed fresh from the wok. "I'd rather have you start and enjoy the food, instead of waiting for me."

Still, I found it hard to start without her. It became a little ritual between us, back and forth at the table. She grew impatient if I waited, wanting me to savor what she cooked at its very best. But I could not stop behaving like the good Chinese son she trained me to be. It was in my blood. I found it hard to ignore my deference and start the meal without her, no matter how many times she urged me.

The second hot dish was braised duck, Shanghai style. Setting the glistening brown bird surrounded by shiitake mushrooms on the table, she hung up her apron and sat across from me.

A smile of satisfaction washed over her face as she watched me down every mouthful of the bamboo shoots and shiitake mushrooms saturated in sweetened soy sauce, typical of the Suzhou and Shanghai cuisine of her own childhood.

"Not even a sip?" I held up the glass toward her.

"I have my jasmine." She took a mouthful from her cup.

Jasmine tea had always been her favorite. An occasional jasmine blossom bobbed above the celadon tea leaves, the subtle shade of Song Dynasty porcelains. The name for the tea in Chinese is *xiang pian,* literally fragrant petals.

She liked to hold up her tea canister to my nose, "Smell this perfume? Can't understand why your father prefers the Iron Goddess."

She never appreciated the bouquet of my father's Courvoisier or the dark liquor of his favorite tea. The first time I took a sip of the famous tea from Southern China, as he held up a tiny cup to my lips, I thought it tasted much like the brew of bitter herbs my mother used to force down me when I was sick. I had to hold my nose to swallow the medicine. It was years later before I began to notice the tea's subtle, sweet after-taste. It took those passing years for me to have the patience to wait for the succor. On the other hand, the fragrance of the Jasmine was hard to miss from the start.

My recent experience with one-hundred percent dark chocolates reminded me of my father's preference for the Napoleon Cognac and Iron Goddess tea. A good friend introduced me to the pure chocolate. The first time I put it in my mouth and chewed it the way we usually eat chocolates, the intensity of the bitter taste made it hard to appreciate. My friend taught me to savor it in my mouth without chewing, like a good lemon drop, letting the flavor slowly permeate my taste buds, then chase it with some sips of freshly picked green tea or spring water at its source. Getting the real flavor of the unadulterated chocolate reminded me of my father's Iron Goddess tea.

As I look back at my parents now, I am taken by their preferences in teas, the close to yin-yang polar opposites of their temperaments and worlds they came from.

Was it the stark difference of polar opposites that pulled them toward each other like magnets? A force that held them together in the face of so many obstacles for so long, until it was no longer enough? Besides a son's desire to know more about my parents' past, there was something deeply touching and perversely intriguing to imagine two people so different coming together.

"Tell me about your early times together." The best time to ask was when my mother was having her cup of jasmine and a Pall Mall close by.

She reached for the red pack beside her. Lit one, and let out a slow, deep breath. A ritual when she finished cooking. To my mother, this part of her routine seemed more important than eating the food she spent all that time making. It ranked second to watching me inhale the favorite foods she prepared.

"Remember the pyramid poem in Cantonese your father wrote for me?"

I could still see my father's words on the long scroll that used to hang in her bedroom in Shanghai. The brush calligraphy from his hand, written in the style of the Master from the Dynasty Jin, Wang Xizhi, came back in front of my eyes. Fluid and graceful as water flowing down a stream but with solid bones, Chinese scholars liked to say, commenting on their favorite art form.

*Tai, king gai, tzo ha teem, bo bui guai zai…*One, two, three, four words, and on it went. The pyramidal construction of his poem with its nine-toned mellow Cantonese rhythms echoed in my head.

6
蛇

"That was one of the things that hurt me most," her voice trailed into a pain that was still palpable, something unexpected for my mother to show. Then she rallied and finished her sentence, "when I discovered he took that scroll with him when he left."

She did not realize he had taken that scroll with him when my mother and I rode with him and my grandmother to see them off at the airport in Tokyo. The Peace Treaty with Japan was signed, my father's work in getting it done came to an end. He decided to return to Taiwan with his mother.

For me, it was a relief that the two years living with my paternal grandmother was over. She did not try to disguise the displeasure she had with my mother. The four of us rode in the car as silent as stones, all the way to the airport. There were no fond and lingering farewells when we parted. I wondered whether this was when my mother started to suspect this was the beginning of the end of her marriage.

From across her kitchen table, my heart went out to her again. My gut knotted in hearing that my father had taken back the talisman of his love for her, after having heard about their bright beginnings earlier.

Some part of me didn't want to believe that my own father was capable of something so cruel. Fighting with my own conflicted feelings, I sat uncomfortably, frozen with feelings, unable to reach over to hug my mother, unable to find the right words to give her some comfort.

As I did on earlier occasions, I held my breath and waited again, uneasily, glued to my chair.

My mother recovered her composure faster than I could sort out my feelings.

"He got me, right from the beginning." She took a sip of her jasmine and wandered back into her memories. "In those short phrases of the poem, your father captured all the things important to me."

Tai, Look! *King gai*, let's chat! *Tzo ha teem*, Stay awhile longer! *Bo bui guai zai!* Precious, obedient son, echoed in my head. I was mentioned in the fourth line of his pyramid. When I was younger, I used to wonder why I wasn't on the top of the pyramid, its first line. I did not realize till later he had to think of the shape of the pyramid, the rhymes, as well as his words of affection and description of my mother's favorite things.

She reached across the table and patted my hand. "You are the one person who has not disappointed me."

Instead of giving her the reassurance she wanted, I squirmed because she was still treating me like a child, even though I had my degree from college. While her words always gave me a feeling of self-importance, I also felt unsettled by them. Replacing my father with me as her object of affection made me feel uneasy.

I shoved in a mouthful of rice and another piece of the duck, so I didn't have to say anything about the conflicting thoughts swirling in my head.

"When Chen Di Qiu visited me that first summer…" my mother finally went back to her early days with my father.

I heard a change in her tone. The earlier edge was now soft and wistful as the early June breezes sweeping over the willows on the banks of Lake Xuan Wu in Nanjing, the city where their love blossomed.

She was using my father's full name, in its familiar form, as if she was presenting him to the public for the first time. The words *Di Qiu* in his name meant the world in Chinese. It was the name he took for himself because it was a close homonym of the number nine in Cantonese dialect. He was the ninth child in a large Cantonese clan in a prosperous suburb of the provincial Capitol.

It became the name by which he was known in the world around him, and my mother liked to use his full name when she talked about him in those early days.

6
蛇

"We used to talk all through the night until we heard the street sweepers starting their work in early dawn."

It was easier for me to hear about the good things that happened in the past between my parents. My shoulders relaxed, and the tension in the air receded into that time of long ago as I sat across from her.

"I was staying with my younger sister in those days," she added.

"Don't remember how many cups of tea I drank, and didn't even notice the sun rising from the corner of the east window." I could see the second line of his poetic tribute to her, *king gai*, coming to life. She liked nothing better than conversations without an end in sight.

"Your father could talk about anything. His high hopes of contributing something to the young Republic, his days in preparatory school and the Imperial Tokyo University. I was very impressed when he told me about his determination to show he could do better than the Japanese in their best schools."

"Didn't Chiang Kai-shek also study in Japan?" I asked, wondering if that was why my father decided to devote himself to the new government.

"Yes, but Old Chiang went to Waseda. Your father went to the First Preparatory School, Yi Gao, and then the Imperial University in Tokyo. Both were the hardest ones to get into, even for the Japanese." Although she rarely liked to give in to my father in arguments, here she was telling me she was more than impressed by his accomplishments. I realized she had found her match when she met him.

My mother never referred to Chiang Kai-shek as President Chiang or Generalissimo Chiang. It was always *Lao Chiang,* Old Chiang. She wasn't using the word old in the way age was revered in China. My mother had neither respect for Chiang's character nor faith in his ability as a leader.

She called him Old Chiang as if she were calling our cook, Old Yu or our driver, Old Leong. When she had good friends over for tea or dinner, she did not hesitate to talk about the corruption in his government, its links to the gangland world of old Shanghai and his connections to the illicit trade of opium from Burma.

"Your father was devoted to the principles of the new republic, the Kuomingtang, founded by Sun Yat-sen," she said with resignation in her voice, when she saw the question forming in my mind. Why was my father associated with this corrupt government?

"Of course, Sun was also Cantonese. You know how the Cantonese always stuck together." I remembered how she used to complain about my father's relatives and friends, chatting away in their animated Cantonese when they came to visit as if she didn't exist. As I grew up and had my own friends, I questioned whether it was a case of male camaraderie and part of the male misogynistic behavior of those days, rather than ostracizing my mother who was not Cantonese.

"When did he ask you to marry him?" I wanted to pull my mother back to her early days with my father, but her thoughts wandered in a different direction, in the details of the early Republic.

"I was at the wedding of Sun Yat-sen and Soong Chingling." In spite of myself, I felt being drawn into what my mother had to say of people I had only read about in books.

"I was not yet ten and in school then. But your Wai Gong worked for the Foreign Ministry, and I could speak French and Russian."

Then she explained. My grandfather used to take her to Russia with him because he was embarrassed to bring my grandmother with bound lotus feet. French flowed in the diplomatic circles and the Russian Court, but Russian was used with the servants at home before the Bolsheviks overthrew the Czar.

I had heard the part about my mother's growing up in Russia before, but with each new telling she focused on a different aspect and dribbled out a bit more about the details.

"Oh, about a year or so later." She finally remembered to answer my question, as she chose a piece of the fish from the least bony portion and put it on my plate. The scare of a fish bone stuck in my throat as a kid, became a fear in my mother's mind I would never to be able to handle fish bones.

"But we really couldn't get married, to each other."

In response to my confused look, she began to unravel the story that led to her clandestine marriage to my father and the enigma of their wedding picture, where there seemed to be two grooms standing next to my mother. One in a formal western morning coat and my father in ceremonial Chinese gown and black satin brocade jacket.

Chapter Seven

馬

"I was staying at my younger sister's, your fifth maternal aunt. Her husband was starting his work at the Ministry of Foreign Affairs in Nanjing." My mother reached for another Pall Mall, noticed I was looking, then put it back down and continued. "I had just finished helping them get married and settling them down close to the Foreign Legations."

I had started to tell her to stop smoking when I began to read the warnings about lung cancers. It was also around the time I was starting medical school. She tried and then started back up the next time I visited her.

She looked at me now, acknowledging my earlier pleadings.

"You see I only smoke a few puffs, then I put it out."

I could see the half-smoked cigarette ends filling her ashtray. As if acceding to my admonitions, she took a sip of from her covered teacup, then continued with her story.

"Your *Waipo* was already dead for a few years by then, and my sister's husband came from very humble beginnings. With my mother gone and my father's money disappearing with the concubine, I paid for everything at their wedding."

I could still hear the satisfaction and pride when she told me what she was able to do for her sister in Nanjing. Yet I also remembered how betrayed my mother had felt when she discovered this same sister and her husband used her funds without her consent when she came to this country a quarter century later.

My mother thought she had found safe shelter in my aunt and uncle's home when we first came to this country.

I remembered staying at their chicken farm in New Jersey that summer for a couple of weeks before going off to college. They had advised her to deposit money into their account shortly after her arrival, but when she asked to withdraw some funds, they told her they had used it for some expenses on their farm.

"We'll give you spending money when you need it." When my mother expressed concern, her sister told her, "Don't worry, we'll pay you back. My husband said to tell you, he won't take your widow's money."

To my mother, this was not only the betrayal, but they were treating her as if she had already lost her husband—when my father did not come with us to this country and stayed in Taiwan. It was another thirteen years before my parents divorced and close to thirty before my father died.

It was a betrayal my mother could never forgive. She did not mention this when it happened, but I remember being surprised when I got her call from New York telling me she had moved from their home.

My own memories of that short stay at my aunt's chicken farm were quite different from my mother's. One of my cousins introduced me to some pleasures of my body I had not experienced with other boys before. It started in the outdoor shower in back of their barn after I helped him with the chicken feed and continued in the attic where we slept at night. I was looking forward to spending more time at his home for our first Christmas in the New World.

My mother, needing a place to live, turned to her old friend now living in New York. This was the same friend who was protective of her the night they went dancing with friends in the ballroom of the Peking Hotel when she met the Last Emperor and noticed my father at a different table.

The friend found a room for my mother in a safe home close to Columbia University after she told him she could no longer stay with her sister. When I visited her over the Christmas holidays from school, he invited us to lunch at the Hotel Pierre off Fifth Avenue.

Still dapper past sixty, he had peppered hair combed straight back, and was impeccably dressed in a well-tailored jacket and trousers with a kerchief in his breast pocket. My mother told me to call him Uncle Ju. His voice was soft and low, with a grand-fatherly cadence and reassurance. I was touched by and can still remember his solicitous attention to my mother and me throughout the afternoon.

When we got back to my mother's place by the taxi he paid, my mother anticipated the question in my mind, after being treated to such luxury. The last time I was in such a sumptuous setting was when she took me to the Park Hotel in Shanghai, after the Japanese surrender at the end of the War.

"Uncle Ju is still working as the personal secretary of T. V. Soong." My mother said in a hushed voice, not wanting her land-lady to hear.

"T. V. Soong?" I tried to understand.

"Madame Chiang Kai-shek's brother and once Premier of China." She answered in a tone as if that was a fact everybody should know, a little annoyed that I didn't lower my voice enough.

"How long has he been Soong's secretary?" I asked after we got into my mother's room and shut the door.

"That's a long story." My mother took off her heels and got into her slippers. "It started with the Xian Incident and the Young Marshal."

I remembered reading about the man nicknamed the "Young Marshal" and how he instigated the famous Xian Incident, which played a significant role in the contemporary Chinese history and made him a folk hero in the minds of many Chinese.

Between cups of jasmine tea in the covered cup she bought in New York's Chinatown, the first item she bought after settling into her rented room, my mother filled in the details on the political soap opera with serious consequences, which affected Uncle Ju directly.

Young Marshal Zhang, dashing and with a reputation of having stirred the hearts of many eligible young women of the day, stepped into his father's shoes in 1928. His powerful warlord father, who ruled most of Manchuria, was assassinated by the Japanese in the well-known bombing incident of his railway car at Huanggutun. He had to be eliminated in the island nation's grand scheme to take over China's Northeast.

After their success in killing Zhang's father, it was not hard for them to entice the naive and inexperienced Last Emperor, who was from the dynasty of Manchurian origins, living in exile in Tientsin to become the Puppet Ruler of Manchuria, establishing it as a separate country of Manchukoku. This gave the Japanese easy access to their continued push into the Chinese heartland.

My mother's intimate knowledge of this era captivated me as if watching a grainy, old film of the war, which I remembered only through the eyes of a young child. I relived this history through her experience with people she had known personally, and I was captivated by the immediacy of her descriptions.

"Why didn't Chiang Kai-shek want to fight the Japanese?" I asked, remembering having read about his reluctance from descriptions of the Xian Incident.

"He barely consolidated his control of the government in the South." Then she added, "Old Chiang always put his own interests and power above everything else. He wanted to eradicate Mao Zedong's communists who were regrouping themselves in the northwestern provinces, after he almost decimated them in a coup of 1927."

In the case of the Xian Incident, she explained what occurred behind the scenes while Chiang was going against strong popular support for a United Front in face of the Japanese invasion. "He consented to a meeting in Xian, brokered by the Young Marshal, between Chiang's KMT and Mao Zedong's communists. Old Chiang had initially hoped to convince the Young Marshal and the local warlord, who had control of the ancient Tang Dynasty capitol, Xian, and the Eastern end of the old Silk Road, to come over to his side and help eliminate Mao's communists instead of defending China against the Japanese invaders."

During the night in Xian, Chiang was caught by surprise when the Young Marshal's soldiers overcame his guards and dragged him out from the hillside compound where he was staying.

"Old Chiang was woken up in his sleep and tried to escape out of a window, leaving his dentures behind." I could see my mother's pleasure in retelling the humiliation of the man she always regarded as a corrupt opportunist who married Soong Mei-ling, the younger sister of the widow of the republic's founding father, to advance his own career.

"He was caught and brought in front of the Young Marshal, disheveled and toothless. Chiang was then forced to sign an agreement of cooperation with the communists to build a united front to fight the Japanese."

Her pleasure was short lived. The Young Marshal guaranteed Chiang's safe return by accompanying the man back to the Southern Capitol, Nanjing. On arrival in his own territory, Chiang promptly arrested the young man and wanted to have him executed for treason.

"That's when Uncle Ju went to work for T. V. Soong."

"Why?" I wanted to hear more of details, not fathoming the interconnections between these people and the incident in Xian.

"T. V. Soong was American-educated and sympathetic to the fate of the Young Marshal. He was also Madame Chiang's brother." My mother explained it was rumored that he resigned from Chiang's

7

馬

government in protest because of Chiang's reluctance to fight the Japanese, and the Incident in Xian was popularly considered a very brave and patriotic act by the Young Marshal.

After Chiang had arrested the Marshal, in sympathy, Soong decided to hire the Young Marshal's right-hand man to be his personal secretary. He was my mother's old friend, and Uncle Ju was to work for Soong over more than three decades.

My mother picked up her teacup, but her desire to continue with the story overtook that for her jasmine.

"Soong Mei-ling, or Mme. Chiang as Americans call her, and her brother prevented Old Chiang from killing Young Marshal Zhang because they were both sympathetic to him, but for different reasons. She was rumored to have been a secret admirer of the dashing Young Marshal herself before her marriage of mutual convenience to Chiang. Uncle Ju started working for T. V. Soong shortly after that Xian Incident in 1936. The year I married your father."

Many years later, on a visit to my father in Taiwan, I was at the same table with the Young Marshal and his wife. The daring young man of history was nearly eighty but still under house arrest and could not leave the island. A mutual friend had asked me to deliver a memento to him. He was very gracious, and his wife was sociable throughout the dinner with the other women sitting at the table. I remembered my mother had told me the wives of the Young Marshal and Uncle Ju were both well-known figures in the society pages of their times. I saw no hint of the flamboyance in an often-quoted line in a poem satirizing their earlier lives in the thirties, *Zhao Si Feng Liu, Zhu Wu Kuang*. Zhao was the Marshal's last wife who was at the dinner table, and Zhu was the wife of Uncle Ju. Zhu was also the undercover messenger for a letter from the late Chinese Premier Zhou En-lai, who was concerned about the well-being of the Young Marshall in Taiwan. The premier admired the Young Marshall's courage when they were both in Xian at the time of the incident.

After Old Chiang and his son who succeeded him in the KMT both died, the man who followed them as President in Taiwan, permitted the old man who was once the Young Marshal to leave the island. By then he was already in the ninth decade of his long life. My father had also passed away and I no reason to visit Taiwan regularly. But I read that with his wife's consent the Young Marshal was able to come to the U. S. and be reunited for a few months with an old admirer of his. The admirer was a friend of my mother's at the mahjong table from time to time and the stepmother of the architect I. M. Pei. They all shared a common hometown of Suzhou. There is a folk saying in China, *Suzhou chu mei ren*, beauties come from Suzhou.

My mother stood up and hurriedly emptied her ashtray into the trash bin under the kitchen sink as if to get rid of the evidence of her smoking. Before she went back to telling more about her early days with my father, I saw the satisfied smile on her face as she noticed how much I was enjoying her food during my breaks from school.

From her apartment near Columbia University, she was now working and studying hard to keep up with graduate school in education herself. Two years later, she got her Master's degree and was chosen to present a bouquet to the prima ballerina absoluta Galina Ulanova who was visiting New York and honored at Columbia. My mother spoke to Ulanova in fluent Russian and talked about St. Petersburg when they were both younger. But I should not digress from what I wanted to hear about my parents.

"My room in Nanjing was the upstairs study of my sister's home. Tall, corner windows and a view of the street below, lined with French sycamores." That was almost a quarter century before the time we went to stay at her sister's chicken farm when we first arrived in America.

7
馬

"'You see the car parked at a distance down the street?' your father asked one evening when he came to visit me. 'It's keeping an eye on your front door.' He pointed out I was being watched by the Blue Shirts."

"The Blue Shirts?" I asked.

"They were Old Chiang's feared Secret Police headed by Dai Li."

Dai Li, that was a name I could not forget. It was only a few months after the War ended in Shanghai of 1945.

My mother moved us into a larger apartment. She hired new help and a cook, hung up old family scrolls, and bought new hardwood furniture.

It was as if our household woke up from hibernation overnight to become a place overflowing with friends and strangers. My father was not the first to return after the end of the Japanese Occupation.

One night after dinner, my mother said it was time for me to go to bed. "But it's too early for my bedtime," I protested.

"Then I want you to stay in your room."

"But why?" Being an only child without the company of sisters or brothers, I was not used to being excluded from her friends and visitors.

"I will explain later." My mother said in a tone I understood left no room for negotiation.

I heard my mother instruct the servants she was not to be disturbed after they served the tea and cut fruit.

This made me all the more curious. I plastered my ears against the side door from the hallway into the living room. The maid saw me and tried to pull me away, but I wasn't going to listen to her.

It felt like an hour, but probably only ten minutes later I could hear a series of footsteps on the hard wood floor from the direction of the front entrance into the living room, followed by men's voices I had never heard before.

I couldn't catch what they were saying. I was getting bored in the hallway when suddenly I heard footsteps coming toward the door next to me. I barely had time to duck back, before it opened. I had to pretend I was on my way to use the bathroom. The same kind of quick subterfuge I had become adept, if my mother suddenly popped into my room and caught me playing with myself.

Leaving my bedroom door open was at my own bidding in the beginning. As a toddler, I was afraid of being left in a room by myself, but later I suspect it was my mother's way of checking up on me when she discovered I was doing something she thought would ruin my mind.

My mother thought of herself as thoroughly modern, but Victorian ideas of child upbringing from the West were still considered the most up to date in the China of those days. Self-abuse characterized pretty well parental attitude on the subject, with emphasis on the last word.

A thin man about mother's height, dressed in an open-collared shirt and dark trousers, followed my mother to the doorway. I noticed his unusually high receding hairline and ashen complexion as if he just stepped off the couch of an opium den. I had seen my mother's old friend, Auntie Lu, using it when we paid our respects at her home on Chinese New Year. The man's eyes fixed on me like searchlights in the night when sirens shrieked to warn us of unexpected airplane raids toward the end of the War.

"Address him as Big Uncle Dai!" My mother told me.

"He looks like you." I heard the man say.

He didn't say anything to me. But I remembered the chill of his hand on mine, like the time our cook let me touch a dead fish on the chopping board, just cleaned out and ready for dinner that evening. I did not like his strange, crooked smile, further distorting the dark shadows on his face. My mother had the right words

7

馬

for it. *Pi xiao ro bu xiao.* A grimace that barely moves surface skin but none of the underlying flesh.

He knew my mother well enough to call her, San Mei, meaning Number Three Younger Sister. He continued to ignore me, as I stood around awkwardly. I was glad he didn't linger too long next to me.

I noticed the other men still standing as if at attention on the other side of the living room. None of them came over to me. My mother soon called for the maid to put me to bed.

She did not mention anything more about Big Uncle Dai at breakfast the next morning. He and his men came several more times. Always when the streets outside were dark and never with much notice ahead of time. Above all, I resented being hustled off to bed early.

One of the men who usually came with him showed up unannounced one afternoon after their visit the evening before. I was not hustled out of the room that day.

He talked to my mother in a hushed voice that I could hardly hear, and I saw the color drain from my mother's face.

After the man had left, I asked my mother what happened. She said Dai Li's plane crashed after he left us the evening before.

Being accustomed to her usual calm even when there was trouble, I was concerned by the loss of composure on my mother's face.

"Is he dead?" I asked.

"And the people with him on their plane." Her muffled answer.

I remembered thinking it was something terrible when my mother told me the poet, Xu Zhimo, had died in a plane crash, after we visited his widow, Auntie Lu, and I thought about the faces of those men around him the night before. Somber, no nonsense serious, and one of them as young and good looking as a cousin of mine who was beginning his studies at St. Johns' University in Shanghai.

The man who brought the news remained a friend. He and his wife met my mother again in the Bay Area many years later.

The couple chose the same cemetery as my mother. Every year on *Qing Ming,* Chinese Memorial Day, when we bring my mother's favorite foods and fruits to her grave, I see the gravestone of that couple next to my mother's. The husband was the lucky one who got away and ended his old age in peace.

7
馬

"I thought you were friends," I asked my mother at the kitchen table. She had said earlier Dai Li was the other reason she could only marry my father clandestinely. Puzzled, I looked at her, chopsticks still in my hand holding a piece of chilled cucumber from the dish in front of me. She was waiting for me to have another mouthful of her Shanghai duck.

"Yes. But he also wanted to marry me." I put the cucumber into my mouth and felt embroiled in the suspense and complicated plot lines worthy of an Alfred Hitchcock film.

"But why does that mean you can't marry Diedi?"

I had heard the simpler version of this from my mother when I was younger. They were like other scenes in the floating world of a childhood puzzle which had not coalesced into anything coherent, and I had never really tried to figure out the pieces. In that distant world of my childhood, I took everything my mother said at face value, without trying to understand anything beyond the words. From her standpoint, it was probably also too complicated to explain all the details to a child of eight or ten.

Across the kitchen table from her that night, I still could not disentangle her convoluted reasoning, yet like a child listening to a favorite bedtime ghost story, I wanted to hear it again, hoping to finally understand the connection between my mother's clandestine marriage and the dark figure of Dai Li.

"In those days in Nanjing, I was working as an unofficial interpreter for the French ambassador, and there were quite a few men after me. Dai Li was one of them," she continued, straightening up her back. I also detected the subtle change of satisfaction in the tone of her voice.

While I still seemed confused, she looked at me with a hint of impatience, "My darling son. You're still too innocent and have become accustomed to the simple, straight forward ways of the Western world." I realized these were similar to words her good friend said to her at the Peking Hotel after her return from many early years spent outside of China.

She took in a breath and relit the Pall Mall she was fingering.

"You see, I don't inhale that much." That was her comeback to my continued pleas for her to stop smoking." It keeps me company."

When I pushed harder, her pat answer was she would stop when I moved in with her after I finished my education.

"I suppose it was my fault to bring you here when you were so young."

She stepped into her parental role again, which always annoyed me but I held my tongue. The desire to hear more was stronger, about that world of Nanjing, the early Capitol of the KMT, filled with deals and betrayals, eliminations by assassination.

"Dai Li threatened to get rid of whomever I would marry if I didn't marry him."

A two-volume biography of this man had come out a few years earlier, a man who has been called the Heinrich Himmler of Chiang's regime.

I read when Sun Yat-sen, the founder of First Republic died, he left the KMT, the party he founded, in the hands of three people. Chiang was one of the triumvirate. When he decided quickly he had to get rid of his rivals, he recruited Dai Li to do the job.

Dai excelled in quietly decimating Chiang's opposition and was named the head of Chiang's Secret Service. I thought how apt he chose the Chinese character *Li* for his own name when I looked up its meaning: the hooded veil of an assassin.

"He had a reputation. *Sha ren bu zha yen*," my mother continued about Dai Li.

Killing without batting an eye. The dark figure who came to our home after night fall in Shanghai seemed to be standing in front of me again, with that grimace, masking any movement of his facial muscles of expression.

"He was in charge of the Blue Shirts, modeled after the Nazi's Brown Shirts. Everybody was afraid of them."

"But you got married anyway." I thought of the picture of the hooded assassin and the wedding photo of my parents.

"No." Then quickly, she corrected herself, "Yes. Yes, I married him. But publicly I married his assistant, Mr. Zhou."

Mr. Zhou was the man in the Western morning coat in the wedding portrait, the one I was calling Baba till I was eight. After my father returned from the War, he became Uncle Zhou to me.

Her story still didn't completely unravel the mystery of their marriage to me. I continued to listen and waited for her to reveal more layers and details in the story.

"Your father was the one who thought of the plan." I heard the tenderness in her tone of admiration of my father. "The night before the wedding, he sent out invitations announcing my marriage to his good friend and assistant, Mr. Zhou. These were hand delivered by people who worked for them at the Ministry of Railways."

"Because his assistant would not be a recognized name socially, very few people would notice, and your father gambled it wouldn't catch Dai Li's attention."

She finally took in a mouthful of rice with a piece of duck breast, then lit another cigarette, and I heard more about how my father out maneuvered the man whose name was known to send shivers down people's spine in Chiang's China from the late thirties to the forties.

"At the same time, your father secretly arranged for a special Pullman car, to be attached to the night freight train, waiting at a station just outside of the city of Nanjing. He wanted to avert any possibility of encountering Dai's Blue Shirts swarming over the main train station in the capitol. Right after the ceremony, we were driven to the Pullman, and the train took off as soon as we got on."

"But was Uncle Zhou left behind? Couldn't Dai Li have killed him?" Dai Li was well known for his ruthless and relentless elimination of Chiang Kai-shek's opposition. I was puzzled how Uncle Zhou was able to live with us for four years under the Japanese Occupation in Shanghai afterward.

"By the time the news got out, I was already married. *Mi yi cheng zhou.* The rice was already cooked, and your father's assistant was not a big enough figure for Dai Li to bother with. I was also relieved to hear he got involved with Hu Die."

"Who is Hu Die?" My mother's conversation often sprinkled with names I had to ask for details to fully comprehend.

"Haven't heard of Hu Die?" She didn't seem to realize that was her glittering world before the war started and I never lived in. She had to explain the woman was probably the first movie star of the Chinese screen.

"Anyway," she continued, "Luckily, the whole country's attention was soon diverted by the Marco Polo Bridge Incident in July 1937, when the Japanese started their attack and all-out war erupted in the North. Chiang's attention and the whole country focused on the war effort. It overtook everything and everybody's life."

That was about all I could absorb for the evening.

Seeing my eyelids droop, she got up from her chair and started to clear the table. I offered to wash the dishes.

"You look tired from the trip. Go to bed."

When she saw my hesitation, she added, "I can do them much faster."

I said good night and headed toward the bathroom. As I walked past her bedroom, I noticed the new biography of Dai Li on top of a pile of Chinese books on the bedside table.

I wondered whether she found herself in those volumes. But I never got a chance to ask. Now the book is stacked in the back row of my bookshelf, among the books in Chinese she left behind after she died.

My mother didn't get around to tell me more what was bothering her lately when I first walked in that evening. The past seemed to have overtaken the present in her telling.

Head on my pillow that night, I imagined a black sedan with curtains drawn in the back and my father's chauffeur dashing and dodging through the poorly lit side streets and alleys of Nanjing that evening of their wedding, always watching in the rear view for Dai Li's Blue Shirts in pursuit, until he finally got to the small railway stop outside of the city. My parents rushed into the Pullman attached to the back of the night train, and the conductor was told to take off immediately.

To this day, I have a special attraction for overnight train rides, even if a private Pullman car would have to be purely a pipe dream. I like to believe I was conceived on that night train ride out of Nanjing.

I wasn't sure if the lightheadedness I felt when I tossed and turned under the bedcover was from an overload of information from my mother or the sips of Courvoisier throughout the evening. Unhappily I had inherited my mother's intolerance of alcohol, not my father's oversized ability to put away liquor. He'd told me stories about the sake drinking contests of his days at the Imperial University in Tokyo. The ability to hold down liquor was considered a measure of the man.

As I was drifting off that night, I wondered how my mother let a man like Dai Li get so close to her, yet able to keep him at bay from forcing her to marry him. Was she intimidated by his ruthless reputation, or was there some subconscious attraction to the sinister power he wielded?

I remembered Dai Li calling my mother *San Mei*, a younger sister, a term associated with some affection, used between close friends or family. I remembered my mother's loss of composure when she got the news of his plane crash. It was not an expression of good riddance but more of profound loss of someone dear to her.

It was not until the next morning that she got to the reason for what had been bothering her when I arrived the night before. An air letter stamped from Taiwan was on the breakfast table. I recognized my father's calligraphy on the envelope, every elegant stroke executed with deliberation.

On an earlier visit, my mother told me about rumors he had another woman in his life. A woman my mother once considered a friend, who had even given my mother an elegant piece of soft British wool for a dress when she visited us on a trip from Hong Kong.

"Her husband used to work for your father." My mother added with a touch of bitterness. "Before that, he worked for Chennault. When Chennault left China, your father gave him a job."

Heretofore Claire Chennault was a name I often heard mentioned in my father's conversations with his friends about their work in transport and supplies for the interior war effort in China. My father was in charge of the supply route from Burma. Chennault started the Flying Tigers, the fledgling Air Force of China, which was not only involved in combat with the Japanese, but also in the war time transport of supplies. Later his Chinese wife became quite an operator in the Chinese lobby of Washington D. C. on behalf of the KMT.

Next to her cup of morning coffee, I could see such a raging fire in my mother's eyes that I had never seen before as she waited for me to read my father's letter. She tapped the ashes of her Pall Mall into the ashtray as if she was trying to tamp down the flames within herself.

I followed the lines of his calligraphy, remembering how carefully he usually chose his words. The words were not at all like those of the Cantonese love poem he once wrote about her.

Down the middle of the page, I came across the line,

I have doubts he is my son.

The rest of his lines became a blur. I could hardly raise my eyes to meet my mother's. I felt stabbed and discarded by the man I once looked up to so much. This was quickly followed by the realization that I was therefore illegitimate. I was a bastard. There was no place for me in the world I was brought up.

I did not want to be in front of anybody at that moment, not even my mother. Deep down I felt she was involved in putting me in that place.

I did not want to look at my mother, but I couldn't avoid her eyes. The fire in them had liquefied into a tearful veil over her eyes.

She finally collected herself and said, "That was why I took an overdose in Shanghai."

Chapter Eight

"You are looking more like your father!" Adele pointed to the picture of him at sixty on my bookshelf. He was sitting in a wicker armchair in his tropical Taipei garden. The photo captured a rare smile, taken ten years before my parents' divorce. Smiles were considered frivolous in front of a camera, especially for men who took themselves seriously.

Meant as a compliment from Adele, I was not sure whether I liked the comparison to my father. I never thought of him as good looking.

Looks belonged to my mother. Secretly, I always preferred the warm reflection from the glow of her radiant presence.

Er zi xiang niang, jing zi da qiang is a Chinese folk saying in Mandarin my mother liked hearing. Gold bricks for walls when the son looks like his mother was an image my mother's friends liked to say in front of her, nodding their heads in fervent affirmation like at a revival meeting. In the hand-colored picture from our family album with me, at six-years old, standing obediently beside my mother seated in an armchair, the resemblance was unmistakable.

Yet, when I was first told this man was my real father, I wanted to be like him. My real father, down to every detail.

I was eight, tucked in for the night inside a mosquito net reaching all the way to the tall ceiling. A small floor fan hummed in the corner, making a soft cackle as it changed direction when it reached one end of its cycle. The fan made barely tolerable those hot muggy July nights of Shanghai when the humidity rose as high as the mercury in the thermometer dangling from the wall, and only those who have lived through them firsthand could have appreciated. Americans had not yet brought in the miracle insecticide DDT to post World War II Shanghai, which was once considered the Paris of Asia and its most modern city.

A shaved head, back lit by the hallway light into a huge incandescent halo, loomed outside the filmy, bridal veil folds of the mosquito net over my bed. Startled, I opened my eyes. Only the big smile on my mother's face behind this abrupt apparition and the familiarity of the blossoms on the apple-green Western house dress she liked to wear at home when no outsiders were around assured me this was not a late summer evening ghost story coming to life.

"Your father is back!" I heard my mother's voice, but it was overly enthusiastic. A tone I was familiar with, when she wanted me to comply with her wishes.

Rubbing my eyes, trying to make sense out of the confusion whirling in my half awakening world, I wondered what happened to the man I called 'Baba' for as far back as my memory could carry? Even he was like a phantom, appearing suddenly every few months, then just as quietly disappeared for many months on end. I learned not to ask too many questions, during those years of our submerged lives under the Japanese Occupation.

The full meaning of the haloed figure outside my mosquito net was almost too much for my eight-year-old mind to fathom, awakened from a dream on that midsummer night.

"*Jiao Day-dee!*" My mother's voice again, this time urging me to address that apparition.

"*Di-E.*" I managed to mumble the words for father in Mandarin.

"He's only half awake." I heard the strange, mellow voice say to my mother. "Let him sleep!"

Di-E-di was what I started to call him. Pidgin English for Daddy, adapted by Chinese into Western ways in the Shanghai of those days. *Maa-mi* was pidgin for Mommie, what I called my mother, instead of Ma, Ma-ma or Niang, more familiar in traditional China.

My father's arrival coincided with the end of the eight-year Sino-Japanese War, the last four years are better known as the Second World War in the West after the Japanese bombed Pearl Harbor. Before that Japan thought it had China close to its knees in the four years of steady advance from Manchuria in the northeastern part of China against a poorly equipped Chinese army and sometimes factionalized government.

The war's end was a year full of flourishes for my mother. We moved from our place of seclusion to a large, airy flat owned by a White Russian near the center of the French Concession.

My mother bought a new bedroom set of mahogany, with a huge three-paneled mirror above the vanity, as if to reassure herself it was now safe to see ourselves and the whole world more clearly, after our years of subterranean existence in the occupied city under assumed names.

She brought out her silks and embroidered gowns, mothballed during years in storage.

I got a new name, *Shao Qiu*, from the man who was my new father. The second character in the name, *Qiu*, was part of the name he chose for himself, which meant a globe, or more simply, ball. The first character, *Shao*, was a Chinese homonym for Junior. So I became the Junior Globe or Little Ball. The Little Ball of me wanted to be like him, the Big Ball, in every way.

The morning after his apparition outside of my mosquito net, I found my new father surrounded by men in our sitting room. Many of them spoke in a dialect foreign to me, unlike the Mandarin I used with my mother, and unlike the dialect of the local Shanghai people. To me, they sounded as if they were speaking with their noses pinched between their fingers.

One of his friends started to tease me. "You'll have to learn to speak Cantonese, if you're going to be the Little Ball and follow in his footsteps."

My father decided to ask his old friend to start my education in Cantonese through poetry. Uncle Lu, the good friend, chanted the lines the way they were taught as little boys. One of the first pieces chosen for me was the *Chu Shi Biao*, an ode written by the famous Zhuge Liang to the young, last descendant of the Han Dynasty before the prime minister set out for battle to reclaim the realm of the Han.

Clearing his throat after a sip of Iron Goddess, the strong, dark, liquor-like Fukienese tea favored by my father and his friends, lines of the long poem rolled off Uncle Lu's tongue like verses to the music and rhythms of Cantonese Opera.

"Tsen leong yeen:
Seen dai tsong yip mei boon,
yee zong tou bun tsou.
Gum teen haa sam fen . . ."

Seeing that I didn't understand a word, he proceeded to explain the meaning of every line, then had me follow him as his voice danced up and down those strange nasal rhythms, round after round.

That was how I first learned to speak my father's tongue. The undulating melody of that ode in Cantonese came back into my ears over half a century later, when I saw its lines carved in stone steles at the tomb of this legendary Prime Minister of the last Han Dynasty ruler, when Adele and I visited China's western province of Sichuan. I wanted to linger longer in front of those words carved in stone, to relive that short golden period of my childhood when my father came into my life. Not knowing its significance to me, the tour group rushed us ahead to see the next site.

My mother used to tease my father about his Mandarin, spoken with a strong Cantonese accent. *Tian bu pa, di bu pa, jiu pa guang dong ren shuo guan hua.* This was a common put down of the Cantonese Southerners trying to speak the official Northern dialect.

My father maintained his customary calm composure, when the words at his expense echoed through the room: Fear not the heavens above, nor the earth below, but do fear the Cantonese speaking Mandarin. Then one day I heard him tease my mother back with evidence the famous Tang Dynasty poems rhymed much smoother in Cantonese than in Mandarin.

"This indicated the southern Cantonese dialect had firmer and older roots than your Mandarin from the North." He had the last word in that conversation with my mother, fortified, no doubt by the studies of Chinese historical linguistics published by Bernhard Karlgren, the pioneering linguistic sinologist of early twentieth century.

Early mornings my father sought to pull me into his passion for Chinese calligraphy— sitting upright next to me at a long, dark wood table, commonly seen in the study of Chinese scholars, dressed in a soft silk shirt, worn by men in China over a millennium.

With patience and deliberation, he guided my hand in preparing the black ink for Chinese calligraphy, slowly grinding the coal black ink stick, which gradually released its faint, freshly burnt pine perfume. The circular motions made full moons in the dark emerging ink on a large stone with carvings of scrolls and seal script along its sides.

Even now, every time I pick up a calligraphy brush to write something in Chinese, the delicate scent of slightly burnt pine wood comes back to me, as well as the way I learned to slowly

grind the bottom of that ink stick onto the wet stone while droplets of water were dribbled slowly onto its smooth, slick surface.

"It's going to strengthen those muscles you will need to practice calligraphy properly," he explained when he saw me getting
bored by the repetitive arm and wrist motion.

"Also, it will teach you patience and deliberation." And later,
I learned those exercises were supposed to light the way on the art
of living my life. It was my father's way to teach by example, not
just words.

For my father, patience and deliberation were two character-
istics he honed to near perfection.

*Even if a large loaded truck ran over your father, he would not let
out a bubble of flatus,* was another way my mother liked to describe
him to her friends, and to me as I got older, when she got frustrated
by his calmness and imperturbability. That description in her perfectly inflected Pekinese dialect, with its hint of derision and impro-
priety in her choice of words, always made me giggle, and its rip-
pling effect would make her lose herself and laugh alongside me.

With my new name meaning a smaller version of my real father, I wanted to emulate him in every detail, the details I could
see as an eight-year-old.

I shaved my head and begged my mother to have an outfit
made for me like his. The *zhong shan zhuan,* was the uniform for
all government officials then, just as the dark suit and tie are for
Wall Street workers of today. It was named after the founder of
the First Republic, Sun Yat-sen, the name by which he is known
to the West. But in China, he is known as Sun Zhong Shan.

I have wondered what Chairman Mao thought years later,
waving his plump hand and fingers from the reviewing terrace
where Imperial Mandarins used to stand high above the gates of
the Forbidden City in Beijing, while wearing the outfit originally
named after the founder of the First Republic and the KMT, the

party Mao fought against before overtaking it in 1949. In the West, the uniform later became better known as the Mao jacket, along with the little Red Book of the Chairman's sayings.

In those months following my father's return, I became a puppy dog at his heels. He gave me the nickname, *Gau Zai*, puppy in Cantonese.

From the time of his Southern ancestors, there was the custom of naming a coveted child after a house pet or domestic animal, to shield it from the envy and anger of the Gods and hopefully, the various challenges of childhood. To the Chinese, perfection could bring about misfortune. Years later, I learned the Native American tribe Mimbres in the Southwest deliberately broke the bottoms of their exquisitely painted pottery to allow spirits to escape. But I am not sure this had anything to do with my father's choice. He was a man who ridiculed old Chinese superstitions when my mother brought them up.

My mother liked to bring up the apprehensions of the French doctor who delivered me about my health, as well as the warnings of the blind soothsayer she consulted. I suspect it was her way of subtly taking credit for having brought me up well despite these ominous odds.

Her perceived delicacy about me must have also imbued a sense of deep disappointment to my father, a man who prided himself on his physique, endurance and ability to out drink his peers when he was a student in pre-War Imperial Japan. I am certain it had something to do with his regarding me early on as a sissy.

Chapter Nine

猴

Aunt Fu, my mother's youngest sister, shook me awake. "I'm bringing you to the hospital." Thus began the early fall night, several months after my real father's return to Shanghai.

Instead of the beautiful Mandarin dresses she usually wore made from fashionable American prints her husband sent back from overseas, I noticed my aunt's clothes were hurriedly pulled on, her hair barely combed.

"Your mother is in the hospital." Then she quickly added, by way of reassurance. "But she is alright." I really didn't understand what she was trying to tell me, but she seemed frazzled, and I sensed she was grasping for words to comfort me.

The last time I saw my mother when she came into my room to make sure I was tucked into bed that evening, she looked no different to me. We had had a simple dinner that night because my father had gone to the Capitol, and my mother had the cook bring in some deep fried stinky tofu from the vendor. It was something my father hated as much as my mother disliked his strong cheeses from overseas.

I liked Aunt Fu the moment she came into my life, at the end of the War and the Japanese Occupation of Shanghai. To my eyes at eight, if there was anyone more beautiful than my mother, it would be my Aunt Fu. She spoke to me in a voice as soft and gentle as a lamb, the same Chinese zodiac sign under which my mother was born. We were barely eighteen years apart, but she became my security blanket when my mother was not around.

I thought of the night we were alone together, when my mother was out for the evening. An early summer thunderstorm struck. Bolts of lightning flashed, and rolling waves of thunder rumbled and crashed outside our windows, shaking the whole living room we were huddled in. She gripped my hands as tightly as I was hugging her. The realization that she was just as frightened as I felt drew me closer to her, more than any other of my grown-up relatives.

Several years ago, on the fortieth anniversary of her suicide during the Cultural Revolution, which had convulsed Mainland China to its core as Chairman Mao intended, I sent a remembrance to her daughter in Beijing. She wrote me back that she lit the poem in front of her mother's image in the columbarium, as an offering. The Chinese believed a burnt offering will reach the world of the deceased loved one.

That night when Aunt Fu hustled me out of bed, it was pitch black in the stairwell outside. She guided me down the stairs to the car, one hand over mine, the other holding a flickering flashlight. I was still trying to clear the webs of sleep in front of my eyes. Our driver was waiting, holding the door open to the back seat of our car. I could tell he had also been roused abruptly from his bed on our back balcony, still in his pajama pants and night shirt, instead of a regular shirt and proper trousers. I didn't have time to wonder when and how my mother got to the hospital.

I had never seen the streets of the French Concession of Shanghai so deserted and dark. The French sycamores, so alive during the day with their distinct patch-worked bark highlighted by filtered sunlight, were now murky shadows hovering ominously overhead. No one on the sidewalks, filled with chattering crowds during the day since the end of the war. No vendor on the corner hawking chestnuts from his large iron wok with the sweet smell of roasting molasses in the sand, heated by the glowing charcoals in his portable brazier.

In the backseat of the car, my aunt pulled my hands close. "Don't worry. Your mother is alright." She was saying it like a mantra, and I wondered what was happening to my mother.

The hospital itself was not unfamiliar to me. Its owner, Dr. King, was a friend of the family, and I often went to play in the large garden next to it. His youngest daughter was two years younger than me, and my favorite playmate. When we had our tonsils out on the same day, I was put in her suite of rooms on the top floor of the hospital where the family lived.

It was common in those days for children of close family friends to have their tonsils removed together. Ice cream was a rare treat for a special birthday before the war ended, but we could have as much as we wanted the day after our surgery. Even though Dr. King was a close friend, my mother liked to tell her friends, my hospital stay cost her a nugget of pure twenty-four-carat gold.

The hospital in darkness did not look familiar or friendly when we pulled up to its front entrance. I shuddered when we got out of the car. There was a chill in the damp night air, the few dim lights inside reminded me eerily of fireflies flickering in the dark at the end of ghost stories, the ones told by the governess when I stayed overnight with Dr. King's children in their summer home outside the city.

A nurse came out to meet us. The clock in the black square box was ticking on the wall. I could barely make out 2:55, the lights were so dim. The woman gave me a smile of reassurance. I recognized her as one of the nurses who took care of me after my tonsil surgery. After I was home from the procedure, my mother and I brought presents for many of them to thank them for taking such good care of me.

I took the nurse's reassurance now as yet another grownup trying to avoid telling me something ominous, while I just wanted to see my mother's face again.

She led us into the elevator, and I could hear its cables cranking us up slowly until it finally stopped on the third floor.

The upper hallway was even darker than the entry, only one small cone of light spread out from the room toward the end. My aunt continued to hold onto my hand and gave it a tighter squeeze. I turned my head to look at her for reassurance, but I couldn't make out her face clearly in the darkness.

When we stepped into the lit doorway, I could finally see my mother. She was propped up on the hospital bed, much higher than ours at home. My aunt cried out, "*San Jie!*" and rushed toward her Third Elder Sister.

When she realized she had let go of my hand she turned back to me. I could see tears filling her eyes.

Then I heard my mother's voice: "I'll be alright. Don't worry, my darling son!" The weak smile on her face looked forced, and her voice was not the bright, booming sound I was used to hearing. It was just above a whisper, so unlike her, as if she were trying to say sorry to me.

But, why was she sorry? I couldn't understand. I felt the same confusion in my head when I encountered the apparition over my bed a few months earlier and was told the man was my real father.

On that earlier occasion, at least I saw my mother's familiar green housedress and reassuring smile. Now I found myself standing in a completely cold, unfamiliar room.

My mother held out her hand, and I ran toward it. My aunt went around to the far side of the bed and took the other hand into hers. She stared at the tubes running out of my mother's arm. I saw her lips tremble and tears welled up her eyes again.

Six decades later, in a hospital bed after surviving a serious complication from an angioplasty in San Francisco, when my daughter stepped into my room, I finally understood the comfort and relief my mother must have felt on seeing me in her hospital room that night in Shanghai.

The hospital owner's wife, Mrs. King, appeared in the doorway as if she'd materialized out of thin air.

"So sorry to disturb your whole hospital at this hour!" I heard my mother say. Her voice was feeble as if she was trying to catch her breath.

That's when I noticed the bed linen under my mother was stained dark with blood. How I knew it was blood that night, I can't even now, many years later, explain. Although I had been in the hospital for my own surgery earlier, I had never seen so much blood in one place.

"Has her husband been notified?" Mrs. King turned her attention to address my aunt.

"He's on the way here by train from Nanjing." My aunt answered in a formal manner, which told me she was not pleased.

The woman then noticed the stained linen and quickly gave orders to the nurses, who herded us out of the room. On our way out, I heard one of the nurses telling Mrs. King in a low voice, "Don't worry. It'll wash out. She's having her period."

I didn't understand what the nurse said. But, growing up as an only child, I had always been more aware of the behavior of grownups around me, and I sensed Mrs. King was more concerned about something else instead of my mother's condition.

I remembered hearing the nurses grumble to my mother that the owner's new wife treated the staff very poorly ever since she married him. They confided in my mother they much preferred the first wife who was a physician herself and always treated the staff as professionals with respect and courtesy.

My aunt shepherded me out of the room by my hand toward the elevator. "We'll come back tomorrow. Your mother is really doing fine, and Dr. King is her close friend." She forced a smile for me.

In the back seat of our car, I sensed my aunt was more relaxed. But she told me she was not happy the owner's wife was more concerned about the soiled linens, instead of my mother's condition.

I asked my aunt why my mother was in the hospital. She motioned me with her finger to her lips to keep quiet. Then said in a low voice, "She took some wrong pills."

I wanted to ask what kind of pills. She made a familiar gesture. It meant I should hush up, and I understood she wasn't going to say anything more.

That night she stayed with me and slept in the guest room. The next morning, my father was back from the capitol. The servants scurried about their chores in hushed tones and seemed to be avoiding me, as if afraid of answering questions I might have.

But I overheard the words, "*Fu Du*," as they were talking amongst themselves. When they saw me, they quickly stopped what they were saying.

I asked my aunt what Fu Du meant. She asked me where I'd heard it. I told her from the servants' hushed conversation. "Don't listen to their gossip. They don't know anything."

The following days were a blur of buzzing activity. Trips to and from the hospital with my father who didn't have much to say to me, or my aunt choosing changes of clothing for my mother, bringing personal toiletries and things she needed, the foods she liked prepared by our cook at home, and being brought back home for my nap in the afternoon which my mother insisted I still needed.

I waited for the day she could come home, and things would be back to normal again. Although the servants and my aunt took care of everything I needed, without my mother at home, the place felt hollowed out, as if I was in the furniture section of the large Wing On department store downtown on the road to the Bund, all the pieces and fixtures were there, but they were waiting there alone, in unfeeling silence.

The day my father brought her home, my mother's face was as pale as the painted face of a Chinese opera singer. She walked in holding onto my father's arm. None of the bounce I was used to seeing, as if she left it behind, in the hospital.

There was a dullness in her eyes I'd never seen before. My father hovered over her with more attentiveness than I had ever noticed and treated her as if she was dying. He told the servants to prepare special foods for her to build up her strength.

I saw beautiful glass topped, brocade boxes with an ivory-colored root looking like a thin dried up carrot brought to the dining room table. The Cantonese maid said it was Korean ginseng to be steeped for hours for my mother to drink, instead of her favorite jasmine. She also made Cantonese soups with black-boned chickens the size of guinea hens, snapping turtles and packets of herbs from the herbalist in the old Chinese section of town, which our cook from Yangzhou was not familiar with preparing.

Over a few weeks my mother improved, and she started to venture out of bed. Seeing the worried look on my face, she drew me close and told me. "Don't worry, my darling son. I'll get well because of you."

Her voice softened, almost to a breaking point, then she hugged me tightly. I didn't comprehend everything she was trying to tell me. But I knew she loved me and would try to get well as quickly as possible.

The sight of the dark bloodstain on her bed not far from my mind and all those tubes on her arms, for the first time I realized I might have really lost the closest person in my life. But now she was back, and I felt a great sense of relief and welling up of love for her and the feeling that I had the greatest mother in the world.

It would take a much longer time for the sparkle in my mother's eyes to return. I could not remember how long it took in real time. It was something that came back gradually and then I realized she seemed to be her old self again.

Chapter Ten

雞

A month after my mother came home from the hospital, my father left for Manchuria to take over the Manchurian Railways, which had been controlled by the Japanese Occupation. It was the most challenging job in the Ministry of Transportation immediately after the war, because the Russians to the north were already secretly helping the Chinese Communist guerrilla forces to try and overtake that area. With his experience of managing the transport of supplies from the Burma Road during the war, he was felt to be the best person to take on the job.

In our home in Shanghai, late autumn was the best time of the year. The sycamores lining the streets of the French Concession were still providing shelter from the sun. Their stippled leaves, large enough to be used as fans for delicate ladies, helped the occasional breeze coming in from the mouth of Yangtze River as it empties into the East China Sea. Their colors, from gold to rust, added to the palette of their already well-decorated trunks.

My mother found a tutor for me during the day, to start my education in Chinese literature, history, and geography.

"You will like him. He is a classmate of your favorite cousin." My mother sought to reassure me because these were going to be the first formal lessons I ever had. During the Japanese Occupation my mother was afraid of sending me to public schools, afraid our identity would be discovered by the Japanese. Now she refrained from sending me to a public school because she was going to join my father in the North and won't be home to see how I would fit into a regular school regimen.

The cousin my mother referred to was the youngest of three sons in his family, the tallest and best looking. He was active in progressive student politics at St. John's University and sometimes dropped by to talk to my mother and ask for her advice. His own mother was an ideal wife of the old tradition, superbly skilled in maneuvering and managing their complicated household but didn't have any formal education. My mother had first been educated abroad and then at one of the prestigious universities in Beijing and he knew she had strong opinions about the corrupt government. When he came to our home, he always had a big smile for me.

From our first meeting, I liked the tutor my cousin recommended. I called him Ruan Laoshi. Teacher Ruan's gentle manner and sympathetic eyes made me feel he was a friend. He never raised his voice with me.

"Today we'll talk about the last Ruler of the Han Dynasty." He always made me feel I was going to hear a good story. He first introduced the historical context, then meticulously filled in the details of the battles and maneuvers. Soon he had me entranced in a continuous series of interconnected tales. The unexpected plot turns and intrigue between rulers and usurpers, loyalists and treacherous courtiers could easily rival the historical soap operas on BBC today.

We started at the end of the Han Dynasty, two-hundred-twenty A. D. when China was split into Three Kingdoms. The dynasty has a legendary quality for the Chinese. Even today I often hear Chinese referring to themselves as the People of Han. It was a period of many battles, bonding and betrayals, the worlds of Star Wars and Harry Potter combined for me as a preteen Chinese boy.

At eight, I thought the most intriguing hero of the Three Kingdom period was Zhuge Liang. He was an Obi Kenobi-like figure coaxed out of his hermitage by the last descendant of the Han Dynasty to become the premier and help defend the kingdom, which had already splintered into three fiefdoms.

I was already familiar with the premier's famous ode when my father's friend initiated me in singsong Cantonese during my first lessons learning to speak the dialect of my father's South. My tutor further elaborated on Zhuge Liang's Solomon-like wisdom and wizardry passed down through the centuries. For a few pennies, Chinese school children could sit on little bamboo stools by the street stalls and read about some of the more spectacular feats in little books for children.

Teacher Ruan was an accomplished student of Chinese history. He turned the famous battles into numerous webs of mystery. With each lesson, he spun the yarn of one episode, the characters involved and their background, the terrain of the battles, the layout of the courts, the interconnections of the characters.

One episode was called 'Borrowing the wind from the east. '

"How could that happen?" I was mesmerized and puzzled.

"Among the many facets of his knowledge, Zhuge Liang was a serious student of meteorology," my tutor then explained assiduously.

"From the stars and their movement and positions, he could calculate and foretell the change in wind direction and pattern." Wide-eyed, I waited to hear how the sorcerer pulled off his magical trick.

"But he also carefully staged elaborate religious rites to make people believe he indeed had magical powers to sway the Gods and change the elements. Thus, he sailed his much smaller fleet of boats against a much larger enemy armada. With a combination of knowledge and surprise attack when the wind direction shifted suddenly he was able to destroy the stronger naval forces his kingdom was facing. From that victory, people attributed magical powers to this last premier of his kingdom."

I was hooked and looked forward to Teacher Ruan's arrival every morning, ready for him to pull out my lesson from the blue cotton bag he carried with him. It was like being at an early version of an unending soap opera of different historical episodes and intrigues in my own study and it made my learning how the dynasties and emperors flowed from one into the next a pleasure instead of a drudging pain.

When my mother joined my father in Manchuria a month later, my attention was well diverted by the mornings with Teacher Ruan. In the evenings, my favorite aunt joined me for dinner and stayed till past my bedtime.

"Please stay with me overnight," I begged Aunt Fu when she put me to bed.

"I have to be with your cousins Qin and Mei because they don't have anybody to stay with them at night." In her soft and soothing voice, she made me see how lucky I was to have the servants around me all the time and if she stayed, her daughters would be left alone overnight. "Then, can I go home with you?" I asked.

"Yes, I'll bring you to play with them on weekends," she promised.

Her apartment was in the old British Concession of Shanghai, the dark brick houses crowded together. When I saw an illustrated translation of Dicken's London, I was reminded of them. My cousins were both younger and looked up to me as a big brother. My aunt allowed me to rig up traps for catching sparrows on her veranda, something my mother would never have allowed me to do at home.

Once, I even tried to cook the bird in soy sauce. I had seen sparrows on skewers once being sold in the market, but I didn't realize I first had to remove the feathers and clean the bird. When

I brought it to the table, my aunt had a pained look and told her maid to take it away.

"That was not a good idea," she said in a firm tone, although she did not seem to be angry with me. Her gentle disapproval made me lose interest in trying to do it again.

Many other things in her home could occupy my cousins and me. Card games, mahjong tiles, and manual string games, and even a set of Monopoly, which her husband had sent from the United States. I hated the end of the weekend when I had to go back home.

Although once I got home, I was happy when I realized Teacher Ruan had another story waiting.

During one of my lessons, I asked him, "What's the meaning of *Fu Du?*"

He looked at me for a moment in surprise, as if they were words that should not come out of the mouth of someone not quite nine years old, but he did not show any anger, the way my mother did when I repeated something crude that I had heard from the cook in the kitchen.

Teacher Ruan was silent for a moment, then he said quietly, the words *Fu Du* meant literally, to take poison.

My mother lying in the hospital bed with the blood stain on her linens, late that night in February, came back instantly in front of my eyes. I wondered what had made her do it. My tutor noticed the changes on my face and looked concerned.

"From where did you hear those words?" He asked.

"Oh, I heard the servants gossiping. They didn't want to tell me the meaning of the words," I said, trying to cover.

"Some words are too complicated for someone your age to bother with. They were probably talking about something that happened in the newspapers," he added thoughtfully, before directing my attention to the new lesson for the day.

His patient explanation only made me more curious. Years later I found out my tutor became a writer and scholar studying the role of Buddhism in China.

In my eight-year old world, I could not understand why someone I loved above anyone else would take poison and leave me. And how could someone who loved me so much be driven to take poison? In my mind, the idea of taking poison was only something dark and dangerous, but I really had no idea what it meant.

I already knew Aunt Fu wasn't going to tell me anything more, even if I begged. It was like when I came down with measles and whooping cough, when I felt I was being torn apart and the coughing was so bad it made me vomit. But I gradually got better, and the pain faded away into the cellars of my memory.

Late spring the following year, my mother brought home a Chinese folding album. Its antique, brocaded covers were framed in rosewood. On its front were four characters in old intricate Chinese seal script, *Mei Yi Yan Nian*, words wishing my parents many happy years together.

The album opened up onto many contiguous leaves of sumi, and watercolor paintings of plum blossoms and bamboo, symbols of happiness and durability, magpies for joy and Chinese calligraphy by well-known contemporary Chinese artists, with dedications celebrating the announcement of my parents' marriage. It was an album celebrating their union.

Years later I learned to read my father's grass-style calligraphy on the first two leaves. He used the occasion of my mother's fortieth birthday as a public revelation of their clandestine marriage ten years earlier. It had to be kept secret because of the special circumstances at that time.

On the same page, he also expressed his gratitude to Uncle Zhou who took care of us during my father's absence in those years under the Japanese Occupation. On the third and fourth leaves was Uncle Zhou's response in his own words.

A large black and white photograph, stuck between the yellowing leaves of the frayed, family album recorded the event around a long T- shaped table packed to overflowing with people and flowers at a formal banquet.

My mother was at the center of the picture making the first cut into a many-tiered birthday cake. The large embroidered rose below my mother's Mandarin collar stood out in the shimmering softness of her silk dress. I remembered she had that pale green gown made by her tailor in Shanghai before she left to join my father in Manchuria. He was seated next to her at the head of the table, looking up at her with a look of affection and adoration.

Thus began my slow process to piece together and understand the complicated arrangement and circumstances of my parent's marriage.

"That was the reason I took an overdose." My mother was finally explaining to me her act of *Fu Du*.

Over the years, her words from across the breakfast table of her New York apartment, when she showed me my father's letter denying paternity, have continued to percolate. It had churned inside me like a vat of soured soy milk.

Pieces of the mystery in her marriage and her overdose before the final public announcement gradually began to fit into the puzzle. But why was the question of my paternity connected with her *Fu Du* that night in Shanghai when I was eight? I still could not completely disentangle this in my mind.

I tried to remember Aunt Fu's words, when I asked her for a second time, a few days after she brought me to see my mother at the Hospital. Your mother was trying to protect your good name. I didn't understand those words then, but I felt I was somehow responsible for my mother's action. She did it for me.

Even though she was saved by her sister's call late that night when there was no answer on her phone, why did my mother have to risk her life to protect my good name?

From early childhood, I have seen my mother's visceral reaction against concubines. She blamed the death of her own mother on the First Concubine my grandfather brought into the family. I could imagine, in my mother's eyes, to be a concubine was to descend into the lowest level of human existence.

From the words in the brocaded album, I realized her own marriage to my father was not made known to the world for over a decade. Before that moment of public declaration, she must have felt my legitimacy was left up in the air. Her overdose and the bloodied linen at the hospital must have forced my father's hand into making the public acknowledgement in Manchuria of their earlier, clandestine marriage.

She never intended to kill herself. And did her actions that night really save me from being a bastard son?

In the Chinese novels, I read from the time as a teenager, a son was always recognized by the family or clan. In the stories of dynastic China I came across, the sons of the Emperor were always acknowledged as possible heirs to the throne, even when their birth mother was not the empress.

I understand now what my mother really accomplished with her overdose. It forced my father to make the public declaration of their marriage, which made her the legitimate wife and not a concubine.

My mother might have believed that she overdosed for my sake, but to this day I remain uncertain of her motive. In Chinese history, even the sons of a concubine were given the father's name. It's a mystery I will have to learn to live with. But I don't think she would be displeased to be remembered as a woman of mystery.

There were things in her life that I did not find out until the last years of her life, such as I had a half-sister ten years before I was born. Some other stories, not till years after I had buried her, and probably many will have to wait for their unraveling, and I will have to rely on my own imagination to fathom.

10

雞

Chapter Eleven

狗

"Is everything going alright?" I was excited and overjoyed to hear my mother's voice on the phone, long distance from Manchuria. She had tried several times earlier before we were connected successfully. Once I barely heard her voice, and our line was broken. But when we finally got connected, all I could answer to her question was, "Yes."

I didn't know how to tell her how much I missed her, even though I liked my lessons with my tutor and Aunt Fu was doing her best to give me everything I needed.

The weather was beginning to get warm in Shanghai, and I could hear the sparrows beginning to chatter in the trees again. Letters from my mother twice a week arrived irregularly. Delivery was sometimes interrupted when rail lines were disrupted by the communist guerilla forces in the oncoming civil war.

My tutor made sure I wrote to my parents every week, but by the time they got the letter, things I wrote were already something way past.

"Make sure you put on a sweater when you go outside. There is still some snow left on the ground here in Shenyang." My mother tried to tell me something about the northern country where she was staying.

I had a vague idea it was even north of Beijing. But my lessons in geography had not yet extended to that part of China.

"Is it cold then?"

"No. We have our fur coats and quilted jackets here."

"When are you coming home?"

"Very soon. How are your lessons with Teacher Ruan?"

"Good."

"Are you eating properly?"

"Yes."

"We'll see you very soon."

"Okay."

11
狗

My answers were short and mostly monosyllabic because I was also afraid to use my voice. It was beginning to crack at the higher registers and always seemed to happen unexpectedly when I was in the middle of saying something. The maid noticed it and tried to suppress a giggle when it happened, which made me more self-conscious and embarrassed.

Part of her job had also been to help me with my baths. My mother wanted to be sure I cleaned myself thoroughly. This became more and more uncomfortable when I also noticed changes in other parts of my body.

When she finally showed up, I almost cried with joy in seeing her again. I was also excited that she was going to take me up to Manchuria with her.

"We'll have a short stay in Beijing before we go to Manchuria." I often heard her talk about Beijing with my aunt and their family home.

"Will we be at your old home there?"

"No, my uncle is staying there now. We'll go visit him someday when we're there. But I'll take you to see the old Forbidden City."

"Will Diedi join us in Beijing?"

"Yes, for a week or so. He can't be away from his work too long."

"Then we'll meet him in Manchuria later?" I wanted to see the place my mother had been talking about on the telephone.

"Yes, don't worry. We'll go to Manchuria together."

My father decided the safest way to get us from Beijing to Shenyang was by plane. Remembering the wonderful trip he took us on the railways near Shanghai, I was hoping to go by rail. But the railways in the Northeast were getting more unreliable and could be bombed or disrupted by guerrilla forces.

The twin propeller plane taking us out of Beijing in late October also doubled as military transport. It wasn't like the DC4 passenger plane, which took us from Shanghai to Beijing. Its mustard green cabin was more like the back of a truck for hauling livestock.

The plane sputtered and shook before finally getting in the air. I felt the temperature in the cabin drop close to freezing. Luckily my mother brought along earmuffs, gloves, and a heavy coat for me. I was not at all prepared for the turbulence of an early winter storm in Manchuria. Swallowing hard, I tried to steady the churning building in my stomach.

"Take deep breaths!" My mother saw my face turning green and tried her best to soothe me. I followed what she said and held her hand. I held on until we finally managed to land in Shenyang, once called Mukden by the Manchus and the old capitol of Manchuria.

When we stepped off the plane, I felt a little unsteady and greeted my father and his friends who came to meet us by throwing up everything I had tried to hold down on the plane. I could not help registering the dismay on my father's face.

I was sure my failure to appreciate the most up-to-date transportation available in China at that time was another confirmation that

I was a weakling in my father's mind. Gloved hands folded tight, I sat sheepishly next to him in the back of the car on the trip to my new home in the northern country. Ashamed by the stain left by the vomitus on the lapel of my new coat, but too frazzled to really care, I was reassured only by mother's presence on the other side.

My new home was a westernized Japanese house with a manicured garden in front and a larger Japanese one in the back. It was once the residence of the Japanese director the Manchurian rail operations under the puppet Manchukoku regime, which was essentially under Japanese Occupation and control.

The staff was waiting at the entrance when we arrived. Their uniforms and formality reminded me of the time my mother took me to the Park Hotel for my birthday. I followed my parents sheepishly into the mansion.

The main floor was built in quasi-French colonial style, with chandeliers glittering above the entry hall and dining room. The hardwood floors were like polished mirrors. But the bedrooms on the second floor all had a side chamber behind sliding shoji doors, and the floors were covered in Japanese tatami. I smelled the faint scent of day-old grass, at the end of spring given off by these pristine straw mats.

On the ground floor, I discovered something I had never seen before, a Japanese *furo*. It was a suite of three rooms, a large room in front for changing clothes with wooden benches and towels, a second room for washing up and scrubbing, and a backroom filled with steam pouring out like a heavy mist from the surface of a large, heated wooden tub that was almost my height.

This Japanese steam bath was my father's favorite part of the house, a custom he acquired from his student days in Japan. The week after our arrival the temperature outdoors dropped to below freezing. He thought it would be a perfect time to enjoy the benefits of our private *furo*.

The maids had already laid out the towels and robes for the family. My father undressed first to show us the whole bathing procedure. He washed with soap and warm water from the wooden buckets and basins in the middle room. Then he stepped into the steaming tub in the backroom.

"Come on in, the hot water is wonderful!" He called out to us. "What's taking you so long?"

My mother was helping me get undressed in the colder dressing room. I did not feel the discomfort with the maid helping me in Shanghai. Maybe because she had helped me for as long as I could remember and she never gave me a feeling of uneasiness undressed. We followed my father's example of washing up first. He was already beckoning for me to join him.

I gingerly tested the water with my fingers and was surprised how very hot the water was. I was scared the steaming bath water would turn me into boiled meat.

My father's strong arms pulled me in.

I yelled out.

"Don't be afraid! The hot water is good for you."

I clawed myself back to the edge and tried to climb out of the tub toward my mother who was standing on the outside. Instead of helping me to get out, I thought there was only a grimace on her face.

Suddenly my father emerged from the steamy water surface and lifted me up to the edge of the tub. I couldn't help feel he was disgusted with me in the rough way he grabbed my shaking body. Facing him in front of me, I became acutely aware of the rivulets of water running down his muscular upper body. For the first time, I realized how big he was. I pulled my eyes away from him, stung in equal measure by secret envy of his manliness and shame for my own inadequacy by comparison.

I can't remember how I scrambled out of the boiling tub and ran for a towel. I heard my mother saying, "You can try again tomorrow. I'll stay here with Diedi a little longer."

I was only too glad to be able to run up to my own room, away from my father, away from both of them. Even from my mother, because she was siding with him in my distress and humiliation.

My father didn't try to get me into the hot bath again. He didn't mention what happened that day. He never said much to me anyway. Recently I had a Japanese style *furo* specially built into our bathroom with a view from the Golden Gateway on the west to Mount Diablo on the east. It has taken me seven decades to appreciate fully what my father wanted me to experience in Manchuria.

As the three of us settled into our house in Shenyang, I felt the distance between my father and me widening. The attacks on the railway lines by the *Ba Lu Jun*, Mao's famous guerrilla Eighth Army, became a daily occurrence. Railway ties were being bombed faster than the linemen could repair them. I saw the frustration and anger on my father's face every time he got the report. He took the bombings as if they were personal attacks on him. Chiang Kai-shek had to send one of his most capable generals, Chen Cheng, to defend China's Northeast, its center of industries left by the Japanese Occupation.

It was during this precarious period of Chiang's hold on Manchuria that brought my father into an abiding friendship with the general sent there to defend it.

"He was an honest man!" my father said. I could understand his words better now. He omitted what he was unwilling to say. Most of the men in Chiang's government were corrupt and inept.

When Chiang lost the mainland and retreated to the island of Taiwan, a portrait of the general hung outside the Presidential Palace in Taiwan, alongside the portrait of Chiang himself.

My mother smirked when her friend told her about it. "Old Chiang needed a vice president known for his rare qualities of honesty and incorruptibility to bolster the government's failing image."

The general was put into a western suit and tie. It did not change the earnest look in his eyes and the neatly combed white mane above a high forehead, the sign of wisdom to his countrymen.

When I had an attic room in a home for students in Cambridge, Massachusetts, the general's son was a close neighbor. He did not have his father's eyes, which seemed to allow you to look into his soul. But the son had a graceful hand in Chinese calligraphy, unlike the rigid formality of his father's calligraphy, which I saw on the dedication of the scroll, his gift honoring my father's seventieth birthday.

I steered way from talking Chinese politics with the son, presuming him to be loyal to Chiang's KMT. I heard enough from my mother about Chiang's reputation and had just read Edgar Snow's *Red Star Over China*, describing Mao Zedong and his comrades in close to saintly terms.

My father and the general shared another common bond, aside from their mutual distrust of communist ideology. They both had a love for classical Chinese calligraphy. The general's father in law was a well-known scholar and collector who supported the founder of the Republic, Sun Yat sen.

The scroll from the general's family collection given to my father now hangs in the entry hall of my home. It was not only a gesture honoring my father's birthday but also alluded to their friendship as comrades in arms, one formed during the days of their last stand against the communists in Manchuria.

In Shenyang that year, my father stayed late at his work for longer and longer hours, as Mao's Red Army forces became more emboldened and successful. I saw less and less of him. Even when he was home, there were often meetings in the living room downstairs, behind closed doors and I was told to stay away. It stirred ominous memories of the night visits to our home in Shanghai by Dai Li, before his plane crash.

He found a tutor for me. The young man's father was my father's fellow Cantonese and a diplomat of the early republic sent to America. Teacher Lee was educated in America. He taught me American English in the morning and took me outdoors in the afternoon for that summer through early fall for lessons on earthworms, tree frogs, and lizards we found in the neighboring woodlands, which he let me bring home and keep by the pond in the Japanese garden.

Reading an interview of the octogenarian, Japanese conductor, Seiji Ozawa, he mentioned fondly his memories of being born in Shenyang. Mukden to him, the city during its height of Japanese Occupation. It made me think of those idyllic sun dappled summer explorations in the woods with my tutor.

Mao's guerrilla forces became more and more successful in cutting the supply lines for rice from the southern provinces, and we had to switch from rice at the table to eating soybeans. My mother did not complain. Only when close friends came to dinner, I heard her apologize for what she had to ask the kitchen to serve.

"You would think at the dinner table of the director we would not have to resort to soybeans!" Soybeans were generally used for feeding pigs in China of those days.

But my father believed in showing others by his own example. He told my mother we would only serve soybeans and no rice on our table until rice came back to the public market.

Hardship brought out my mother's resourcefulness. She used it to survive our years under Japanese Occupation. Faced with the cut off of rice from the South by the Red Army, she thought of new ways for the kitchen to cook soybeans.

Her recipe of the spicy, pickled Chinese green called *xuelihong* with slowly braised soybeans became a favorite of mine.

11
狗

Looking back, *xuelihong*, which meant Red-in-the-Snow literally, was an ominously prescient choice on my mother's part. Mao's Red Army was soon to take over Manchuria, where snow covered the earth for many months of the year.

Whether it was my mother's ingenuity in making our limited food supply always palatable and I had no memory of real suffering under the Red Army siege of the city or because she never complained or said anything bad about Mao's guerrillas, I did not develop any of the strong anti-Communist feelings of my father.

A man of few words, even when the last caller was out our front door after one of their marathon meetings, he never told me why he had such strong anti-Communist convictions. I thought the principles by which he lived and the lessons he taught me were closer to true communism than the regime he devoted his life to supporting.

My mother was frustrated by, what was to her mind, his lonely fight against the pervasive corruption she saw in Chiang Kai-shek's government. What difference, she thought, would our little soybean dinners make while other officials were serving rice? It made us stand out like sore thumbs or worse as if we were trying to do better than others. My father was never one who followed convention, but my mother felt Old Chiang only paid lip service but never carried out the words of Sun Yat-sen, the founder of the Republic.

Years later, safely out of the grasp of the KMT, I asked my mother how she knew about all the corruption in Chiang's government, she told me it was Dai Li who told her in confidence.

Being the head of Chiang's secret police, he was in charge of the behind-the- scenes opium trade from Burma, the deals with the gang boss of old Shanghai, Du Yuesheng, not to mention the assassinations of Chiang's political enemies.

"I know too much." He confided in her the last time he had visited before he died.

"He told me about his fears that his knowledge of all these behind the scene deals made him a target for elimination by his suspicious boss." My mother said, "He was beginning to suspect Old Chiang was planning to get rid of him and bury all the dirty work before the Americans arrived after the war. He knew Madame Chiang was weary and wanted him out of the way, when American generals and advisors questioned about the dirty work he did for her husband's government."

I remembered the name, Du Yuesheng. Flipping through an old family album, my mother once pointed him out in a group picture taken in the home of one of the most influential men of the early Republic. He was an old colleague of my mother's father from the time of the ancien régime. She was sitting off to the side in that birthday celebration. In the same row, next to her uncle, front, and center, was the gang boss who controlled the underground drug traffic.

My father was always silent when my mother complained about Chiang. He did not like to counter her arguments openly when he didn't have to. She was smart enough not to make her criticisms in public. And he was not deterred and continued to do the work for the government he felt he had to do. Better to lead by what you do, not by what you say. Turning to me he added, "You should remember that when you grow up!"

Following this dictum to the end, he insisted we stay in the city of Shenyang, even when the guerrilla forces were closing in. Finally, he conceded to leave, and we got on the last plane before Mao's forces took over the airport.

Chapter Twelve

豬

With Manchuria taken over by Mao, we retreated to our home in Shanghai. My parents decided it was time to focus attention on my formal education in public school.

Much as I liked my earlier tutors, Teacher Ruan in Shanghai, then Teacher Lee in Manchuria, my father thought I should have more interaction with people my own age. He excelled in rigorous Japanese schools he attended, and thought my upbringing had been much too sheltered. He convinced my mother to find a school with a good academic record, as well as a reputation for rigorous development of a youngster's body.

The boys in my class were already very familiar with each other. The school year had started two months earlier. The principal, who was introduced by a family friend, thought I could be put into one of their fourth-grade classes. I was an outsider from the first day. There were no girls in that school. Heretofore, they were the only playmates I knew. My classmates had already formed their groups at recess, playing soccer and games in the schoolyard. It didn't help that I had never kicked a soccer ball in my life.

I was also plunged into some complicated math homework. It was the first time I was given math problems such as, if there were twenty coins in my hand, made up of five, ten and twenty cent denominations and the total amount was fifty yuan, how many of each coin was I holding.

My mother noticed that I became more and more anxious about going to school and asked my father to help me.

He tried. I was not really able to tell him what exactly was bothering me, other than I hated going to school. He told me about his early days as a young man from Canton enrolled in the college prep school in Tokyo, one with a reputation for having the toughest curriculum. Their graduates had a straight shot into the prestigious Imperial University, now known as Tokyo University.

He and his brother were among a wave of Chinese students, moved by the cause of their fellow Cantonese, Dr. Sun Yat-sen who overthrew the Manchu Dynasty. Along with promising young men across the country, they were sent abroad to be trained as future leaders of the young Chinese Republic, some to Europe, others went to Japan. I see him now, stiff and serious, in his Japanese student's uniform, a four-cornered black cap on his head, when I raise my head to his picture in a jade frame above my desk.

"You have to beat them at their own game," he said, "Become better than what they are good at!" He put in extra hours every day to practice the martial arts of jujitsu and at the end of the year beat the top man in his class. "I was not going to let them think that Chinese are weaklings!"

Grabbing hold of my spindly arm, he looked at me. "You've got to develop better muscles! Don't be tagged as a weakling!" He rolled up his sleeve, flexed his biceps and put my hand on it. It was a big lump, and hard as a rock.

A review of a book on the history of the Sino-Japanese Wars I have read recently detailed the preoccupation and national Chinese obsession to overcome the label of being a weakling, after the series of defeats at foreign hands, one after another, from the mid-eighteen-hundreds.

The British were the first to crack the façade of the Paper Tiger Chinese Empire when it handily overcame the declining Manchu

Dynasty and forced opium through its ports. Many countries followed suit, including China's neighbor, Japan. As a sheltered nine-year old, I was not well-versed enough on the national sentiments for them to be helpful in dealing with the very personal problems I was having in school.

His pep talk did not make me feel better, only more ashamed that I could not live up to what he was expecting me to do. I had no idea how to get into the soccer games, feeling scissor legged when I got on the soccer field, much less in trying to be better at it. I would rather be doodling at my desk, or trying to catch tree frogs in the woods and butterflies in the garden, as I had done with my teacher Lee in Shenyang.

One Sunday afternoon when I was struggling with another one of the convoluted math problems, I asked my mother for help.

"Your father is a whiz at math," she said and sent me to him.

He tried to make me see how I could solve the problem by first eliminating the unlikely combinations and then trying to come up with the correct one at the end. After half an hour's effort of different approaches, I was still unable to grasp what he was trying to help me extricate.

"We'll try some other problems after tea." I could tell from his tone and expression that my father was at the end of his patience as he withdrew himself from the study.

I happened to walk by my parents' bedroom and overheard his words, "The kid is just too stupid. I can't teach him anything." I couldn't make out what my mother said.

I tiptoed back into my room and shut the door. *Shame.* I was crushed to have disappointed my father again.

Dinnertime that evening my mother came into my room. I could not look her in the eye without breaking down, I told her I had an upset stomach and didn't feel like eating. She put her hand on my forehead to see if I had a fever.

"Good thing you don't have a fever," she always prided herself for being able to detect my fevers better than a thermometer, "I'll have the cook make some rice porridge with red dates for you." The fragrance of the slowly cooked rice and the mildly sweet dates were my favorite when I was sick.

I was relieved she didn't linger too long. Cocooning myself inside my blanket, I kept my face turned toward the wall. It was too painful even to admit to myself that I didn't think I could ever live up to my father's standards.

12
豬

When I was close to fifty, about my father's age when he showed up in my life, I found myself sitting in front of my therapist in Northern California. He asked me during one of our sessions, "Now that you have a degree in chemical engineering from the best engineering school in the country and a doctorate in medicine, do you still believe what your father said was true?"

I could still hear a nine-year-old boy's voice inside me, echoing those early words of my father.

It was around the time of my parents' divorce that the strain between my father and me came close to a complete break.

I was visiting my mother in her one-bedroom apartment on the edge of Harlem, at that point she was renting out the bedroom to make ends meet while getting her master's degree from Columbia. My father had returned to Taiwan with his mother fifteen years earlier, after his work in signing the peace treaty with Japan was accomplished. Through her friends, my mother heard he was involved with another woman.

She wrote to me she was seeking a divorce. On a break from my classes in Boston, I visited her in her apartment. When I walked into the kitchen, I found her usual warm welcome a little muted, even though she prepared some of my favorite dishes for dinner.

She waited till after breakfast the following morning to go into the details, "Your father really knows how to get to me!"

She nervously tapped her Pall Mall on the ashtray, already half filled. "Just look at what he wrote!"

As she handed me the letter, her hands close to trembling. I recognized the elegant calligraphy. In the letter, my father denied his paternity of me.

That was over half a century ago. With the idealism of youth and the insecurity of my own identity, I was not prepared to acquiesce to the fate of being labeled a bastard. My mother's words later on that afternoon, when she saw how upset I was, hardly registered in my ears.

"Remember, he is still your father!"

I struck back impulsively, as only a young man in his early twenties could do. When I got back to school, I wrote a hasty note to the man I once embraced so doggedly, from top to bottom, from his shaved Yul Brynner haircut to his passion for Chinese calligraphy. I told him because he was doubting that he was my father, he no longer needed to consider me his son, and essentially, I declared he was no longer to be my father. The thought that he had betrayed my mother in getting involved with another woman after what she had endured, as well as being, what I felt, hopelessly blind in persisting to support Chiang's government in Taiwan made my decision easier.

I found solace and comfort by imagining a kinship with all the illegitimate sons who overcame their shame and surpassed their father's accomplishments. Marching into the local library, I asked the librarian's help in researching illegitimacy regarding any of the founding fathers of this country. Alexander Hamilton's illegitimacy was not well known as it has become today with the wildly popular musical.

I even began to dream about the glamour in a life lived at the edge of society, and fantasized about having the higher intelligence I once overheard my mother say illegitimate sons often possessed.

A parade of my mother's old suitors and paramours marched across my reviewing stand. The list of those who sought her hand seemed endless.

When she thought I was old enough to understand, I remembered marveling that almost every other old friend who came to visit her, had once been in pursuit.

There was Uncle Zhou in his English wool suit and spats. He was my father's secretary who stood next to my parents in their wedding portrait. Handsome and debonair, someone I would not mind resembling when I put on another thirty years, even though my mother never said he was a suitor. Dark and mysterious Dai Li, the man killed in the plane crash and held in his palm the fate of men living in China during those years. He had threatened to kill anyone who was anyone who dared to marry my mother. There was Uncle Mao, the younger brother of Chiang's first wife. He was fluent in French and circulated in the diplomatic circles of Nanjing, the new Capitol of the First Republic, but my mother thought he was not much of an intellectual challenge for her to consider him seriously.

I could accept anyone of them as a paternal alternate, I told myself, with the exception of Dai Li, whose dark, Gestapo persona was hard for me to forget from the glimpse I had when he came into our living room those late nights before his plane went down.

I did not tell anyone about my fantasies. I was ashamed to bring it up with my friends in school. My rage of what I felt on the surface only served to cover for what was too painful for me to admit or examine more deeply.

True to himself, my father was silent and did not utter a word on his own behalf. As my mother always said, even if run over by a ten-ton truck, he would not let out any gas.

He did not retaliate by disowning me. He side-stepped my heated declaration and continued to send me letters as if nothing had happened between us. I did not open them. They sat in the bottom of my desk drawer, but somehow between my moments of rage, hurt and deep-seated confusion, I fell short of destroying them.

Recently, when I was cleaning out my old papers, I found them again. The calligraphy on the pieces of yellowing rice paper aged more gracefully than my years. There was not a word about what he said to my mother.

It never occurred to me to ask my father directly, when there was still time for us. I realized later my mother's views were not always unbiased after she forced me to cancel my wedding, seven days before the scheduled ceremonies because she felt she was insulted by my bride's father.

But I remembered her words. My father was still my father. I started on my visits to his bedside when he was hospitalized in Taipei, once, sometimes twice a year when I took time off from my work. When my children were old enough, I brought them to visit their grandfather. For the last six years of his life, I went straight from the International Airport to the hospital.

He stayed in a section of the hospital which was relatively quiet, at the end of a long corridor. There was a waiting area outside, a smaller room for the nurse, a small kitchen, the larger room with his hospital bed, armchairs, and a sitting area toward the window, with a round table in the middle and chairs around where he sometimes sat up and conducted meetings for the first few years when he was still capable.

His nurse always ushered me to the chair closest to his hospital bed. The physical distance was easier to bridge than the silence between us.

We talked about other things—the grandchildren, my medical practice, his medical treatment. Never about what lay deep in my heart and mind, about what was between us. It was like the secret chambers of a temple, hidden from view, not to be penetrated, not destined to see the light of day.

Now that I have lived past his age, the age when he wrote that letter to my mother, I have noticed my hands and fingers seemed to have grown into his mold. Even the nail on the ring finger of my right hand has developed a crack in the middle like his. Was it another stigma from him, showing up before my own eyes?

Having now been through a divorce myself, I tried stepping into his shoes. Hurtful things were said that should not have seen the page and even less so shown to a son. But at my age now, even the prospect of being called a bastard no longer carried the same sharp shrill it once sounded to my ears.

On one of my last visits to him at the hospital, he was short of breath, making words more difficult for him. Plastic cannulas went into his nostrils to give him extra oxygen. When I stood up to leave, he did manage in a voice I had to strain to hear, "Be good to your mother. I am much indebted to her."

His words still bring tears to my eyes, when I think about the affection he still had for the woman he once married against all odds. He married despite the strong will of his own mother. Despite the threat of being assassinated by Chiang's secret police. The love between my parents, defying family objection and tradition, then enduring the hardship of long separation of the war years, must have been a powerful one.

Even though that bond had dissipated like footprints in the sand, enough of it still remained.

From that midnight behind my mosquito net in Shanghai to the tropical sun at high noon under which I waited for his ashes at the crematorium in the foothills of Taipei, we lived under the same roof for a total of about four years. His other eighty-five years were like looking through the mist of China's Mt. Lu, made famous by the Chinese folk saying, one can never see the real face of that mysterious mountain.

Closer to me in my home in San Francisco, it's like the blanket of fog that often rolls over the hill across the window of my study, shielding me from the summer heat, maybe it has kept me away from things better not seen too close. Maybe it's a mystery between father and son that is always hard to fathom completely.

Those fifty months, fifteen hundred days, I had with my father I hold tight in my palm and close to my heart, unfolding and refolding them like a box of heirloom origami, fraying but no less treasured.

As I sat alone now by that window in my study, I noticed the lights across the hill flickering almost like the fireflies in the garden on summer nights in the countryside of Shanghai, when I was eight, before he came into my life.

Chapter Thirteen

鼠

Jan tiptoed to the operating table and tapped me lightly on the shoulder. She didn't want to disturb the concentration of the young doctor I was helping in the removal of a tumor from a Chinese woman's face.

It was now hard for me to tell the woman was Chinese, only part of her face was exposed. The rest of her was covered in surgical blue, with the paper drapes effectively removing any personal identity. I wondered whether it was the anonymity and loss of human identity that made it possible for me to cut into a fellow human being.

Two hours ago, I had held her thin wrist and told her I would do my best. Her eyes hung on to mine, conveying what she didn't put into words, *I'm putting my trust in you!* as she let the anesthetist clamp on the gas mask putting her to sleep. It was a delicate balance between the cold precision of the surgical knife and the touch of warm humanity that I tried to tread.

Getting the room ready for the operation, before we started the surgery that afternoon, Jan asked about my mother when we were alone for a few moments. Several days earlier, when we were in the operating room, I told her about the coma.

She was not really the best circulating nurse I'd come across over the years. Sometimes, her mind seemed to be preoccupied with her many other entanglements in life, rather than getting everything I needed for surgery. But over the years, our mutual interests, in and out of the hospital, drew us together and to an occasional dinner after work.

She confided her troubles with the married professor she was seeing, and I told her about the men in my life. We traded barbs about people we disliked at work: peacock surgeons, men, and a few women, who treated nurses like serfs, and the nurses who sucked up to them. We rolled our eyes about every new regulation handed down, ones designed to make our work in the operating room unnecessarily tedious and more time consuming. We were trying to get things done as efficiently as possible, unwilling to concede occasionally that regulations were put in for legitimate concerns.

I had a warm and cozy feeling whenever Jan was assigned to my operating room, like Linus with his security blanket. In the middle of the heightened vigilance with a patient on the operating table, under glare of the surgical spotlights and droning sighs of the respirator pumping, I found relief in the moments we caught one another smiling at something perceived simultaneously.

One year we bumped into each other at Civic Center plaza in a futile protest against the invasion of Iraq, when Joan Baez's pure soprano came over the loudspeaker with "We Shall Overcome."

I turned my head to read the note Jan was holding up discreetly at my eye level, "Mom stopped breathing 5 min. ago."

The overhead halogen lights struck the steel retractor in my hands and shot back like a laser into my eyes. I was blinded for a split second. The fragile nerve we had carefully laid out and were trying to preserve on the Chinese woman's face zoomed in and out of my focus. I forced myself to snap back to the patient who had put her faith in me.

The news did not come as a total surprise. My mother drifted into a morphine coma a week earlier. I was beginning to get used to it, but I couldn't forget the last words she mumbled to me. "You're not going to overdose me with the pills, are you?" I gave her the morphine drops myself, although I hired Filipina caretakers to stay 24/7 in her bedroom. She had developed a special rapport with her doctor of many years, bringing him chicken feet from her familiar poultry shop in Chinatown, which his wife enjoyed. When he told her about the seriousness of her condition, she told him firmly she wanted to remain in her own home till the end.

Before I left for the hospital that morning, I stood by her bedside, and she was hardly stirring. Never a large woman, she had shriveled even more over the four months since her lung cancer was diagnosed. Under the pale pink covers, she was breathing quietly like a child. I thought of the times when she used to tiptoe to my bedside, making sure I was covered on cold nights.

As I backed away from her bed, I told myself this might go on for weeks, or even months, remembering the comatose young woman I took care of when I was still an intern. The coma was the result of injuries from a car accident ten years earlier. Her boyfriend who survived showed up every day after work at her bedside, holding her hand for hours. Her name, a murmur on his lips from time to time.

I could have asked a colleague to take my place in supervising the young doctor- in-training to do the surgery. But schedules had to be rearranged, and chances of my mother dying that day were not any more likely than a week or two later. My mother had always been a fighter, never one to give up. I told myself, she was in a coma, she didn't even know I was there, throwing up science as my alibi. She could also stop breathing the moment I went to use the bathroom, even if I stayed with her all day.

Were these just excuses I clung to, I ask myself now. I did not want to admit I simply did not feel like holding my mother's hand

13

鼠

the way the boyfriend stood vigil beside his comatose girlfriend. Or even as I held the Chinese woman's wrist to assure her before she was put to sleep. Didn't I realize there was the possibility that my mother might have felt the hand most dear to her? Why did this not occur to me before it was too late, I ask myself now, along with my general sense of not having done enough of what my mother would have liked when she was still alive.

Nor did sadness hit me when I read the held up note. I just felt numbed and dazed, except for the slow realization, like thin ice crackling on a near frozen lake, with her gone I would now be the next in line.

It was hard for me to admit, I failed in her last wish. She wanted me to be there with her. She told me many times, "The only thing I want from you is your promise to be here when I take my last breath!"

I failed her.

She wanted me to move into her apartment when her doctor told her the cancer in her lung was not operable.

"Maybe six months." Was the answer her doctor gave when she refused treatment by irradiation.

"I don't want any treatment if it's not going to cure me," she said.

I resisted her request, insisted I could only take care of her by visiting her after work every day. The thought of listening to stories I heard many times before and endless justifications of why she stopped my wedding plans would open up black holes from years ago where I did not want to go. Filipina nurses, waiting to get their license in this country, stayed with my mother, filling the role I could not make myself do until she lost consciousness.

The young doctor looked up sympathetically after we got through the critical areas. "I can close up here if you want to go."

He had already been with us for several months. This was his last year of training before hanging up his own shingle. After his first week with us, I wrote down in my evaluation that the young man had a skillful pair of hands. Still, I could not bring myself to accept his offer.

"I'll stay till the skins are closed," I said. I thought of the trust the Chinese woman had put in me when she held my hand before she went to sleep, while I had just failed my own mother.

The room became noticeably quiet. I felt as if everyone was expecting me to say something more. The light banter between the anesthetist and the nurse helping us at the operating table had stopped.

The regular beeps of the Chinese woman's heart on the cardiac monitor and the steady sighs of the respirator pump, delivering oxygen and anesthetic gases into her lungs were the only sounds to our ears.

"First sponge count is correct." Jan's voice broke our silence.

"Thank you." My answer clicked in automatically, like so many times before, near the end of surgery before skin incisions were closed.

"3-0 chromic on a cutting and your fast absorbing 5-0 for skins?"

I understood that nurses always had to check to make sure that I hadn't changed my mind on a particular case, but I could feel myself getting annoyed. The fact that the operating room could not manage to keep a record of each surgeon's specific needs so that the question had to be asked every time was an annoyance I found particularly hard to bear that afternoon.

I held my tongue, remembering Jan's gripes about intemperate surgeons.

As I was walking out of the operating room, she came up close.

"Take care," she said. A whispered breath of our friendship.

Outside, the cool early evening air of late January stung my cheeks. Refreshing, it made me notice the half-moon lighting the doctor's parking lot, tucked in back of the hospital. It was the evening before Chinese New Year. No stars in that steely gray sky.

I knew I should hurry to get to my mother, before rigor mortis set in. There were nine layers of funerary garments I must pull onto her stiffening limbs.

I put the car into gear without thinking and drove through the older part of the mid-peninsula town where the hospital was located.

Four months earlier I was driving after work under the same oak umbrellas of this road just past the old business area, on my way to visit my mother. Suddenly I was startled by what felt like giant hailstones pummeling the roof of my car. Then I saw acorns from the aged oaks raining around me, and the SUV in front was weaving as if shimmying in shallow water.

Sudden silence over the radio. When the announcer from KPFA came back, I heard, "There has just been an earthquake, magnitude of…"

That was only a few weeks after the doctor told us the shadow on my mother's chest X-Ray was probably a tumor. The earth's trembling felt like an omen. When I reached the City, the lights were out. It was deserted as a ghost town.

Now, when I approached the hill where my mother lived, I had the same feeling of loss and desolation the evening of the earthquake. I was surprised to see the lights were lit on her street and people were rushing to make the curtain call in the theaters below.

I had to concentrate to get my Toyota into the parking space designated for my mother's apartment. Gingerly, I touched the button for the elevator to her floor, as if to make sure it was still there.

I had pressed that button many times before. Visiting her after work, when she had my favorite dishes ready for dinner. The crisp Suzhou fish smothered in soy, ginger and green onions, or a plate of refreshingly chilled daikon, julienned and sprinkled with diced, browned scallions and sesame.

Or bringing a boyfriend to meet her and watching out for any sign of hidden disapproval. Because I could not believe that she truly accepted me the way I really was, although she did not seem to be ruffled when I told her, at the time of my divorce.

She even went on to ask me whether I remembered the time she took me to visit the brother of a retired prime minister and friend of the family. I was nearly nine, on my first visit to Beijing, the city where my mother was brought up. The man received us in a woman's kimono in his ancestral mansion. I realized my mother's conception of a gay man might not be quite the same as mine when I told her about myself.

It was also the same elevator when I brought the children to visit her on weekends after my divorce, and she took them to Chinatown on the other side of the hill.

That evening, when I stepped off the elevator and stood at her door, I hesitated to turn the key and push it open. I knew there would not be the familiar greeting. '*Er Zah…*' in her perfect pitched, Peking dialect.

The two syllables for 'son' in Mandarin, drawn out into an aria of lamentation and longing, love and nuanced incrimination of perceived neglect. I would never hear those words again, except as an echo in my mind, impossible to erase, even if I wanted to. It hit me again as it did when I read the note at the operating table, that imperceptible veil between me and my own mortality has been quietly removed and vanished.

The apartment was dark but for a large red candle in the hallway and another one flickering from her bedroom. My friend, who had been more attentive to her daily needs than her own

13

鼠

son, had come earlier to close her eyelids and opened a crack in the window.

I inched forward in the stillness as if I might wake her from her sleep. Kneeling by her bedside, I picked up her hand and held it. It was cool but not yet cadaver-cold. My throat tightened, but no tears came.

The reflection of the row of French perfumes which followed her from Shanghai to Taipei, Taipei to Tokyo, then finally from New York to her last home faced me in the mirror of her long dressing table close to her bed. Her favorite bottle of *Fleur de Rocaille* by Caron was near empty. She always preferred its milder fragrance to the stronger and better-known Chanels. When she found it hard to find the old perfume of her younger days, she treasured her last bottle even more.

I held onto her fingers for a while, as if they might warm to my touch. Then I wakened to the beginning of its stiffness and the need to get those layers of funerary clothing on as quickly as possible.

Her garment chest was brought up from storage when she went into the coma. A whiff of the camphor wood caught my nostrils like incense when I lifted the lid. I set aside the brocaded gowns and found the soft silk undergarments in the bottom.

She had shown these to me when she first found out and instructed me the sequence in which the garments should be put on. Light summer wear over undergarments, then lined spring and autumn clothing, and finally, quilted and brocaded winter gowns trimmed in fur, reminding her of her early days in Russia.

Tentatively I lifted off the light blanket that was covering her as if she might be chilled from its removal. I set the cream-colored silk undershirt next to her and put my arm under her to lift her body.

She let go of a deep sigh. Startled, I dropped the torso and stared at her face. Her eyelids were still closed. Her look peaceful.

"I'm so sorry," I couldn't help saying.

Then I realized the movement of my lifting her had made her expel the last bit of residual air from her chest. Was she really waiting for me to let out her final breath? The stiffness setting into her was the hard fact I had to accept. She was no longer alive.

The rooms would no longer echo her footsteps, fast paced always, at least up to the last two months. The scent of her French perfumed handkerchiefs and the flavors of her cooking would no longer fill the air I breathed.

13

鼠

Intermezzo

As I flipped through snapshots of my parents' lives, I have reflected not only on them but also about myself and the crossways I have come to pass. My parents were a study in contrasts, coming from vastly different backgrounds, having even greater differences of temperament. They were like fire and water. Hard to ignore the amperage when my mother entered a ballroom, while for my father it was hard to make a ripple in his still waters.

Born into a family from the Ming Dynasty center of literati and culture in Suzhou on her father's side, and into a prominent family living in the new commercial center of Shanghai on her mother's side, my mother spent her developing years in Czarist Russia with her father and stayed through the Bolshevik Revolution. She inhaled European culture along with the crisp air of the Siberian forests on bareback horses in her childhood.

When she returned to China after her mother's death, she had to find her own place to fit in a country going through rapid transitions, from an end-of-millennia dynastic rule to its first republic. Often, she found herself teased and chided. Her directness in expression and open ways were not customary for traditional China, and in particular for women.

It was the traditional role of the woman that I believe my mother had the most trouble accepting. Was it because, as Uncle Ju, her old friend suggested, she had imbibed too much of western ink and influence to accept her father's dictates? After all, she divorced the man he had forced her to marry as soon as her mother died. My mother consented to the marriage when her mother pleaded with her. She needed to obey; otherwise, her father would have beaten her mother to death.

Divorces were close to scandalous in the early twenties, but my mother walked out of her father's grasp and never looked back. Yet strong men continued to appear in her life, some as sinister as Dai Li. Was it because she was fearless in facing strong men (beginning with her authoritarian father), or was it because she attracted them with the bewitching sparkle and fire in her eyes? I will never know.

At the same time, I cannot help but think of the pain she tried to hide from me, allowing only a glimpse when she thought the moment ripe. She gave up her first child, the only thing she had at that time, to get out of her forced marriage. She brought me up virtually single-handed after her clandestine union of love with my father, an act made more difficult due to the war and times they lived in, as well as the strong objection of his matriarch. In the end, she had to give up even that love and be on her own in an alien country where she knew only a few words of its language.

Yet, she never let on she felt sorry for herself. I think that was why she fell right in step with the civil rights movement and their marching cry of "We shall overcome!"

My father, on the other hand, did not encounter foreign influences till he went to Tokyo for his high school and university education. Japanese culture was not as alien as what my mother faced—being basically still Far Eastern in philosophy and thought. Yet, Japan after the Meiji Restoration, with its underlying old samurai culture, was considerably different from his boyhood in Canton. His grandfather had achieved the highest honors in the Imperial Examinations of the Manchu Dynasty Qing, but his own father died young, and his widowed mother had to rely on the relatives for support of her children.

He could never forget the hardships his mother endured. It made him cater to her wishes throughout his life. When she chose her favorite niece as his bride against his will, he went into a monastery and shaved his head, but eventually consented to go through with the marriage in name. He never shared a bed with the woman who eventually decided to embrace Jesus as her savior.

Even when my father found his true love in my mother later, he had to marry her without telling his mother. He was afraid the elderly matriarch would not survive the news. In the Confucian tradition that he was brought up, that would be unforgivable. But in the end, he decided to live with and care for his aging mother in Taiwan and separate from the woman he married against the matriarch's wishes. A man of very few words, he would have appreciated his contemporary across the ocean, Marianne Moore. In "Silence," a poem about her own father, she wrote, "The deepest feeling always shows itself in silence;/ not in silence, but restraint." When he felt the end approaching, my father did manage to find his voice and tell me he was in debt to my mother.

Both of my parents grew up at a time when China was at its weakest, an era of unprecedented defeats in its long history, after multiple and repeated wars brought on by foreign invaders trying to gain access to a closed Chinese world. They witnessed the concessions forced on a defenseless country against far superior firepower and gunships, and had to learn to adapt to the changes they faced.

Their lives continued to change with the turmoil of civil war between Chiang Kai-shek and the Chinese communists which followed in quick order, forcing them to leave behind the lives they were used to and go to the island of Taiwan for refuge. For my mother, she did not feel any sense of safety until she was out of Taiwan and able to come to the United States. She had always lived in fear that Chiang Kai-shek's Taiwanese regime held her suspect due to her many years in Russia and her strong affinity to its culture.

For me, I am left with many indelible legacies from my parents, along with their contradictions. My mother gave me her spirit of overcoming the seemingly insurmountable; my father, his love of Chinese calligraphy, beginning from the day he held my hand around the brush. When my father gave me a framed fan with calligraphy from our fifth-generation ancestor, he said, "This is the most valuable testament I am leaving to you." Later I realized the ancient roots of our family originate from Shaoxing, the city of Wang Xizhi, the Chinese sage of fluid and graceful calligraphy.

Recently, while strolling through a retrospective

of Richard Diebenkorn's works, which included his unforgettable West Coast landscapes of vast greens and blues of the seventies and his stark, richly colored portraits, I was touched by the thoughts attributed to the painter about his changes in life direction, from early abstract painting to figurative expressions, then back to abstraction. He thought of influences he had received and his own independence. Somehow things gradually happened in his artistic career, even though he could not pinpoint the details of when and how.

I considered how his words could be a metaphor for the unpredictable course of my parents' lives. And I wondered if I could ever really understand them, even though my mother had once thought I would understand better when I had my own children.

But after many years trying to be in my parents' shoes in writing about them, and coursing through the maze and tributaries of their decisions and indecisions, much of their lives still feel like mysteries. As the son of Odysseus realized in Homer's epic, "No one truly knows his own begetting." It is not really possible to fathom if the paths my parents chose were shaped by their own will or the times they lived through. And this, I am coming to realize, can also be said of the life of my own.

PART II

Chapter Fourteen

牛

A few blocks to the east of the school where I started junior high was Adele's family home in Taipei, overlooking the city's Central Park, a toy version of the one in New York. The trees in this fairly new park were beginning to provide some shelter when the tropical sun baked the earth. Even in early February.

Neon lit shops of all kinds have replaced the rice fields where I used to hunt for duck eggs on my way home, ones for my mother to pickle in salt and rice wine, a favorite accompaniment to rice porridge for weekend breakfasts.

Specialty Northern Chinese dumpling shops and fashionable vegetarian quick food. Gucci-like boutiques and discount outlets with piles of sweatpants at a dollar fifty a pair. They all jostled with each other for space. An occasional storefront served traditional Taiwanese cuisine, fixed up to remind me of my school days over half a century ago. A mere specter now of the old, colonial Japanese town where my mother shopped at the stalls selling meat and vegetables, our Taiwanese maid helping bargain because we didn't speak the local dialect. I looked around for the old man with his little stand renting old books of Chinese folk heroes practicing *Wu Shu* or *Gong Fu*.

Once an occasional water buffalo trudged along the rice paddies, pulling its plow, followed by a farmer in his cone-shaped straw hat dressed in rolled-up thin cotton pants, with a whip of strong hemp to urge the beast along. Now there are sounds of two-story cranes and heavy machinery for the construction below street level, making way for a multileveled mass transit system.

Buddhist prayers, *A-mi-tuo-Fo*, *A-mi-tuo-Fo*, *A-mi-tuo-Fo...*, rhythmic as Gregorian chants are flowing out with the faint fragrance of offered incense from Adele's mother's bedroom.

Monks and nuns from the local temple had placed a shimmering yellow shawl decorated with bright red Sanskrit over her small, stilled body. In another month, Adele's mother would be ninety-nine according to the traditional Chinese way of counting age, adding twelve months after the new Lunar Year.

At the foot of her bed was an altar table with a gold, painted Buddha in the center accompanied by two bodhisattvas, red and yellow votive candles, three small teacups of water, a celadon urn for the offered incense, and four plates of fresh tropical fruit.

The traditional forty-nine days of Buddhist chanting after death have been adapted to fit the pace of modern Taipei. The chanting would only continue for eight hours. Then her body could be removed to the funeral home, which had previously taken care of Adele's father and grandmother. The Buddhist monks and nuns, heads shaven, wearing saffron robes held in place with maroon ties at the waist, echoing the love for red by Chinese for most occasions, led the family in chanting the mantra of prayers, while Adele's mother's body lay motionless at the head of the room.

I sat next to Adele, close to her mother's deathbed, following the words and rhythms of the mantra. The guide from the Temple showed us how each syllable of *A-mi-tuo Fo* was almost drawn out into a sentence and chanted in a rising tone with each syllable for the first round. By the middle of the next two mantras, I was floating on the waves of a warm and caressing sea. In the fourth round, the tone softened, almost into a whisper, close to breathless, signaling a kind of closure. This chanting cycle started over again, and again as if repeating the course of a long life. Cycle after cycle of the Chinese zodiac. Lifetime after lifetime.

14
牛

This was what my mother had wanted and written for herself, seventeen years earlier in her Will and Last Testament, a formal Buddhist ceremony.

I called the Buddhist Temple in San Francisco after I finished putting on the layers of her funerary clothing for all the seasons of the year. There was no answer at the temple at first. I called again, and again, until finally a woman picked up the phone, sounding irritated that I had persisted.

"How much can you pay?" was her first question in answering my request of a Buddhist ceremony on my mother's behalf.

I was taken aback. It was not what I expected from what I had always thought about Buddhist philosophy: giving alms, saving lives, helping people through difficulties, helping them transcend this life cycle on Earth.

The woman continued after the hesitation on my side of the line, "Besides, do you know this is the Lunar New Year's Eve?"

Chinese New Year's Eve. A time for celebration, feasts, family gathering. Not a time to talk about funerals.

I had not realized that when I was calling, not having checked the Chinese calendar on my mother's kitchen wall. I did not even own a calendar with the lunar months and significant days of the year, such as the Harvest Moon Festival, the Lunar New Year, and the Dragon Boat Festival in May commemorating the early patriotic poet Qu Yuan from the state of Chu.

"We do not go out of the temple for fifteen days after the New Year," she added. She probably took my hesitation to mean I did not have the money for a Buddhist ceremony.

"I'll see what I can do." My devoted Thai-Chinese friend came to the rescue again. When my mother was hospitalized years ago and wanted hot water at her bedside, instead of the usual pitcher of water with ice, he offered to bring her a hot thermos every morning. Over the years, he has become a treasured member of the family and the son who catered to her every wish, the kind of son my mother always wanted.

He was able to get the monks from the local Thai Buddhist Temple to preside at my mother's funeral. They came in their formal robes and chanted in Thai at the funeral. I could have only hoped it was close enough to the Chinese Buddhist ceremony my mother wanted for me to arrange in her Last Will.

I thought of the final months after she was diagnosed with inoperable lung cancer. Among her last requests was her repeated wish for me to move in with her, but in the end, I did not even fulfill her wish that I be by her side when she took her last breath.

As the mesmerizing rhythms of the mantras continued throughout the day next to Adele's mother's body, the portrait of her on the Buddhist altar seemed to merge with one of my own mother. I could not help seeing the life of my mother unfolding, replaying scene by scene, year after year, in front of my closed eyelids. Involuntarily my eyes moistened, blurring the scenes of the life I remembered.

We were in the large garden in the back of a friend's French colonial summer house on the outskirts of old Shanghai. I could still see her dashing across the well-manicured lawn to hover over me, a lioness over her cub, when a baseball from an older boys' game struck me accidentally. I finally stopped crying, but I could not admit to myself the measure of embarrassment that I was acting like a sissy boy from the looks on the other children.

I could see my mother lingering over piles of her Russian heirloom silverware and sterling services, which she had brought over to this tropical island of Taiwan from Mainland China. She had arranged them on little tables like mounds of incense offered to her ancestors, but it was for a garage sale in our Japanese garden. She was trying to build a nest egg for my college education in faraway America, which she thought would give me the best future she could imagine. I was still a student in my first year of junior high school.

Then on a sharper screen closer to home, a memory when she was already in her seventies. Because she tinted her hair, I had more gray than she did. I was taking her to Mother's Day lunch at the Carnelian Room, and I should have known better than to carelessly shut the car door over her finger in the parking garage. She did not cry out, I only saw her eyes water. Her silent tears stung me more deeply than if she had cried out in pain.

And on the last image in front of me, I saw her lying motionless in her apartment, yellowing shoji screens shuttered and candles flickering from the crack of the window opened at the foot of her bed, waiting for me to put on her ceremonial funerary clothing. A duty for the son that she had made sure I remembered, when she knew her days were numbered. I could feel the onset of rigidity in her body and the coolness of her skin where warm blood had stopped flowing. She had been waiting for several hours for me to come from the hospital where I was finishing my work in the operating room. I realized I had failed her again.

The mantras continued, undulating and urging me on, rhythms calm as a maternal lullaby when the sun disappeared from the horizon, *A-mi-tuo-Fo, A-mi--tuo---Fo, A-mi--tuo---Fo, A-mi-tuo--Fo*...My eyes closed, my breathing slowed, the words I heard gradually became— *Ma--mi--tuo--Fo, Ma---mi---tuo---Fo, Mommy----tuo----Fo.*

The tears for my mother finally flooded my eyes, and I could not stop myself.

Chapter Fifteen

虎

We inched along the road where I used to live, a copy of a newly published tourist guide to the old French Concession of Shanghai in my shoulder bag. I had decided, a year ago, to rent an apartment on the old Avenue Joffre, now renamed Huaihai Lu, not far from my earlier home. Treading in the footsteps of my childhood, I wanted to show Adele the part of the city I remembered.

By stroke of luck, they kept the old name of the road where I used to live, *Mao Ming Nan Lu*, a name alluding to exuberance. Other roads of my childhood, *Xia Fei Lu* or Avenue Joffre, *Pei Dang Lu* or Avenue Petain, *Mei Er Xi Ai Lu* or Rue de Cardinal Mercier, all have different names now. Without its old name and the neighboring street names all changed, it would have taken me hours to find the quiet residential street lushly lined with French sycamores, once filled with the chattering sparrows at sunset and the golden yellow, maple shaped leaves on the sidewalks in early autumn. It was in my home on this street after World War II, from behind the ceiling high gauzy mosquito net, where I remembered seeing my father for the first time.

Now the street was full of specialty shops selling the latest fashions in ready-made silk or cashmere women's wear and boutiques offering quick, made-to-order men's suits in British wools, as well as shirts in Chinese silks and Egyptian cotton. Only a smattering of the old sycamores survived. The sparrows did not, following

Mao's orders to rid the country of birds because they were thought to harm the farmer's crops. Wedged in between the high fashion, young men and women sat in bars decorated with posters of Moulin Rouge and Montmartre or ordered sushi from chefs in Japanese happy coats. The home where I used to live was nowhere in sight.

On the street corner, a middle-aged man who could have been a Red Guard of the Cultural Revolution thirty years earlier was bellowing, *tang chao li zi, tang chao li zi.* The nickel-sized, sweet, fragrant Tianjin chestnut roasted in hot sand, darkened by a touch of molasses, was the only thing reminding me of the street when I was eight. I remembered staying close to my mother and her younger sister in their flower-printed dresses, carrying leather purses and wearing high heels, considered the height of fashion in post-World War II Shanghai.

The man's words were in Mandarin now, words somehow lacking the sweet rhythms imprinted in my memory; the same phrases sung in the local Shanghai dialect of my childhood when customers not speaking the local dialect were often charged a higher price.

I remembered hearing a stream of words, *tso na niang ge bi,* so lively and mellifluous in Shanghai dialect from the street to my eight-year-old ears of nascent curiosity, that I repeated them in front of my mother at the dinner table, only to be stunned by a slap across my cheek.

"Don't you ever repeat those words again! Do you hear me?" It was the only occasion I could remember of my mother striking me on the face. She never explained their meaning, and I didn't dare ask, knowing they must have been riven with something terribly forbidden. I didn't find out till I was in college and met a fellow student who grew up in Shanghai.

"No wonder your mother slapped you!" he said, doubling up with laughter. "Those words meant, 'Go fuck your mother!'"

"You were too sheltered in your upbringing," he said, chiding my lack of exposure and savvy to common street lingo.

Yet my mother was not upset when I repeated the words of our driver. When my father returned, he brought along an old Ford sedan and the Cantonese driver who was with him through the years of the war. The driver tried to satisfy my curiosity about the car, which was not a common object at that time even for Shanghai.

In the process of trying to educate me about automobiles, he said Lincolns were at the top, then Buicks and Packards, Oldsmobiles in the middle, and our Ford was at the bottom. The word for Oldsmobile was quite a mouthful. To make it easy for me and probably for himself as well, because he did not speak English either, he said, just remember *O Si O Niu*. That made it unforgettable for me. When I repeated those words in Cantonese at the dinner table, my mother did not laugh, but I could hardly contain my giggle because they meant to defecate and urinate in Cantonese. After I came to this country for college and found myself face to face with a real Oldsmobile, those words in Cantonese would precede its proper English pronunciation.

Today Mandarin is taught in schools and has become the compulsory national tongue, a singular achievement of Mao Zedong's Communist Revolution, which his predecessor, Chiang Kai-shek was unable to accomplish, but for the risk of pushing innumerable regional dialects into oblivion.

"We couldn't have missed it!" Adele was sure we checked every house number and every storefront on this section of *Mao Ming Nan Lu*.

She did not live in Shanghai as a child. Her passion for traveling played a major part in bringing us together. For as long as we have known each other she exuded the same confidence in finding an obscure piazzetta with its own framed corner Madonna, as the first time she showed me her favorite Florence in Tuscany or some hidden cobblestone path climbing up a hill town of Umbria. She had no doubts we would find the house where I used to live.

My mother and I weren't able to live in Shanghai under our real names. The Japanese had already occupied the city, which surrendered without much resistance after the news spread about the massacre in Nanking, the other end of the Nanking-Shanghai Railway line. They would have dragged us into jail or worse, if they found out my father's role in ChungKing, the wartime Capitol for Chiang Kai-shek's KMT.

The flat on *Mao Ming Nan Lu* my mother rented was owned by a White Russian émigré. Marshall Stalin did not join the Allied war effort until the very end, and Russians were more or less left alone by the Japanese.

Our landlord felt an instant kinship with my mother who spoke to him in Russian and reminisced about old St. Petersburg and Moscow, when they were both younger and under better circumstances. She had me call him *Dzyadzenka*. I was quite accustomed to addressing my mother's men friends as Uncle, and this seemed to have endeared ourselves to our landlord forever. My mother also felt he was less likely to find out about the nuances behind our assumed names.

Dzyadzenka's house was in the first block up from the street leading to the old French Park, a leisurely ten-minute walk to the park where my nurse took us mornings when the sun lit up the remaining dew on the grass lawns. The Japanese left the old colonial sign up which read, *No Dogs, Bicycles or Chinese Allowed.* But the rule was no longer enforced.

"Why don't we start over from the old French Park?" It was close to noon and Adele thought we could also take a break there.

Its front entrance on the newly named *Chende Lu* was wide open. As I was trying to point out where the old French sign used to be, we passed through the open gates. A voice yelled at us from a small office, half hidden behind the stone gateposts.

"Where are you going?"

I was startled, not careful enough to notice the small sign about the entrance fee partially hidden behind the gate. "We're just taking a walk in the park," I was conciliatory in my tone because I knew it was still better not to argue with authorities in Mainland China, although things had improved a great deal from the time of my first trip—shortly after it reopened to visitors. At that time, I could not walk around much on my own without being followed by a guide, even though I did not need an interpreter like some foreign tourists.

"I used to come here as a child," I added in Shanghai dialect, when I overheard the woman speaking in that dialect to her friend sitting beside her on a wooden stool.

"There is a two yuan charge for use of the park." Her voice softened from the initial authoritarian bark.

We paid the equivalent of a quarter for the two of us and the woman became helpful in pointing out the way toward the lake. I remembered it being one of my favorite places as a child and could see flowering bushes and tall evergreens in the background. A pavilion for tea stood on one side.

The tune of *Tea for Two* serenaded us as we got closer, and I was eight again, when my mother brought me to hear the band at the Park Hotel. In those days, the twenty-four-storied art deco edifice was the tallest building in the Orient, and its ballroom felt huge to me then, as enormous as Radio City Music Hall when I first visited Rockefeller Center while on vacation from college.

Adele and I walked toward the back entrance of the park. A vendor had yo-yo's and shuttlecocks from a bamboo rack strapped to his bicycle. A little girl in a pink-striped outfit with a cat and mouse appliqué, begged her mother to buy one. I was about her age when my nurse held my hand while we had our morning walks here on sunny days.

As we passed the exit gates now, I couldn't help looking back at the girl. She succeeded in persuading her mother and was happily kicking up her new toy. I had noticed earlier that parents from Mainland China were very indulgent, the one child policy made them tolerate unruly behavior unseen in days when I was young.

We took a side street and noticed a sign for Sun Yat-sen's old home.

"Not finding your old home," Adele said brightly, "shall we take a look at the Founder's of the Republic?"

The house was on a street a block away from *Mao Ming Nan Lu*. A road sign indicated it was now a historical monument, but I was still intent on finding some trace of my old home.

We passed several large brick houses with fences low enough for us to peek over and see the well-kept gardens. I spotted the entrance portico to a French colonial mansion. The fine lines of its old self were still discernable. Now there were about seven or eight mailboxes tacked onto the doorway.

The house was like the one of Auntie Lu in the older part of the city, where artists and writers made their homes in the Thirties.

I had just past my sixth birthday two months earlier and was dressed in my Chinese New Year's best. Once a year my mother relaxed her vigilance of keeping a low profile under the Japanese occupation, and we celebrated and welcomed the New Year.

It was also the year of the Lamb, marking of the beginnings of the third cycle of her life on the Chinese zodiac. Auntie Lu, a good friend from their earlier days in Beijing, shared that distinction on the zodiac, but she was one cycle ahead of my mother. Now widowed, she was still living in the large colonial mansion she once shared with her husband. My mother was holding my hand when we were ushered into her inner chambers.

The curtains were drawn except for one window at the far end of the chamber. The early winter afternoon light from that window filtered through the haze hovering over the vast, intricately carved bed, known in China as the *luohan kang*, literally, a platform of repose for arhats and bodhisattvas.

The slightly sweet and musty smell of something burnt, which I learned later was opium, wafted back into my nose. The drapes were drawn except for one window at the far end of the chamber. A single ray of light from that window beamed onto the little terrier, head cocked toward the Victrola on the RCA logo in one corner.

My eyes caught a small dark figure reclining in the recesses of the cavernous *kang*, half hidden by the partially drawn embroidered silk curtains.

"*Guo lai*," the tiny sparrow like creature's bony fingers motioned for me to come closer. I was a little apprehensive to approach her. Dressed in dark ruby colored crushed velvet Mandarin gown with embroidered collar and sleeves, and a bright jade ornament shiny like a search light in a miner's tunnel pinned to her forehead. She looked as if she were on the stage of a Peking Opera.

My mother shoved me forward to accept the red envelope held out to me. It was for the New Year, my mother explained, after telling me to call the fragile figure Auntie Lu.

"You don't have to kowtow in front of me. Just a bow will do." Her voice was a bit hoarse, but gentle. In her other hand, she was still holding a long pipe with a small brass scoop at the end, darkened from use.

"Don't get up." My mother said. "We can just visit like this."

"Time for me to get up and stretch these old bones a little. I've been going over his poems all day." With that, she pushed a large pile of books into the darker recesses of the bed. My mother stepped forward to help Auntie down from the bed into her slippers with tiny heels.

I had seen my mother's embroidered slippers, but never any with heels.

Even with her heels and standing up, Auntie Lu still looked diminutive and crouched like a crow. Wearing a crooked smile as if to reassure me, she shuffled around us. I noticed some of her teeth were darkened and a few were missing.

"How old is Auntie Lu?" I asked my mother when we were in the rickshaw taking us home.

"Only a few years older than I."

"She looks really old."

"She's been through a lot." My mother thought for a moment and decided to explain further. "She was known as the Beauty of Qingdao before she married the poet, Xu Zhimo. He was killed in a plane crash some years ago." My mother made it sound like something terrible, but I didn't know what to die in a plane crash really meant.

"What was she smoking?" The image of Auntie Lu bent over with her long pipe kept popping in front of my six-year-old eyes, as the rickshaw rolled along the road.

"Shh!" My mother held her fingers against her mouth and pointed to the old straining rickshaw puller in front of us, even though we were separated from him by a heavy curtain put up for the winter months.

"Why was she holding that long pipe?" I had to know, as soon as we got inside our house.

"When you are older, I'll explain."

"She used to have a good voice for Peking Opera, and she's a good painter too." I was not dissuaded by my mother's attempt to distract me from the direction of my curiosity.

When I was a little older, my mother explained Auntie Lu was one of the few people the government looked aside, permitting her the crutch of opiates after the tragic loss of her celebrated husband. Opium use was a capital offense from the time of the founding of the First Republic, and plane rides were a rare and perilous undertaking in 1931.

Her husband was a romantic poet and essayist, considered to be the Keats of early twentieth century China. When I was a student in Cambridge, Massachusetts, I picked up a volume of his poems. His "Goodbye Again to Cambridge" was my favorite, even though his adieu was dedicated to the other Cambridge, across the Atlantic.

A refrain from that poem echoes in my ears every time I read it, I can't help but also see Auntie Lu in her crushed velvet and bright jade cabochon again. Several years ago, I read a marble plaque in the poet's memory had been installed on the grounds of Kings College, Cambridge, England in 2008.

A gray-haired man emerged from the shadows behind the portico of the old house, as Adele and I hesitated outside its gate.

"Are you tourists?" He noticed the book, in English, I was holding.

"I used to live on the next street over," I answered in Mandarin. I decided to tell him because his tone was gentle and his English had an old-school accent, almost British.

"How long ago?" he smiled and switched to Mandarin tinged with a Shanghai accent.

"Ah…Almost sixty years ago." I did some mental arithmetic and switched to Shanghai dialect.

"A lot has changed," the gentleman said thoughtfully, decades seemingly passing across his eyes.

"Have you always lived here?" I was curious.

"No," he shook his head, "I moved here after the Cultural Revolution." He switched back to English, sotto voce.

"The house was abandoned by its owners and my family lost our own home. So, we moved into one of the rooms in this house."

It sounded almost too painful for him to recount the details, although I wanted to ask him where he learned his English. Instead, I just said, "You speak English so well!"

"I used to teach it." He straightened himself up a bit from his stoop. "That's why I try to speak it whenever I see tourists going by."

"A lot of tourists in this area?"

"Ever since that Guide to Old Shanghai came out." He looked at the book I held in my hand.

15
虎

"What happened to the old homes on Mao Ming Nan Lu?" I thought he might have the answer.

"It's a shame what happened to that street," I could see the corner of his eyes drooping in resignation, "first a few bars opened up. Now it's full of bars and shops. They have torn down the old buildings because the businesses offered more money. It's made this area so noisy now, especially at night."

"We couldn't find my old home," I commiserated with his sentiments.

"Which one was it?"

"It was a three-storied white building in the middle of the last block before you turn onto the street for the old French park." I could almost see the old sycamores shading the front.

"Was it the one that used to be owned by an old Russian man?"

"You know it?"

"Had a row of pigeon coops in the back garden."

"I used to live in the flat on the second floor. You've been inside the house?"

"I used to teach the Russian boy English," his thoughts were churning back sixty years, "before the family immigrated to America."

I figured he must have just gotten out of college then. He must have read my thoughts, because he added, "I was just in my last year at St. John's."

I remembered an older cousin who had studied there, a college in Shanghai where students could speak English by the time they graduated.

My cousin was already a strapping, handsome young man at the end of the war. He was also my mother's favorite, the third among three boys in his family. Several times he appeared suddenly, late at night, blood drained out of the healthy cheeks I was accustomed to seeing.

"You've got to help me, Auntie," he pleaded.

My mother would set up an extra cot for him in my room, but he was always gone by the next morning.

"Where's *San Ge?*" I asked when I woke.

"Don't mention it to anybody that he was here," my mother cautioned.

Years after we left Shanghai and I was a high school student in Tokyo, I heard he was high up in the government after the Communists took over and I asked my mother whether she knew.

"Yes, he was hiding from Old Chiang's secret police, and he knew they would not look for him in our home because of your father's work with Old Chiang's Government."

"You hear from that family anymore?" I asked the old gentlemen, although I didn't think it likely with everything that's happened. During the Cultural Revolution, any contact with the United States was an automatic prison sentence or worse.

His brows came together, and I didn't know what he was going to say, "I didn't expect it. But, last year the young boy was here with a tour group. He was asking just like you are now. And..." his voice trailed a bit, and I thought I could see his eyes moistening.

"It was almost like a miracle. I had to tell him they tore down the old building five years ago."

I felt a little thickening in my throat, "Thank you for telling us all this," I managed to say.

The deep roots of the few surviving French sycamores on that street and this old gentleman in front of me were the only ones with memories of those days now. There had been a directive by the government to cut down the trees and eliminate the birds' habitat.

I gave him my calling card and told him to look me up if he should ever come to California, even though I knew it was unlikely.

"Come back again!" He seemed to stand up taller than when he first appeared at the portico, as if he was about to gesture with a bow, then waved as he retreated into the shadows of his doorway.

15

虎

Chapter Sixteen

兔

My golden age in Shanghai was when I was six.

Fireflies in the rear garden of our friends' home in Hongqiao. The countryside outside Shanghai, rice patties dotting the two-lane road, our pedicabs along the ox-carts, now the site of the second largest international airport and many skyscrapers.

Jen-Jen, my favorite playmate, her older sister and I were gathered around the knees of her governess, *Shui Xiao Jie,* Miss Shui. Their father owned a private hospital favored by the Western-trained doctors. We were introduced to them probably through my mother's first cousin on her father's side, the first Chinese woman gynecologist trained at Johns Hopkins.

Miss Shui was the children's favorite, a woman soft and wide as the waters of the sea, which was her family name. Her nose sat on an open face like a flowering cabbage, her smile was warmer than the quilted jacket my mother insisted I wear after sundown.

On balmy evenings, the children huddled around her ample bosom eager for her tales of ghosts and spirits from the classic, *Liao Zhai Zhi Yi.* Another governess, *Zhu Xiao Jie,* whose last name Zhu was a homonym for pig, sat in the back, trying to keep the mosquitoes away by slowing waving a fan of palm leaves. The fireflies and the summer moon were our lanterns at dusk.

Miss Shui timed the stories so that they ended just when cooler night breezes crept in from the fields behind us and swept away the fireflies.

"Time to go to bed," she gathered us up to our feet, "the fire-flies know when the ghosts are coming, that's why they have put out their lights."

In truth, my first introduction to Shanghai was the gray wharf with the black hull of our ship docked alongside, which carried us north on the East China Sea from Hong Kong, then up the River Huangpu to the city of my maternal grandmother's ancestors.

My mother had decided to return to the city more familiar to her, where she had friends and family, not far from Suzhou where she spent her early childhood. Although Shanghai had already fallen to the Japanese, she did not want to remain in unfamiliar, Cantonese-speaking Hong Kong, which was soon going to follow into their hands. Her friends told her the Fall of Shanghai was not as brutal as that of the massacre in Nanking. Shanghai was also a city used to foreign intervention, from the time China lost the Opium Wars, a century earlier. The Japanese Occupation more or less left the Foreign Concessions alone in the beginning, especially the French one, although they controlled most everything else during the occupation.

As soon as we entered Shanghai's harbor, the grip of my mother's right hand on my blue wool mittens was firm, letting me know we were now on uncertain grounds. I clung to her reassuring grip on that mid-January afternoon of cold pewter sky. Her other hand was tucked into a huge furry purse, common in the early forties, used to ward off some of the chill.

People around us shuffled along in long gray coats over their ankle length mandarin gowns. A few wore western clothes, the dark trouser legs distinguishing them from the more traditional. The few women there dressed in somber colors for fear of attracting attention from the Japanese military.

Coolies, pedicabs and rickshaw pullers hovered and hustled for business, the only ones seemingly unaffected by the gloom.

"Can we get on one of those?" I tugged at my mother's hand and pointed to a rickshaw, not having seen one before in Hong Kong.

"Shhh!" She lowered her voice and stooped to my ear, "You should keep quiet, or the Japanese soldiers will come and get you!" She pointed to one not far away, but not within earshot, bayonet flashing like a warning signal in the waning afternoon light. My mother's warning voice and expression of alarm somehow made me more frightened than the actual sight of the bayonet. I did not yet comprehend the harm it was capable of inflicting.

Her old friend found us and stepped forward from the crowd.

"Address her as Auntie Chu." My mother pointed me toward the woman with dark complexion and a little taller than herself, and she acknowledged me with a quiet smile of welcome.

Chu was her maiden name. It was an acknowledgement of their old days at *Beida*, the familiar name they used to describe the old Beijing University, when my mother was still Miss Guan and her friend Miss Chu. My mother was active in the diplomatic circles and spoke both French and Russian, while her friend was already rumored to have caught the eye of chair of the Department of Chinese Classics, a man known for his elegant calligraphy.

Auntie Chu arranged for us and our luggage to be taken in three pedicabs to her home. I was tucked between my mother and her friend in the first cab, an old blanket across our legs and an oil cloth as windshield over our front against the chill. The little gaps in the cloth loosely fastened on the sides of the cab allowed me peeks of the bustle and traffic on the streets passing by, more than I was used to seeing in Repulse Bay of Hong Kong. Auntie Chu's maid rode in the last cab with our lighter luggage while the heavier trunks and suitcases went on top of the middle cab.

"You've got to be careful in Shanghai." Auntie Chu whispered to my mother like a big sister, "The city is not what it used to be when you and I were younger. If you're not careful, the other cab could run off with your luggage." Then she cautioned further, "Don't ever let Didi go out alone, there are kidnappers who will get a child and disembowel it for drug smuggling!"

She referred to me as little brother, the affectionate way of calling her old friend's four-year-old boy, and I felt my mother's hand tighten around my own.

The ride seemed to have taken the better part of what was left of the afternoon, partly because I could not see much from inside the cab. Later, I learned that the driver had taken a longer route in order to avoid the headquarters of the Japanese militia; the wharf was not as far away from the English Concession where Auntie Chu lived, as it seemed on that first ride.

Auntie's house was located on a small street off the main road. At dusk, the three-level brick structure that stood in front of me looked very dark, and not just from years of wood and coal burning in the neighborhood. In retrospect, I could see it in a Dickens' London, with Chinese mahogany interiors, in sharp contrast to our home in Hong Kong which was an airy, cream colored two-story stucco with lacquered, blond-wood furniture, a block up from the sandy beach of Repulse Bay.

My mother gave me a tug as I hesitated to step in the front door, not sure of what to expect. A long, narrow stairway led to the floor above from the back of the entryway. The living room had sturdy, traditional Chinese chairs and tables, all in dark mahogany. Two long scrolls of matched Chinese calligraphy in large formal characters faced me as I looked into the room.

"Those are by Uncle Shen," my mother pointed out. I didn't know enough to sing praises as expected. The famous calligrapher, who was Auntie Chu's husband, my mother explained. "Uncle Shen is a great calligrapher! And Auntie Chu as well."

Great calligraphy was just a bunch of wiggly black lines to me at the time. It was to be four more years before my father first came into my life, when he held my hand and initiated me into the art of Chinese brush calligraphy.

In the somber, coldness that permeated Auntie Chu's home, I stuck closely to my mother's side. I thought of one of the side rooms of an old Chinese temple to which my mother had taken me once, across the bay of Hong Kong.

Ding-zi-geh was the room we were put in, a room between the ground and second floor, just above the kitchen. In Shanghai dialect, a pavilion room was euphemism for, more accurately, a garden shed. The French have a good word for it, *entresol*, a low-ceilinged space between what they called the first floor and the ground level.

Many poor students rented these rooms when they could not afford better accommodations, luckily it was never cold because of its location above the kitchen, but along with the warmth, all the smoke and odors also found their way into the niche.

Auntie's room was on the floor above, and she was good enough to share the bathroom with us. On the third floor, in the front was a studio for Uncle Shen's books and more of his calligraphy; although he had followed the university and its students in the mass retreat from the Japanese, into Chungking in the southwestern interiors of China.

My mother was grateful to her friend that we were allowed to stay there, but also realized very soon we needed to find our own place as quickly as possible.

Not long after we settled in, Auntie Chu hinted to my mother we were putting her family at risk, knowing my father worked for the KMT government in Chungking, and she was already afraid of being discovered, given that her husband was also KMT. The Japanese Occupation was brutal with people if they found out they were harboring anyone with connections to the KMT. In addition to ending up in jail for giving us shelter, Auntie Chu could lose her house in the process.

My mother shielded me from what she heard about the Nanking Massacre, where the KMT Army tried to defend its Capitol. News spread underground of Japanese soldiers using babies for bayonet practice, women raped en mass regardless of how young or how old, and people forced to dig their own graves before being shot or bayoneted.

I was not to find out the details until I read Iris Chang's book, *The Rape of Nanking*. The fragility of the author's emotional state could not survive when faced with these terrifying details and the onslaught of Japanese criticism of her afterward, in their attempt to deny the facts she uncovered. She took her own life eight years after the book was published.

Auntie Chu and my mother were both lucky. The Japanese never found out about us. Uncle Shen, like my father, also returned to Shanghai at the end of the War, but he was discouraged by the corruption he saw in Chiang's regime and decided to dissociate himself by resigning from all his positions and live by selling his calligraphy and books of poetry and essays he wrote. Later, I read when Mao took over the Mainland, Uncle Shen was honored with the position of Vice Cultural Minister and his calligraphy hung in Mao and Zhou En-lai's private offices.

My mother found her old friend when the Mainland was reopened after the rapprochement negotiated by Kissinger and Nixon. Auntie Chu had become known for her own calligraphy and succeeded her husband in the Cultural Ministry after he died. She gave my mother a scroll with the calligraphy she had done of her husband's poetry.

When I look at this memento in Auntie Chu's hand now hanging in the study of my apartment in Italy, I can almost see the woman who gave me a kind smile in Shanghai harbor over seventy years ago.

My mother could not shield me from everything during the Japanese Occupation. One of her friends took us to see a film. It was past my usual bedtime, but I was wide awake and excited, never having seen a movie before.

We walked along a dimly lit street to a building looking like a discarded warehouse. There were no lights from the windows. The friend tapped on a side door, and a man appeared from behind a black curtain. He hustled us in, then quickly shut the door.

Inside were rows of wooden benches and there was a large white sheet at the front end of the room, which was used as the screen. The man pointed to some seats on the far side. The room was already nearly full. My mother lifted me onto her lap in order for me to see the front.

The film was grainy, in black and white. From time to time I heard a loud snap, and the picture went blurry like snowflakes, then stopped. I could hear someone cranking something in the back and then the jerky picture came back. The sound track was harsh like a badly scratched record on a Victrola.

On the white sheet, I saw a woman about my mother's age being forced to be nice to a rich businessman collaborating with the Japanese. The slight wavy motion of the sheet made the woman look more fragile and unstable. She was able to feed her family with the money she got from him, and she passed on information she gathered from the man to the Underground. Eventually, she was discovered, dragged out, and tortured. My mother covered my eyes, when the woman was shot by police working for the Japanese Occupation, leaving behind her mother and child.

The room was very quiet at the end, and we all slid out through the black curtain like mice into the night. My mother put her finger to her lips for me to keep quiet when I tried to have her explain why the woman was killed.

From the extra tight hold of my hand, as we walked briskly away from the place, I knew my mother was not only trying to reassure me, but as frightened as I was, and feeling safe only after we finally got behind our front door. In the middle of the night,

I woke up screaming, I thought the police were coming to get us, until my mother came to my bed and reassured me everything as all right.

Several months later, when I was getting ready for bed, there was a knock on our door. My mother went to open it.

The man I called BaBa, or father, was bent over and almost fell into the room. His hair ruffled, his overcoat disheveled and unbuttoned. His shoes untied. He hobbled in and collapsed onto the kitchen chair.

Under the light, I could see his face. On one side, his eye was shut and puffy, and his cheek, bruised like a rotting eggplant. My mother helped him out of his coat, and I saw his shirt and pants were soiled and torn. She led him into the bathroom and shut the door.

I heard the water faucet running. When my mother opened the door to get something from the bedroom, she shooed me away. But I was able to get a glimpse of BaBa in the bathtub.

Bruises covered him. Then I noticed his scrotum was an over-sized burnt *mantou*, the large steamed bread-like bun my mother made on special occasions. He tried to cover it with his hand when he saw me staring.

Neither he nor my mother said anything to me later or the next day.

But from bits of conversations I caught between the grown-ups, I found out he was beaten by Japanese border patrol on his way back from a trip to Chungking.

He was lucky not to have gotten worse treatment. A man my mother knew worked for the Japanese Occupation. He intervened when the Japanese soldiers were still kicking BaBa on the ground, with their boots and striking him with their rifle butts. He had to guarantee that BaBa was only a businessman travelling back from inland and not a spy. After the war, I learned, in truth, several times a year he was risking his own life carrying information about us in Occupied Shanghai to my real father in Chungking.

A large black and white photo in the old Family Album of my mother's fortieth birthday celebration after the War, recorded the occasion when my father thanked this good friend for letting us use his surname as a shield when my mother and I lived under the Occupation. My mother was afraid I could not be trusted as a child with the truth and thus told me to call him BaBa.

The man who saved him visited us several times near the end of the War. My mother told me to call him Uncle Lo.

He confided in my mother he was disillusioned by his work collaborating with the Japanese Occupation. After the War, he was tried as a traitor but spared the death sentence given to some of his co-collaborators, because he had helped some people against the atrocities of the Occupation.

My mother never told me whether she was one of the people who pleaded leniency for him. But I saw the pain in her eyes when she told me he died during the Cultural Revolution in a Mainland jail. The Communist regime did not treat him kindly, she said.

I will never forget the day I was taken to the Railway Station to pick up my maternal grandfather, Wai Gong, for Chinese New Year.

He lived in Suzhou. Half a day by train in those days, but only 27 minutes away when I visited with Adele two months ago. The city was once called the Venice of China.

Before his arrival my mother told me firmly, to be polite but never to call the woman he was bringing with him, Wai Po. Maternal grandmother in Mandarin. Eavesdropping on the conversations between my mother and her brother, my Fourth Maternal Uncle, I learned, the woman was grandfather's Fifth Concubine. From my mother's tone of voice, this was not a person deserving respect.

The pedicab driver dropped us close to the front of the Station. He was not allowed to approach the Main Entrance. Rolls of barbed wire, bayonets, and Japanese soldiers barricaded the path. The station was a slow-moving sea of cotton rags and patched quilted clothing, people carrying packages in hands and bags tied onto shoulders and backs, for Chinese New Year.

I walked between my mother and the maidservant who came with us to help with the luggage. From my mother's vice-like grip, I knew I was supposed to stick close.

I felt the relief in my mother's grip when we got by the soldiers without having to have everything inspected. Some people had their belongings strewn all over the ground while the soldiers picked at them with the points of their bayonets.

We gradually edged our way inside with the crowd and looked for the platform for the train from Suzhou.

Jammed in like fish caught in a net, people were packed against one another everywhere. Bayonets drawn, soldiers goose stepped back and forth, poking at the scared and shuffling travelers from time to time.

One woman with a face like a shriveled beet root had a baby papoosed on her back. Suddenly I saw the flash of a bayonet. A soldier ran its sharp point straight into the baby. There was no cry, no blood. I instinctively folded into my mother and shuddered.

Next, I saw the woman yanked out of the line by her hair. The soldier kicked her on the side and woman started to beg for her life.

My mother and the maid quickly pulled me away.

"Why?" I looked at my mother.

She shook her head and gave me the look to shut up.

Seeing I was still puzzled, the maid whispered into my ear. "That was not a live baby." With an even lower voice, she added, *"Ze si."* The way she said it made the words for smuggling in Shanghai dialect sound like the worst crime in history.

Then I remembered Auntie Chu's words in the pedicab from the wharf when we first arrived. Smugglers kidnapped children and stuffed their bodies with drugs. Instinctively I squeezed the two hands that were holding me on each side, as tightly as I could.

"Didn't know you had such a tight grip." The maid looked at me, trying to make me relax.

Wai Gong was just getting off the train when we got to the platform. He was in a dark traditional Chinese gentleman's gown, black-rimmed spectacles and shoes made of heavy black cotton and white soles, just the way I had seen him in one of his photographs. In his right hand was his walking stick with a silver top, and his left hand held onto a young girl a little shorter than myself. A woman, plainly dressed, almost like our maidservant, followed with a small suitcase in her hand.

My mother stepped forward while continuing her hold of my hand and told me to address my maternal grandfather.

The woman quickly came over and addressed my mother.

"*San Xiao Jie, Nin Hao.*" How are you, Third Young Mistress? She addressed my mother in Mandarin as if she were a servant of the family.

My mother gave her a nod of recognition and asked about the young girl.

The woman just as quickly asked her daughter to step forward and address my mother the same way. The young girl was actually my mother's half-sister by this woman.

Once a concubine, forever a concubine. And that goes for their children, too. My mother's harsh words, uttered when she got going about Wai Gong's numerous concubines. She never gave up her deep resentment toward them, because with the first one he brought home, arrived the beginning of her own mother's suffering and the beatings at the hands of my grandfather, which were to become routine until she died. Pictures of my grandmother in the family album showed a petite woman, dignified but defenseless with tiny, bound lotus-feet. Eventually, my mother believed, the abuse led to her early death at age forty-eight, leaving behind ten children.

The woman, carrying the suitcase next to my grandfather at the train station, looked harmless and without guile. Her daughter gave me a timid smile. She could be a playmate like Jen-Jen I thought. She was a year younger than I when my mother asked her mother. She stuck closely to her own mother throughout the visit.

Several months ago, I received a first draft for the updated edition of my mother's family genealogy. My mother never mentioned things about her own father's family or his accomplishments. She could not forget the beatings and abuse her own mother suffered at his hands.

Her family genealogy was like reading the ghost stories I heard on summer nights told by Miss Shui. The people with whom I was familiar—my mother, her sisters, her brothers, her father and his concubines—all are gone now.

My maternal grandfather's distant ancestor, Guan Zhong, was a well-known Prime Minister from the period in Chinese history, called the Spring and Autumn, Warring States. Over two millennia the clan scattered and migrated southward. One branch ended up in Suzhou. I imagined the spirits of these ancestors hovering on a summer night, among the fireflies under the moon.

The only name I recognized in my mother's family genealogy, who is of her generation and still living is my grandfather's youngest child, born in 1938, a year after me and a Tiger by the Chinese zodiac. The little girl, sticking close to her mother when we met at the train station in occupied Shanghai, is listed as a professor in the University in Nanjing. She should be the same age as Adele now.

Chapter Seventeen

龍

If my mother gave me her looks and joie de vivre, I get my bones and marrow from my father. He introduced me to the art of Chinese calligraphy when he showed up in my life. Over the past seven decades, his passion for it has seeped into my blood and soul.

Chinese brush calligraphy has been held up as the center of Chinese arts from the time it was carved into bones of animals. Scholars of Chinese culture have even referred to it as "its elegant backbones." The mother of the folk hero and poet general of the Song Dynasty, Yue Fei, famously tattooed her teachings onto the skin of her son's back in calligraphy. And one of the first folk songs I learned in glee club used his poem as lyrics.

As I sat at the scholar's table, a size my father would have approved for the practice of brush calligraphy, I could feel myself inadvertently straightening the sock and sinews of my spine, holding my elbow off the table with my wrist at right angles to the calligraphy brush, moving the brush with close to balletic pas de deux precision and deliberation, the way my father taught me. It was like practicing a form of Tai Chi at the table. The brushes my father left behind faced me from the brush holder held up by the carved stone chimera at its base.

The scent from the ink stick was unmistakable, as the pitch-black resin bound pigment was slowly ground onto the inkstone from my grandfather. My daughter had playfully thrown the stone against the hard floor when she was barely two, chipping the tail of the carved hare. I felt deeply remiss that something over four centuries old, belonging to the great scholar, painter and calligrapher of the Ming Dynasty, Dong Qichang, and a gift to my father from my maternal grandfather then passed down to me had been damaged under my care, so I had it restored by a woman who also had the DeYoung Museum as her client. It was a very skillful job, but I could always see the damaged corner, like the scar of a damaged heart muscle that could be seen on an electrocardiogram tracing.

Moonlight through the wavy old glass on the Italian veranda doors across my table could have been the first blue light of dawn in the study of my childhood Shanghai home were it not for the silhouette of the church tower which sparked Rafaello Sanzio's career five centuries ago.

My father held my hand, guiding my brush strokes on the rice paper. He had just returned from his job directing the transport of supplies from the Burma Road to China's inland Southwest. This was the main lifeline of survival during the Second World War for the Nationalist KMT government, which had retreated inland when the Japanese attacked from the North, taking over and cutting off the usual routes from the coastal cities and ports.

Along the cobbled alleyways and narrow winding streets of this medieval town in central Italy where I was, on occasion I have come face to face with plaques on the façade of palazzos commemorating the massacred Italian resistance of this town with its ancient towers, the same time that my father was involved with the war effort in China.

"You should sit tall and straight, to make sure your spinal column is well supported so that your shoulders and arms will be able to move freely." I could hear my father's words echo and could almost feel him try to lift my elbow at a ninety-degree angle, "Only like this will you be able to have energy flow down your wrist and fingers onto the rice paper."

17
龍

Now as I dipped the brush into the black sumi ink, my elbow seemed to lift off the table from memory of my father's instructions without further prompting. The words of Tang Dynasty's Li Po flowed onto the yellowing rice paper:

Raising my head, a clear moon by my bed
Could it be frost on the terrace?
Lowering my head,
Memories of my ancestral village.

The words swept me back to my home in Shanghai and my first encounter with an American over six decades ago. When my father introduced him, he bent down and shook my hand so energetically that I thought he was angry with me. His hair sparkled like filaments of gold in the sunlight. He was so tall that my father's head only came to his shoulder, and I could not understand a word of the booming voice directed at me.

Later my father explained what the man said at that first meeting, "That's the way you shake a hand. The American way, my boy!" He had flown with Claire Chennault's Flying Tigers, China's fledgling air force started by the American general who collaborated with my father on the Burma Road.

His wife, Lucy, became a friend of my mother's. We visited their apartment in Victor Sasoon's Cathay Mansions, a few blocks north on the street where we lived, called the Building of Thirteen Stories by the locals. It was turned into the first luxury hotel in Shanghai after the Cultural Revolution, and Nixon was a guest there on his visit of rapprochement with China.

When I took Adele to Shanghai a few years back, I was happy to find the old structure still standing, although my own home was replaced by a neon lit bar and café. Across the street from the old mansions sprouted a new luxury hotel funded by Japanese investors. Its shops on the ground floor included an

Armani boutique and stores stocked with the latest from Hermès to Ferragamo.

When Lucy and her husband were leaving Shanghai to return to their home in California, my mother gave her an embroidered ceremonial gown, an heirloom from my grandfather's days in the old Imperial Court. My mother thought Lucy could make use of it as an evening coat, given that her American friend towered over her by a full head. My father gave them a long scroll of Chinese calligraphy.

"You must bring your mother to come and visit us when you come to America!" Lucy held my hands as she bent down and looked into my eyes warmly as a parting remark.

My mother confided to her, it was her intention of sending her only son to the Land of the Beautiful, as America was called in China. Japanese transliteration, the Land of Rice was more enigmatic.

A quarter of a century later, when I was looking for a place in California to start my medical practice I called on Lucy in La Jolla. It was not too far from where I had an interview.

The high-rise condo building where she lived had some antique Chinese tables and armchairs in its entry vestibule, reminding me of the old Cathay Mansions where she used to live. On one side of the main hallway hung a painting of an ancestral figure wearing ceremonial robes such as the one my mother had given Lucy. Opposite, there was a carved seated wooden Buddha about my height.

Her caretaker opened the door to her apartment for me and ushered me into the living room. The clear December afternoon gave me an unobstructed view of the Pacific horizon and Asia beyond.

When Lucy appeared from behind an inlaid Chinese screen, she was no longer the red headed woman in my memory, a head taller than my mother. She was a little shorter than I, and her back was slightly hunched, but she still held her hair up with a pin. At the end of the hairpin was a piece of emerald green jade, the color prized by Chinese women of means for many centuries. The best jade came through the road to Burma, where her husband used to fly his missions.

She told me her husband passed away a decade earlier, and she lived alone with her caretaker. Their daughter preferred that strange city up north, she said, meaning San Francisco, without bothering to hide her disdain. "She's almost a world away," Lucy added.

Briefly, she inquired about my mother, who was still living in New York at that time. After a few minutes of awkward pleasantries and after I finished my cup of tea, she gave me the feeling it was time for me to leave.

This was the time shortly following the wave of Mainland Chinese refugees into this country, seeking asylum, primarily political, from Mao Ze-Dong's Revolution. Once again, I could not help thinking about the Officer at the Immigration and Naturalization Service in Boston, eyeing my file and records with suspicion and barely disguising his contempt when I tried to renew my visa. The only reason I changed my studies from Engineering to Medicine was to stay in this country, he sneered. It was a comment that made me feel unwanted, like an undesirable alien from another world. Even as I write this now, I can feel the venom of his words, more than half a century later.

I thanked Lucy for her cup of tea and got up. I noticed the long scroll of Chinese calligraphy given to them by my father, off to one side of her large living room. It was an expression and token of his friendship with them during the War when they were in China.

I thought of the sentiments expressed in the strokes of the scroll, combining the soft fluidity of the sumi ink with the solid underlying structure of every individual character.

The distance between my father and me had made it difficult, as well as a gradual and slow process for me to appreciate his passion for Chinese calligraphy. He lived in Taiwan, and I continued my education and training in the U.S. But I have finally come to admire the elegance and feeling embodied in his Chinese characters.

After I came to America, in the absence of his hand to guide me in the art of calligraphy, I used to trace the strokes of the characters in letters he sent me from across the ocean. Over the years, I began to develop a sense of its softness and strengths and the reason my father pursued calligraphy with such a passion throughout his life. Something slowly crept into my own blood, though I was reluctant to face my admiration when still a young man, particularly during the period he denied his paternity while going through a divorce with my mother.

As I walked to my rental car in Lucy's parking area, I felt the chill of the wind on my cheeks. I thought about the difference of what I remembered of her in Shanghai and the reception I was given. There was no trace of acknowledgement of the friendship with my father, embodied in that scroll on her wall. Perhaps Lucy was afraid that as a refugee in this country, I might have come to ask some favor from her.

I looked again at the words of Li Po I had just written on the rice paper. The moonlight on a frosty night made him long for his old ancestral home. I thought about my visit to Lucy and my old home in Shanghai, which was no longer standing. The past was perhaps best left as a memory. It was something much harder to try and recapture.

A saying that I keep on my writing table speaks to what I was feeling:

Gli anni insegnano
Cose che i giorni
non conoscono.

The Italians have a culture as ancient as the Chinese, they understand that only the passage of the years will teach things that a few short days cannot. The intricate brocade of their teachings is as fine as that of my forefathers in China.

Chapter Eighteen

蛇

The journey was planned a year ago, when I finally decided to bring over my father's ashes. They sat on a hill where old banyan trees were threatening to take over the crooked path leading up to the graves. It was the only cemetery with a straight shot toward Taipei's 101, its slick modern tower downtown, until few years ago the tallest in all of Asia.

My annual visits to pay filial respects at the grave were getting less frequent as the trips became more arduous with my own advancing years. The small hill was getting less and less known even to the local drivers. Each time I went, more commercial buildings dwarfed the small streets and alleys, obscuring more of the winding road uphill, even the taxi drivers were telling me it was getting difficult for them to find. I could not reasonably expect my American born children to carry on this tradition, much less, the grandchildren.

Along with my father's remains, there were also my grandmother's, and those of his first wife, who became a devout Christian after my father left her for my mother.

My grandmother's was a whole-body burial, according to ancestral custom in China. She was also a lifelong Buddhist. But a cross was placed on her gravestone because she allowed my father's first wife, who was also her favorite niece, to convince her when she was already semi-conscious, to be a Christian on her deathbed.

"Local gods and spirits must still be consulted." The caretaker at the cemetery was careful to point out, when I asked about having my grandmother's remains cremated and the ashes of all three of them disinterred.

The first time I went to offer incense at my grandmother's grave, this caretaker was still a young woman with a towel wrapped around her head, holding back her sweat from the midday sun of this semi-tropical island. Her son stood by her side now, a young man ready to take over her business.

Auspicious dates had to be selected to harmonize the descendants' astrological signs with the local gods and goddesses, to avoid misfortune in their future lives. There were also regulations about bringing the ashes across international borders to be fulfilled. For me, running from one bureau to another to comply with these official regulations, including buses and trains to nearby townships because a lot of the minor governmental agencies had already been moved out of the city itself, were easier than the unpredictability implied in the consultations with the local gods and spirits.

To no one's surprise, the whole process took the better part of the year of the Water Dragon. Dragons were auspicious creatures to the Chinese. But the Water Dragon year was not an auspicious one. It was predicted to at least foster many changes, from sickness to death. I imagined reinterment of ashes from Taiwan to America must have fallen somewhere in between.

A proper final resting place in the U.S. must be found and purchased. I decided on the same cemetery where my mother was buried, overlooking the Bay and toward the Pacific. For my mother, the most important factor for her choice of a final resting place was its clear and undeterred view of China and the Fragrant Hills of Beijing, where her own mother lay buried for the ages.

For me, I was also fulfilling a subconscious wish to see my parents together again, at least in the same cemetery, even though they had been divorced for many years. And it would also be easier for those coming after me, I thought, to have everyone in the family together.

Adele and I decided to choose a niche for ourselves. She was making a conscious decision not to be with her own ancestors, who occupied an imposing site on a famous hill outside of Taipei.

After our close to two decades together, she was deciding to throw in her lot with me. We chose a square niche in the columbarium beside a small pond with water lilies, at a level below my father and grandmother's remains.

"Think your father might be angry about this move?" Adele wondered aloud when we got back from the reinterment ceremonies at the Hill Top cemetery in El Cerrito. A day earlier, I had placed his ashes next to his mother's into the same niche, those of his first wife into one next to theirs. I wanted to make sure their names carved onto the granite façade in Chinese calligraphy were done without mistakes, and the people at the cemetery did not confuse the placements of the ashes into their separate niches.

I felt a sharp tightening in my gut as Adele's words reverberated in our kitchen. I was more worried if my grandmother would curse me forever, for deciding to have her remains cremated for the journey across the Pacific, but I found some degree of comfort knowing at least the move was not without precedence in my Family Book of Ancestors four centuries earlier.

"Our Fifth Generation Ancestor traveled to Canton to retrieve the remains of his father, the Fourth Generation Ancestor." My father began telling me, as he handed me copies of our family genealogy book he had just finished revising and printing.

In its preface, he continued in giving the details of the story of the ancestor saving a local salt merchant and his family with whom he stayed in Canton from complete financial ruin and

18

蛇

disgrace. He gave his remaining funds to that family, forfeiting his own chances of returning with his father's remains to his hometown of Shanyin in the north and thus starting the southern branch of his own family.

I remembered the long scroll my father hung in his living room, which now hung in mine in San Francisco. It was an old, stone rubbing from the preeminent Buddhist Mountain, Taishan. Its five large characters: 行善无所住, dated back two millennia, to the time of the First Emperor who built the Great Wall.

For a man of few words, I realized these five characters conveyed the principles my father followed from the day he started working for the Republic of Sun Yat-sen. There were no limits to goodwill and charity.

Words from the Book of Ancestors and ancient Buddhist texts were not foremost in my mind when my father was hoping to educate me about our ancestral history.

As a young man, barely out of my medical training, on the way to make a living in the small town outside San Francisco, raising my young family and repaying the debts I owed, preoccupied me more. But the names of the ancestral town Shanyin near Shaoxing must have registered. The wine from Shaoxing was well known to most Chinese households.

In planning the trip to bring back my father's ashes, I wanted to include a visit to Hangzhou on the Mainland of China: the city he took me to visit on our first train trip together.

The black and white, square format pictures he took on that trip with his Rolleiflex camera slung around his neck were held with small cellophane corners in the tattered, green family album. Some of those cellophane corners have become torn, and I could no longer find any replacements for them now.

One picture showed me squeezed between him and my mother in a boat on the famous West Lake, with my back toward the camera, fascinated by the boatman in the back, steering the boat with a paddle and a long pole.

West Lake was man made in the Song Dynasty, when the city was its Capitol. It has been immortalized by poets and painters over many centuries for its unique beauty and serenity and better known recently by Nixon's visit to China. Premier Zhou En-Lai toasted the occasion in the famous restaurant on its shores, Lou Wai Lou, the Pavilion Beyond Pavilions.

But I remembered the trip because I was able to run around inside the carpeted Pullman car, with its wine red, velvet curtains, and upholstered armchairs. My father arranged to put us in the Pullman because he had been managing China's Railways from the time he started working and we had the car all to ourselves.

The childhood trip was an overnight train ride from Shanghai, close to seven decades ago. On this return visit, the fast train covered the same distance in less than an hour.

Our second-class seats were clean and comfortable. We were impressed by the overhead screen announcing the speed we were travelling. A young father chased after his well-dressed toddler who seemed to be having the fun of his life running down the middle of the aisle, the way I did on my first train ride.

The desire to relive those early memories with my father on our first trip together was not incidental. Nor was I sufficiently aware of it when I planned the trip with Adele because I didn't even mention it to her.

"Shaoxing is less than an hour from Hangzhou." Adele looked up at me, pointing to the map in the travel magazine she was reading, pulled out from the seat pocket in front of her.

Shaoxing, Shanying. My father's words floated back like strands tethered to an old tapestry, along with its history of honey colored wines, arias of regional operas lamenting lost love, and fabled tutors hired by the mandarins for their children.

"This says it's also a town of canals rivaling Suzhou, and the home of the writer Lu Xun." She showed me the pictures, but the following text caught my attention in particular.

It was the hometown of Wang Xizhi, the recognized Master and Sage of Chinese calligraphy, and I read, also of the late Premier Zhou En-Lai.

Wang Xizhi's elegant cursive was held up in front of me from the time my father started me on the proper way to hold the calligraphy brush. His large hand steadied my small wrist to slow the grinding of the ink stick on the carved stone tablet. I was eight-years-old again, noticing the faint pine scent from the stick for the first time, as it gradually suffused the study.

He did not tell me the Master was from the same town of his early ancestors, when he mentioned Shaoxing to me. There were so many chambers of his life he did not open up to me, which I have only slowly been discovering on my own. But to omit such an important part of what he admired, the calligraphy he spent hours in the early morning practicing!

Then I thought, my father was always a man of few words. He preferred to let me discover the truth by his own actions. It took me a long time, seven decades, in fact, to discover this part of my ancestral history.

As I felt the cobblestones under my feet on the street where the calligrapher lived a millennia and half ago, famous passages of the master's work greeted me from every street and around every corner.

They were in the same style that my father practiced every morning. The soft flowing cursives, yet anchored with bones of steel, to quote the words of a well-known Chinese art critic, alive as if they could speak from the walls onto which they have been copied. I had the feeling my father was walking alongside me. He wanted me to discover this for myself in this ancient town of my ancestors.

When I looked at the best-known example of his calligraphy, the Preface to the Orchid Pavilion, more closely after I got home, I realized it was a validation of individualism and vulnerability, echoing the insecurities of the four centuries of unrest preceding the Tang Dynasty.

18

蛇

Feeling the cobblestones under my feet that afternoon, I would not have been surprised if someone would suddenly appear in front of me and tell me we had the same father. My mother only told me about my half-sister from her first marriage a year or two before she died, and she was the one who told me she couldn't keep any secrets, while my father was the master of the clandestine hand.

My first stop along the stone path was the calligraphy Master's old home. It was a Temple now, as it had been for several centuries, I read from the plaque on the wall. The sage's domain was not immune to rise and fall of dynastic changes through the centuries.

"The Red Guards took it over during the Cultural Revolution." The caretaker noticed my interest in reading the details of its history. "It was returned to us only a few years ago." He continued and offered more information about the area where the old Master used to roam.

It occurred to me there was an underlying reason for his helpfulness. After the disastrous results of the Cultural Revolution, Deng Xiaoping decided to open the country to some free enterprises. Along with this change, temples were reopened but were expected to earn their own keep.

Years of indoctrination against religious practice had pretty much eliminated any public support of temples, and they now had to find ways to survive on their own.

I noticed the donation box on the side and put in a twenty yuan note. The man thanked me profusely for my three-dollar contribution.

I continued along the cobblestone way and stopped at a shop selling local artists' and calligrapher's work. Long scrolls hung from the walls and folding fans with calligraphy, most of which were done with a hasty hand, not much different from work found in tourist frequented Fisherman's Wharf or around the corner from the Ponte Vecchio of Florence.

"Are some of these your work?" I asked the man behind the desk.

"Yes," he nodded, then added apologetically, "These are for the young tourists who just want something from here.

"Elderly Sir," he used the honorific term to address me, "Are you a collector?"

"Not really." I smiled at him. "But I have enjoyed calligraphy for quite some time. My father was a great admirer of Wang Xizhi."

"Let me show you some of my better works." The man said enthusiastically.

He opened a drawer behind the counter and brought out a fan from a brocaded box.

As he slowly unfolded it, I could tell he had spent considerable time on the work. But it was not the style I preferred. On the desktop in the corner, I saw an inkstone and a brush on its porcelain rest. The ink glistened where the afternoon sun struck the dark stone. There was a very faint scent of pine.

"A very intricate work, indeed." I complimented him but did not extend the compliments to show any further interest in his work.

"Are you from this town?" I diverted the conversation.

"Several generations, Sir. My father was a calligrapher who won the provincial title of Master Calligrapher." He proceeded to tell me how difficult it was to earn a living being a serious artist.

His shop occupied a strategic corner on the long winding street leading up to the famous calligrapher's old home.

Around the corner from him, I noticed the Memorial Museum dedicated to the calligrapher.

"It has only replicas of existing pieces attributed to him around the world." He noticed my attention wandering. I didn't expect to find any originals from the master here. I knew there were none and only very few existing famous copies by later masters, which were exhibited on rare occasions by the museums, holding the pieces like national treasures.

Across the street was a small pagoda erected to commemorate the place where the calligrapher had written on a fan that an elderly vendor was selling, allowing the woman to get a very handsome price when she sold it.

"May I offer you some tea?" I knew it was a ritual in the old days to offer tea to visitors and customers, but I was touched by the man's gesture.

"Thank you. But my wife is waiting for me down the street." I didn't want to go into the details of the relationship between Adele and me.

The words life partner in English have no equivalent in Chinese. *Ai Ren*, a lover, the term used now in proletarian China sounded a little off-color to the old Chinese part of my ear. The English designation was all too complicated for an old town in China, I thought.

But then I remembered our times in Italy after my retirement. I had the same problem. There was no other appropriate word but wife. In many ways, I thought, Italian society had many similarities with the Chinese. It's close-knit families, attention to food, and a long tradition of some degree of endemic corruption! The life depicted in the old movie *Divorce Italian Style* made almost half a century ago, had not changed much.

"My ancestors are from this town. Called Shanying, when they were here," I decided to tell him. Hearing those words echoed in the calligrapher's shop made my throat tighten and eyes cloud over unexpectedly. I was unable to continue.

"That's right." He didn't seem to notice. "Actually, the pavilion where Wang Xizhi wrote his famous poem is in the section of town still called Shanying. It's only about twenty-five minutes by bus from here."

He squinted at his watch. "Elderly Sir," he was again using the honorific form to address me, "You won't be able to make it by closing time. It's already past four-thirty. You can make it tomorrow if you're staying overnight."

"I'll have to come back," I said to the sympathetic and congenial man in front of me, as much as to myself.

Chapter Nineteen

馬

"I was lucky to be alive, Ge Ge." She always called me elder brother, rather than cousin, because we were close like siblings.

Sitting beside her in the taxi, I noticed she hardly had any wrinkles around the corner of her eyes. Many of my patients her age in sun worshipping California wore the stigmas of skin damage like cracked roads under desert sun. Her confinement to mostly indoor activities of reading and teaching because of her disabilities had its blessings.

I marveled the years of living under Communist China did not leave permanent scars on her face. Except her eyes, once the brightest part of her face when we were children together in Shanghai. They were her mother's, my mother's youngest sister and my favorite Aunt Fu.

She had taken Cousin Qin and me to see the film from America called National Velvet. I thought Aunt Fu's eyes were as bright and beautiful as those of the young movie star, Elizabeth Taylor, on the screen in front of us.

Today there was no brightness in those eyes. As if they alone bore witness to her life, a life lived like a frightened sparrow, fortunate to have survived under the reign of Mao Zedong. One political struggle after another, from one anti-this or that campaign to the next, including the direct order from Mao to rid the country of all sparrows which he believed ate the grain seeds and finally the Cultural Revolution, when both of her parents took rat poison and then electrocuted themselves in order to avoid further persecution. Her father, chair of the Engineering Department at the University, got his doctorate from M.I.T. about fifteen years before I graduated there in Chemical Engineering. The killing of all sparrows had the unforeseen consequence of allowing locusts to flourish without its natural predator, which in turn devastated the country's crops and caused countless millions to die of starvation.

Cousin Qin showed me her parents' torn wedding picture. It was returned to her many years after it was confiscated along with everything from their home following their double suicide because their act was considered counter-revolutionary. My cousin patched the old black-and-white studio photo with a piece of tape on the back, but it could not repair the tears in the lives of my cousin's family. Her younger sister who was still in middle school was not allowed home. She had to walk fifty miles to find shelter. Friends and relatives shunned the girl from a condemned family.

Squeezed into the taxi together, my cousin told the driver. "*Wan An Gong Mu!*" Cemetery of Ten Thousand Tranquilities. I was in Beijing on Memorial Day to pay my respects to my maternal grandmother's grave.

I noticed the driver's white cotton gloves and round, peasant face, fairly typical of people on the outskirts of the capitol.

"Not too far beyond the Summer Palace." My cousin added in a voice thirty decibels above what was necessary for most of us to hear, reminding me of my patients with moderately severe hearing loss.

After the bear hug with tears in her eyes at the airport where she came to pick me up, one of the first things she told me was her hearing and balance were permanently damaged by streptomycin so I would have to speak louder for her to hear. She waddled like a duck to keep her stability.

When she was sent to Inner Mongolia to work on a farm, she brought back a head full of lice and tuberculosis, which affected her kidneys. She had to have her hair shorn, and streptomycin was the only thing available to treat a tubercular kidney during the Cultural Revolution.

The cemetery was in the Fragrant Hills, west of the old capitol, and beyond the Old Summer Palace. A twenty-five-minute taxi ride took us from my cousin's home on the university campus to the cemetery. Fifty years earlier, at our grandmother's funeral, the procession took two and a half hours.

Qin glanced over at me in the narrow back cabin of the taxi as if to say everything will be all right. Her eyes seemed to tell me time and again, "How good of you to come!"

I thought to myself, I had to come. My mother would never forgive me if I didn't, even though she was no longer with us herself. She had even chosen her own grave so that she could face in the direction of where her own mother was buried.

I held my cousin's small hands. She was only two years younger but seemed like a toddler next to me when I was eight. Our grandmother's funeral procession was led by twenty monks. Her coffin was covered with white carnations, which spilled over the edges of the open-top car snaking its way behind the monks.

I whispered to my mother who was walking alongside us about the small black dots on their shaved heads. "They're from incense burns," she said. "But why?" I tried to understand. "It shows the level of their devotion." When I still looked puzzled, she told me to be quiet and walked ahead solemnly behind the hearse, in the footsteps of the monks. Their chanting and the pipes and gongs moved us along at a steady pace.

My cousin didn't complain about her feet hurting. We were both excited by the whole spectacle and waiting for the sweet red date-filled delicacies my mother had ordered from the pastry shop near the Old Gate Tower of Qian Men. It was her mother's favorite when she was alive, my mother said.

Qian Men was the only old Gate Tower still standing today, the rest of the massive ancient wall surrounding the old Tartar city felt by some to embody its soul, has been torn down to make way for the new Capitol, in spite of heroic efforts by Liang Sicheng, considered the founder of modern Chinese architecture and his wife Lin Huiyin, also an architect and aunt of Maya Lin, who had both hoped to preserve the best of China's architectural traditions. Mao and his regime were in no mood to heed any advice regarding preservation of ancient Chinese traditions, in fact, he wanted to break down the teachings of Confucius which were in the way of his idea for perpetual revolution.

"Slow down!" My cousin said to the taxi driver. "We'll be making a turn to the left soon, I think." She turned to me and added, "They've been changing the roads around here so many times. Every time I come there's something new."

"Yes, our tour guide when we visited Shanghai told us every time he returned to his home from a trip, he's afraid he won't recognize his old neighborhood." The young man then pointed to the huge cranes all over the city skyline, "That's the National Flower of our New China today."

As we neared the cemetery, I saw a tall, green iron fence, as if the dead needed protection from the still living.

There were no gates when the Buddhist funeral procession brought my grandmother to her final resting place half-a-century ago. The old caretaker shuffled out of his hut and bowed to my mother, then led the procession to the gravesite. His hut was now a neocolonial, two-story building with white marble columns and two stone lions in front, near the front gate.

"That's as far as we can go." the driver opened our doors with his white gloves.

I hurried to pay the cab fare and added five yuan for the long trip.

"You needn't have given the tip." My cousin admonished as we walked away. "No need for taxis or restaurants here."

We explained to the Gate Guard the purpose of our visit. He let us in and pointed toward the receptionist inside the building. A young man behind the desk came out shortly with a large book in his hand. He checked the name of the gravesite our grandmother occupied.

"There's some back rent owed on this account, and there are some late payment penalties." He finally looked at us.

"That's not possible!" My cousin raised her voice. Her usual was high enough because of her hearing loss. "The account was paid for in perpetuity."

She turned toward me and added, "I was here when your mother asked and paid for the account in perpetuity!" My cousin rummaged in the cloth bag she carried for the old receipt. "You have to be prepared for everything here!" she grumbled.

"The rules were changed when the cemetery was reorganized by the government." The young man declared officiously.

"How come I was not notified?" My cousin demanded. I noticed her voice was taking on the tone of the University Professor, the job from which she had just retired.

"It was announced in the *People's Daily News*!" The young official was getting more belligerent.

"I never read the official newspapers anymore! They are just full of useless government propaganda, and I am tired of reading it all these years." She was now frankly lecturing the young man as if all the years of submerged frustration suddenly erupted in front of our eyes. The little sparrow surprised me in her transformation into an eagle. I thought of Nikita Khrushchev pounding his shoe on the table in front of Richard Nixon.

A middle-aged man with graying temples walked out from the inner office.

"I was probably already working here when your relative made the transaction." His tone was calm, and he motioned for us to join him in his inner office.

"I am sorry about the misunderstanding about the old regulations." He motioned his secretary to bring over some tea.

"Please don't trouble." My cousin began to soften her tone.

"No trouble at all." He continued in his conciliatory note. "But nowadays the government has changed its regulations on cemetery ownership countrywide. It's not just our cemetery here. We are now only allowed to rent the lot for a term of twenty years. But it will be renewable at the end of each term."

"Yes, I can see what the government is trying to do!" My cousin resumed her litanies. "Everything is for getting the last penny out of the Old Hundred Names nowadays!" She used the colloquial term, *lao bai xin,* for the common man.

"I can see you have been around here for a long time, Professor." the older man continued with a knowing smile and used the honorific address of Professor because from my cousin's manner of speech he probably surmised she was associated with the universities nearby. Then he glanced over to me to include me in the conversation, "That's what we have to deal with all the time."

"Do have some tea," he urged.

Recognizing the man was trying to be conciliatory, I nodded at him and picked up the teacup in front of me.

"Let me intercede at this juncture. Since it is the new government regulations, we will have to abide by it. Although it seems a little unfair for those, who thought they had bought the rights to the cemetery lot in perpetuity."

My cousin relaxed a little, listening to me, but did not completely change the expression of indignation on her face. The man waited attentively for me to continue after I sipped at the tea.

"I would like to pay the next twenty-year fee as the son of the woman who thought she had paid for her mother's gravesite for all generations to come."

"Ge Ge, I can't allow you to do that! If anything, I should be the one to pay for it because this happened here on my watch." I knew my cousin's retirement income would only be a portion of her original income which was not much, even as a full professor and Chair of the French Department at the university. She once told me the taxi drivers now made several times her income.

"Please don't argue with me on this point. Since you have called me elder brother all these years, I am going to exercise my right as the elder of the family here. Besides, I am fulfilling a duty to my own mother, who is no longer with us."

The old man looked relieved that someone was going to pay the bill without causing him to make more apologies for the governmental changes.

He volunteered, "The penalties will be deleted, of course. That is only reasonable, and I have the authority to do so."

I looked at the account and quickly counted out the bills. My cousin was still protesting, but to her chagrin, she checked her purse and had not brought along enough cash to pay the relatively large sum.

The man counted the bills and turned them over to his secretary. "I will be glad that I will be retiring in two years from this job."

"I just retired from mine at the university last year." My cousin offered in a softer tone.

The secretary presented us with the receipt and the certificate of the next twenty years for our grandmother's cemetery lot. We stood and nodded at the man as a gesture of appreciation.

As we walked out of the building toward the grave, I noticed the walkways were well maintained, the trees lining the paths neatly trimmed. Some graves we passed had names I recognized from recent Chinese history. Perhaps this was the reason for the new tall fence and the large, neocolonial office building with shiny roof tiles.

It was quite a difference from the picture my mother showed me after the Red Guards sacked the place. Tombstones were over-turned, statuaries destroyed, symbols from the old Confucian tradition of ancestral devotion and worship deemed decadent during the Cultural Revolution.

My grandmother's stone, inscribed and carved with my father's calligraphy was broken in two pieces, and the stone flower vases and platforms for offerings were strewn in disarray.

When the Mainland Government was first establishing its presence in the U.S. following Nixon's rapprochement, it tried to get the good will of the overseas Chinese population. My mother decided it was the right time to demand authorization from a sympathetic Consulate Official to supply her with crew and funds to rehabilitate this family site.

Other families had probably done the same, from what I was able to see on the walk.

My cousin and I laid down the flowers we brought when we reached our grandmother's grave. I set about dividing them into the two flower vases at the base of the tombstone.

"Third Auntie always said you have an artistic eye." My cousin always referred to my mother by the order of her birth among her siblings. Aunt Fu, Qin's mother, was the ninth.

Our grandmother's favorite, old pastry shop succumbed to the Cultural Revolution along with many other old shops of the area. My cousin said she has not yet found a shop selling good old-fashioned pastry in her neighborhood and she no longer had the energy to look around the city for the pastry of our childhood. Instead, she brought some fresh fruit in season.

I looked at the dates carved into the restored marble tombstone. Our grandmother was twenty years younger than my cousin and I when she died.

My mother's words flooded back in front of my eyes. Her mother was beaten by our grandfather after he had his first concubine. She was defenseless in her unstable bound feet but bore him one child after another up to a total of ten.

My cousin held onto to me to steady herself as we bowed to our waists to pay our respect. We decided to dispense with the old custom of kneeling on the ground in front of our grandmother and knocking our heads on the ground three times. My cousin had her balance problem, and I was taking a much longer time getting up on bent knees.

As we walked away slowly, letting my cousin hold onto my arm, I heard myself asking, "Who's going to take care of grandmother's grave after we're gone?"

"I've given instructions for my daughter to continue. But after that, I don't know."

In my silence, I knew my own children in America would not even know how to find their paternal great grandmother's gravesite. I felt I was letting my mother down, in not fulfilling her wishes to maintain her mother's grave in perpetuity.

I wondered if each generation was bound to disappoint the preceding. We always tried to do the best for our children, but it didn't seem to work the other way around, not usually in our world of today. That was the way of my Confucian ancestors. To carry through with our parents' wishes like edicts from Heaven. There were still enough of those Confucian sayings etched into my brain.

The taxi driver opened the door for us as he saw us approaching.

"Thank you so much for waiting for us." My cousin knew the meter was running, but she thrust some change into the driver's hand, "That's for your lunch money."

"No need, no need." But unobtrusively, he pocketed the money.

On the way back, we were silent for a long while. My cousin held onto my hand.

Then she looked at me with a smile. It gave me a flicker of its brightness of years ago, but had an equal measure of amusement and embarrassment, which I could not remember seeing her express, "Before today, I bet you couldn't have imagined that I could ever behave like a crazy woman. I wonder what you must think of me."

"If I went through what you did, I don't think I would have survived."

"Ge Ge, how this life has changed me! I don't think I can even recognize myself sometimes."

"You did just fine. I loved seeing you in your professorial role." Although I truly had not imagined my gentle, little cousin capable of the histrionics she displayed. "Besides, it got us to the man in charge. And we didn't have to pay any penalties as the younger man demanded."

"I guess I've learned to act like a devil in front of devils," she sighed. "But don't think I'm going to let you get away with paying the whole bill on this!"

"Let's not argue about that now. But, I'll let you take me to lunch."

Chapter Twenty

After many months, I got a reply to my ad in the Harbin papers looking for my half-sister. The only lead I got after my mother told me about her, two years before she came down with lung cancer. I was ready to give it up for another loss, my mother had told me she tried many times earlier without any success.

I remembered asking her when I was a kid, why I couldn't have a little brother to play with. She told me she lost him when I bounced on her belly. She never mentioned this half-sister. The little girl with small round eyes and a huge ribbon in her hair was a distant relative, I was always told, when those eyes looked at me from the family album.

She would be ten years older than I, my mother said, when she decided to tell me. Her name was Ya Du. Two ideograms in Chinese, short for Siberia and Beijing, chosen by my maternal grandmother because the child was conceived in Siberia and born in the old Capitol, Beijing.

The last time my mother saw Ya Du was in Harbin, near China's northern border with Russia, where she was not allowed to have any further contact with her three-year-old daughter as a stipulation in the divorce.

"I never consented to my first marriage," she said when she decided to tell me more about that marriage and Ya Du.

Then, for someone who has rarely lost her composure, my mother's voice almost shook, when she added, "The wedding night was like a rape."

In response to my surprised look, she explained further. "The man worked under your Wai Gong in the Foreign Ministry, and he was a friend of your grandfather's concubine."

I remembered what she told me about that concubine. Her arrival was the beginning of my grandmother being beaten. My mother blamed her for her own mother's early death.

The first time I heard about the First Concubine was when I was nine. I was taken to the burial of my grandmother after the War with the Japanese ended. Her coffin remained in a Temple in the Western Hills of Beijing for over twenty years. My grandfather did not bother to bury her after she died.

"My mother begged me to obey my father. If I didn't marry the man, Wai Gong would have beaten her to death."

I listened to my mother's story and imagined that world of Confucian teachings and traditions. The sage wrote, in his Book of Rites, "the woman obeys the man. In youth she obeys her father and older brother; after marriage, she obeys her husband. When her husband is dead, she obeys her son." Then I thought about the grandfather I met when he visited us in Shanghai after the war. He was already in his late sixties, ramrod straight, with a full head of gray hair and still a picture of the revered retired diplomat. But he had run out of money and came to ask my mother for help.

"Soon as I got news that my mother died, I decided to get a divorce."

It was the twenties in China. Divorces were rare, especially in respectable families.

This did not deter my mother. Her father disowned her, and she had to give up Ya Du.

The man who answered the ad claimed to be Ya Du's son. His mother was too frail to reply. There was a phone number, and he sounded earnest when I called. Check in with him when I got into my hotel in Harbin, he said.

20

羊

The Russian-made train sat dormant, a dark anaconda on the tracks. Inside its window was a sign in black block Chinese script, Beijing to Harbin – Super Express. On the platform, people pushed and shoved in waves of browns and blues, older men and women bundled in quilted Mao jackets, necks wrapped in hand knit wool scarves with an occasional bright China red grabbing my eye, children held tight by their hands with faces like freshly steamed pork buns, students shivering in thin uniforms, everyone surging toward the cars.

Vendors blocked my way with small plastic bags of boiled tea eggs and peanuts in my face.

"*Bu yao! Bu yao!*" Wei waved them off.

I would have bought the tea eggs. Their marbled insides were so much part of train rides in my childhood. Boiled food was the only thing safe to eat in those days. But Wei was my guide this time. His wife was my childhood friend. She insisted I should not go on the trip alone.

I gave in. Besides, I have always enjoyed being with him, from the first time Jen brought her husband to meet me at the Friendship Hotel when the Mainland reopened to overseas Chinese in the eighties.

We were born the same year, both oxen by the Chinese Zodiac. But he always felt like a cross between a horse and a lamb, to me. Reliable as a horse and gentle as a lamb.

Tall for someone downstream of the River Yangtze, he spoke Mandarin with a heavy southern accent, although he has been away from his hometown for many years. To me, the southern inflection in his Mandarin had a certain charm, evoking the southern poets and scholars of the Ming and Song Dynasties from Suzhou and Hangzhou.

On my earlier trips back to the Mainland, he led me around the antique flea markets, when there were very few buyers from outside of China. He was afraid I had forgotten how to bargain in the old country.

He held my hand when we crossed the bustling streets where stoplights seemed to be more for decoration. I felt like the little brother, although he was only a few months older. And it seemed like the most natural thing to do.

There was none of the squeamishness I felt the first time I walked down Castro Street in San Francisco, trying to hold onto my boyfriend's hand, while he looked around nervously and jerked it away.

Wei was lucky to have gotten tickets in the section with private compartments, usually reserved for party members and official guests from foreign countries. He must have stretched the definition of the latter, using my American passport at the ticket office.

Although I pulled together clothes for this trip to blend in with the locals, Wei still insisted they could tell I was from Overseas within five seconds. "It's in the way you move. The packet of facial tissues you carry in your pocket." He looked at me with all his earnestness. "Even the way your hair is cut!"

In the end, I decided to give up trying and accepted the safety under his wings. I was also happy to be in his company, although not quite ready to admit to myself that I was lonely for some company.

A few months before this trip I stopped seeing Jimmie, my boyfriend of several years who liked seeing me with my children.

He seemed to have gotten along better with my teenagers than myself, during the weekends they spent with me. Then he decided he wanted to have children of his own.

"You must be very careful, Da Ge." Jen cautioned, she called me *Da Ge*, meaning Big Brother. "You don't know the extent to which people scheme to make money nowadays! Ever since Deng Xiaoping said it doesn't matter whether the cat is Communist or Capitalist, as long as it catches mice."

She took the initiative to make the hotel reservation in Harbin for me. "I made it for one room, so Wei can take care of you all the time. You never know when problems might occur."

I remembered when I asked her recommendation for a restaurant on an earlier trip to the Mainland.

"I can only trust the food at McDonald's," she said, "You just don't know what they are doing in the back kitchen. They might be serving you dog or horse meat and calling it lamb. *Gua yang toe, mai go roe!*"

The lights above the platform were turned on at six. It was mid-November. The sky was gray-green, a shade lighter than the trains, the color of the hills surrounding the capitol city of Beijing.

Wei opened the travel bag he was carrying when we settled into our compartment on the train, and offered me the fruit he packed for us.

"Let me peel this for you." He took the tangerine from my hand.

"You're much too *ke qi!* Let me do it myself!" I remembered he was so polite and attentive when my mother visited with me on an earlier trip.

"There's no trouble. I do it all the time."

He did it all the time for Jen. She told me he was a good husband, although I wasn't sure whether she was just saying it because that was what I wanted to hear.

After I finished the tangerine, he gave me a moist hand wipe to clean my hands. The sudden jerk of the train getting started pushed him against me.

I held his hand for a few seconds and looked at him, "Thank you for doing all this for me."

"I could not let myself do otherwise," he said.

"I love being on a train." The first family trip my father took us to visit the gardens and lakes of Suzhou and Hangzhou was by train.

I reminisced about that trip when my parents also invited my friend to go with us.

"Jen said she could never forget that trip with you and your family!"

"Do you like the trains?"

"My experience has not been like yours." Wei put his hand on mine to assure me he was not being critical. "I had to take the hard-backed seats as a student, from the South to the capitol on the overnight train. Sometimes even stood all the way." He continued without any trace of resentment or envy. "A private Pullman car was out of the question for me."

"Mine too, actually. When I was a student in America, I could only afford the buses. Not even the trains." I was trying to minimize the differences of our lives, but also felt I could never truly imagine what he and Jen went through during the Cultural Revolution.

"This is the first time for me in a private compartment." He brightened. "Thanks to you!"

"Thank you for accompanying me!" I touched his hand. Much as I told myself this was not unusual and very natural between men in China, I could not help but also feel there was part of me who was making the best of it.

"I'll take the top berth."

"No, I should take the top. You are a few months older."

"But you came all the way from America."

When he saw I was not quite ready to accept his line of reasoning, he added, "Besides, I'd like to see what it feels like sleeping on the upper berth. I've never had that experience."

"I know I can never win an argument with you. You are always so *ke qi* and kind to me. I can never repay you for everything you're doing."

"You are the one who has been so kind to us. Both you and your mother. Jen told me she can never forget what the two of you have done for us, when you found out her father jumped to his death during the Cultural Revolution."

"My mother felt terrible when she heard about what happened. She blamed herself for not having consented when Jen begged her to leave Shanghai with us."

I saw the little girl in front of my eyes again, listening to ghost stories with me, fireflies lighting our faces. She held onto my mother before we left and I remembered my mother telling me her regret when she heard about what happened to the family who was so close to us, but she said she didn't want to separate Jen from her parents.

"Da Ge," Wei was now calling me Big Brother also, even though he was a few months older by birth. "Jen understands now why your mother didn't want to break up her family."

"I am so happy Jen has you in her life. I feel comforted to see that you are so good to her."

"You embarrass me by saying that. She has been very good to me too."

As if to divert the attention from himself, he said. "Shall I pull down the upper berth?"

I thought of how times have changed. Before the Revolution of 1949, white-uniformed attendants used to come into the compartments to prepare the sleeping berths for the night, when the guests were in the dining room. But now, even under the dim overhead light, I could see the stains in the dark upholstery on the berth and the carpet on the floor.

"*Cha piao! Cha piao!*" The conductor's loud voice echoed down the corridor.

Soon he stood at the doorway. Wei had our tickets ready for inspection. The conductor looked at him, then at me, sizing up our status whether we deserved to be in the compartment.

"*Wai Bing?*" He looked at Wei. I felt a twinge in being designated as a Foreign Guest in the country I was born, as well as being uncertain of my reception. I still remembered from an earlier visit a person in a position of authority such as a ticket seller at the station or a conductor could do as he pleased.

"From *Mei Guo.*" The beautiful country, as the United States was called in China. I wondered whether the title referred to the colorful Stars and Stripe of our flag or whether the *Mei* came from the first syllable of 'Merica in its abbreviated form.

"Sank you!" The conductor used his few words of English and smiled at me.

"*Bu xie!*" I replied in Mandarin.

"Oh, you speak perfect Mandarin."

"*Guo jiang le!*" Much too complimentary, I replied.

"Not only perfect Mandarin, but perfect Peking dialect."

"My mother's old home was in Beijing."

"Welcome back to China!" He clipped our tickets and handed them back to Wei.

"A very polite man," I said to Wei about the surprisingly pleasant exchange.

"You can never tell nowadays. Probably because of your status of honored guest from outside the country."

He proceeded to pull down the upper berth.

"We don't need to pull down the shades, do we?"

"You never know. We might stop at some stations during the night."

There was no word equivalent for privacy in the Chinese language, and yet, Chinese tended to be more timid than westerners when undressing in front of others.

There was a small washbasin and mirror in back of the door, but the toilet was down the hallway.

"I'll go use the toilet first," I told Wei as he laid out our travel bags.

"Good idea to get some rest early so we'll be ready for tomorrow."

He was sitting on the lower berth in his T-shirt and shorts when I returned. He had neatly hung up his clothing on the hook by the berth.

"You don't need to use the toilet?"

"No. We didn't have much to drink tonight."

I started to take off my sweater and shirt in front of him but felt a little self-conscious as he seemed to be watching me. I realized this was just another difference between Chinese and Americans. There was no feeling of intruding into someone's privacy by staring at them. But coming from San Francisco, it was hard for me not to feel as if I was being cruised.

"I waited for you before climbing into the upper berth because I was afraid you might need something."

Ordinarily, I didn't like to sleep with clothes on, an aversion and habit I picked up from my roommate in medical school. But I was not sure how clean the linens were, and I was getting more self-conscious in front of Wei. There was also a tug between enjoying the closeness with Wei and the feeling of guilt I shouldn't be enjoying it. In the end, I decided to keep my underwear on for the night.

When he saw I had finished undressing for the night, he got up and pulled up the sheet and blanket on my bed for me.

"Let me do it myself."

"It's easy. Get in before I dim the lights." I watched him as he turned off the ceiling light and left on the reading lights by the berths.

I slipped under the bed sheets to give him room to climb up. As he used my berth as a step to get himself upward, I saw he had strong legs, fairly heavily covered with dark hairs, unlike his wrists and arms. Then with one swift motion, he pulled himself up.

"*Ming tian jian*," he said as he turned off his reading light.

"See you tomorrow." I echoed him and put out my light. The image of his legs lingered, until the steady motion of the train over the tracks eventually rocked me to sleep.

When I opened my eyes again, a pearly predawn had replaced the pitch darkness outside the thin window shade. I slipped out of bed and pulled on my pants, relieved I didn't have to betray my morning arousal in front of him. But I noticed his pants and shirt were already off the hook. He was so quiet, I did not hear him climb down and slip out of the compartment.

"*Cao*! Did you sleep well?" He stepped in through the door.

"Good morning," I rubbed my eyes and stretched, "Slept like a *Si Zhu*, a dead pig. Something I learned as an intern in surgery. Can sleep standing up when I'm really tired."

"Another forty minutes or so before Harbin. The conductor said looks like it's going to be great weather for us. Clear skies, no snow." Wei seemed to take care of everything.

As our train neared the central station in Harbin, it slowed, sputtered and coughed, fitful as an old chronic smoker's morning chest clearing. The station was Russian, built in the late nineteenth-century with vast, intricate ironwork framing the glass covered façade. It was the period after the Opium Wars, when many nations were carving out parts of China for their own gains. From inside the station, the dawn light barely breaking through the morning mist made the facade resemble two giant opalescent fans placed back to back, juxtaposed against one another.

Wei held onto my hand going through the station as if I might be kidnapped.

An enormous bulletin board glared from above as we entered the main hall. The Chinese characters, Welcome to Harbin, Ten Thousand Years to Chairman Mao, beckoned below the portrait of the puffed, potato-faced man.

"Let's go through the front doors to find a taxi."

I knew he would have taken the city bus himself.

"I can go on the bus with you," I said.

"Let me talk to the driver. It wouldn't cost that much."

I decided to let him take the lead. Besides I thought it would be best to get to our hotel early and contact the man who claimed to be Ya Du's son.

It was a short ride. The city was just awakening. Bicyclists in heavy quilted jackets and felt caps cupping their ears, with white masks strapped on their faces to warm the cold November air, peddled by in slow motion, and they made me think of Lee Majors in the early movie of the bionic man. Pedicabs and pushcarts mingled with streams of cyclists, reminding me of Beijing on my visit several years earlier.

Other than the concrete blocks built during the decade of collaboration with the Russians in the fifties, many of the buildings gave me the feeling of a poorly maintained quarter of old Paris. Our hotel turned out to be one of those concrete rectangles.

Large Chinese characters told me it was The Great Eastern Sea Guest House. Jen told me she made a point of choosing a modest one for us, to avoid giving the wrong impression about me to Ya Du's family.

20

羊

"People here think all overseas Chinese are rich," she had warned me earlier.

Wei shoved the taxi fare into the hands of the driver, when I reached for my wallet.

"You can't take care of everything here," I protested.

"It's our duty to take care of you. I'm only afraid that we haven't done enough for you."

The fare was five yuan, less than a dollar, but his salary as an engineer with Public Utilities was only a few hundred.

He presented his identification at the registration desk, and the clerk asked for mine. "*Wai bing.*" She looked at me when she saw my passport. "Let me check about the room charge."

"He's my first cousin." Wei was fast to come up with the excuse of a family connection.

She hesitated and looked at the reservation made by Jen who worked for the university.

"I'll let it go," she decided. "By rules, we have a different rate for visitors outside the country."

"Thank you so much." Wei bowed for additional emphasis.

"Your room 5025 is on the fifth floor." She handed us the room key as she continued, "turn right after you get out of the elevator and you will see the room numbers on the wall. The porter will help you with your luggage."

"We just have some hand luggage. We'll carry them ourselves." Wei thanked her again and walked toward the elevator.

Our room faced the back of the hotel. A double bed was put close to the bathroom, a chest of drawers doubled as a television stand, a round table with a brocaded tablecloth under a glass top, and two armchairs. The furniture was all painted to resemble mahogany, but the finish was dull with too much brown. The curtains were red-brown damask, framing a window looking onto a large pond in the garden below. I thought that must be the Eastern Sea, which lent the hotel its auspicious name.

"They must have reserved this room for a couple, when Jen called." He pointed to the double bed.

"I don't mind, if you don't."

"I didn't want to ask for more at the desk when the clerk already gave us the local rate."

I nodded in consent.

"I should try to contact Ya Du's son." I found the phone number in my notebook and gave it to Wei.

"*Wey*," he said, getting the hotel operator on the phone, "We'd like to make a local outside call." He repeated the phone number to the operator and waited.

"*Wey*," he said again as the line was connected, "I am calling on behalf of Chen Zong Yuan from America.

"Oh, yes, he is right here." I heard him tell the person who came on the line and handed the receiver to me.

Ya Du's son sounded a little hesitant initially. Chinese tend to be cautious anyway and especially after everything they have been put through the past several decades. Then he remembered our arrangement and brightened up.

"Is PoPo with you?" He asked about my mother and addressed her as grandmother.

"No. She's too ill herself to come with me." I didn't explain to him that my mother came down with pneumonia when we spoke on the phone earlier.

"I'm sorry to hear that PoPo is not in good health. My mother has not been doing well either."

We agreed to meet after lunch in the lobby of the hotel.

I was filled with an equal measure of anticipation and apprehension after I hung up the phone. I was glad to be meeting the son of my half-sister. I was finally a step away from finding her and was hoping to bring some good news about Ya Du back to my mother. Yet the son had somehow not recognized my name right away on the phone, even though I had spoken to him only a few months earlier when we first made contact.

He stood up from the sofa in the small waiting area at the end of the entrance hall, when Wei and I came out of the elevator. A tall man with plain, flat features and small, wide-set eyes like Ya Du's in the only picture I had of her.

"I am Rui bing." He came forward and extended his large hand.

I felt the coarseness of his palm as we shook. "Thank you for coming to meet me. This is Wei, the *Ai Ren* of a close friend who brought me here." I used the term for spouse in the current Mainland Chinese lingo. "And how is your mother?"

"Not very well," his eyebrows furrowed, "she's in the hospital."

"Yes, I remember you had mentioned she was very fragile, the last time we spoke."

"Unfortunately, she has deteriorated over the last month, and we had to take her to the hospital."

"Did the doctors say what was the matter?"

"They think her lungs are failing. She might have lung cancer."

"Was she a smoker?"

"For many years. Actually, for as long as I can remember. Now they say it's affecting her heart as well."

"What are the doctors doing for her?" I asked.

"They are giving her oxygen and watching the amount of fluids she is taking. She is not always conscious." His voice started to trail a little, "They are waiting to get some kind of special X-ray scan of her lungs."

"How long is the wait?"

"Several weeks before there is an opening. My mother's was not considered an emergency." He sounded subdued and resigned. "And she is almost seventy."

"No other hospital can get the scan earlier?" I thought Harbin was not a small town and must have an alternative.

"They said unless we want to pay privately, there is no other way."

"Did they tell you how much?" Wei cut into our conversation.

Rui bing lowered his head and stared at the floor in front of him. "It's much more than we can afford to pay."

"Maybe I can help," I offered.

"We can't let you do that."

"But I would like to help in any way I can."

He looked at me, then at Wei. "They said it would cost about nine hundred yuan."

"I didn't carry so much cash with me." I looked at Wei, "But I suppose I could try to get it from the bank."

"I am really embarrassed that you have to do this for us."

"Please don't feel that way. Your mother is my elder sister. There is an old Chinese saying, an older sister is like a mother."

"We don't know how to thank you and repay you."

"It really comes from my heart. But when can I see your mother?"

"I'll check with the hospital and let you know. She is in a special section of the hospital, and they don't allow too many visitors."

"Maybe you can tell them I came all the way from America to see her."

He nodded in agreement and said he would let me know as soon as he checked at the hospital.

"Have you had lunch yet, Uncle?"

"No, we haven't yet."

"Let me take you out then."

"Don't be too *ke qi*. Wei and I can get some food anywhere. You must have many things to take care of."

"It's only proper, Uncle."

"Don't worry. Actually, I'd prefer you to check at the hospital and let us know when I can visit your mother." After I said it, I realized I had become more Americanized and was cutting through some of the protocol and etiquette of a first meeting with a relative.

"In that case, I'll call you as soon as I can make the arrangements."

I would have liked to ask the hotel clerk for a recommendation of some small local restaurant nearby, but Wei insisted that we eat at the hotel. At least we were guaranteed a certain standard by eating at a place associated with the hotel, he thought. Then I remembered Jen had advised me to go to a MacDonald's for food.

We ordered two dishes, chicken with mushroom and green peppers, and braised tofu and chrysanthemum greens.

The steamed fish sounded enticing on the menu, but I trusted his judgment, when he said, "I never try seafood in a place I don't know." I remembered Jen told me he grew up along a branch of the Yangtze River in Zhejiang province in the South and his preference for the fresh fish from his area.

After lunch, we found the road to the Bank of China, the only bank handling foreign currency accounts. Wei explained my situation to the teller, who consulted with his supervisor. He could only authorize a withdrawal of the maximum daily allowance of one hundred dollars.

I pleaded the urgency of my half-sister's condition, and he called their central office in Beijing. I was finally allowed to withdraw the sum of three hundred dollars over a two-day period from my ATM card.

We thanked the supervisor for all his troubles and his compassion, and he counted out seven-hundred-fifty yuan in front of me, saying to go directly to him the next day for the balance.

I was fortunate the supervisor was sympathetic. He could have taken the official line and refused to bend the rules, which was often the case when dealing with governmental organizations in China.

Back at the hotel, we waited for the call from Ya Du's son.

The early winter sky was darkening outside, and we still hadn't heard anything from him. Wei tried his home, and there was no answer. Around seven-thirty, he suggested we order some soup noodles and Tsingtao beer from the dining room because I did not want to leave and miss the phone call.

Rui bing called at nine. He had been at the hospital all afternoon because his mother's condition worsened further and the doctors advised a tracheotomy. So he stayed there until the surgery was done. But the doctors were unable to arouse her again after the procedure.

I told him I would be able to get the funds for him by the next morning.

"I really do not know how to thank you, Uncle." Then there was a stitch in his voice, and he added, "I just hope we can still help her at this point."

"Let's all hope the heavens are going to help her pull through." I tried to offer something encouraging in what sounded like a dire turn of events.

"I think it's too late for you to go to the hospital tonight. I'll come and fetch you tomorrow morning. Would ten o'clock be too early?"

"That would be fine." It would not make any difference at this point, I thought, now that Ya Du was already comatose and would not be able to speak to me. It would also allow me enough time to go to the bank for the second installment of funds.

Wei noticed I was unsettled by the news over the phone.

"Why don't you take a hot soaking bath or get a massage for relaxation?" A massage for forty yuan was mentioned in the hotel brochure.

I took his suggestion and undressed in the bathroom. When I came out the masseur was already waiting in our room. He looked too young to be an experienced practitioner I thought. But I decided any massage was going to be helpful. Wei retreated into the bathroom to wash up while the young man started to work on me.

I was surprised and relieved his hands were very experienced. He seemed to be able to locate precisely where my muscles were tense.

He worked deeply into my lower back muscles and pelvis as he applied pressure with his firm palms. Then he worked from my calves down to each one of my toes, kneading them between his fingers and making a popping sound as if they were coming out from between his lips.

He bent my legs backward and massaged my thighs. I felt a stir in my groin, but was too relaxed and embarrassed to acknowledge anything.

When he turned me over onto my back, I was glad he put a towel over my middle, because I heard Wei coming back into the room from his bath.

It was a relief that the masseur shifted his attention to my face and shoulders. It gave me the chance to relax and breathe normally again. When he finished, I asked Wei to pay him so that I didn't have to get up from the bed. As Wei sent him to the door, I was able to slip under the bedcovers.

"A good massage?"

"Just what I needed. Thank you for suggesting it. I'm so relaxed I'm going to fall asleep."

I woke up past midnight. Our room was overheated because we turned up the heat for the massage. Wei seemed to be asleep on his side of our bed. I tiptoed slowly from the edge of the bed to the bathroom in the dark, not wanting to wake him.

After flushing the toilet, I thought I heard him turn over in the bed. I slid back under the bedcovers and closed my eyes.

But I thought about Ya Du. She would not be able to talk to me about our mother when she was young, about her own life after our mother divorced her father. Our mother was not allowed to contact her daughter ever again, the toll exacted in order to get her divorce in the twenties.

An aching sense of loss from inside me alternated with a mixed feeling of relief from the massage and concern whether Wei had seen me when I was aroused at the end. I turned and tossed on my side of the bed, wondering what time it was. It was too dark for me to even read the time on my watch. Gradually, exhaustion overtook the thoughts spinning around me, and I drifted into state of semi-oblivion.

I felt his hand on my waist. He must have turned to me in his sleep. I held my breath, too tense to move, wondering whether it was intentional and wishing it might be so.

I have been deeply moved by this sweet, gentle man for whom I have developed a love as a brother, and I also realized I have been trying to withhold any feelings I felt I should not have for him. I could not imagine doing something that might embarrass him or worse—to hurt my childhood friend.

I was suspended in this state of titillation and trepidation, until I thought I finally heard his breathing become regular. I could not bring myself to move or even touch his arm.

How long did I spend in that position? I could not remember.

I got up before the predawn light started to peek through our curtains. Wei was still asleep. I cleaned myself up and shaved, then put on my briefs.

"Did you sleep all right?" Wei was awake when I reentered the room.

"A bit fitfully. Thought about Ya Du, the past and now. Hope I didn't disturb you."

"Oh, no. It was a bit warm last night. Made me a little restless." He paused for a second. "I hope I didn't keep you awake by my turning and stirring."

"Don't worry. I'm sure I'll make it up tonight. But I am sorry that I forgot to turn the heat back down after my massage."

"No, it was actually my fault. You were so relaxed and under the covers. I should have been the one to turn the heat back down."

"You can't take care of everything, Wei."

"But I should."

"I feel like some nice hot porridge and a cup of tea. How does that sound to you?"

"It'll only take me a few minutes, and we can go down for breakfast."

I turned toward the windows to avoid staring at him when he got out from under the bedcovers. When I heard the faucet running in the bathroom, I straightened our sheets and made up the bed.

"There is a phone call for you, Mr. Chen." The desk clerk came to our table in the dining room. "You have to come to the front desk."

"You don't have a portable receiver?" Wei didn't want to have my breakfast interrupted.

"I'm sorry. Our system cannot transfer calls like that."

I anticipated it was Rui bing wanting to let me know when I could visit at the hospital.

"Uncle," he said, then he went silent for a few seconds. "My mother just passed away."

"Oh, no!" I gulped down my own disappointment, instead of saying something to comfort his loss.

I felt the pain my mother must have had, never being able to see her daughter again after being forced to give her up. My own attempts to find Ya Du was partly trying to fulfill a wish of my mother's. In the end, all these years and attempts, all these miles of travel, had come to nothing.

"I can come and fetch you to the hospital if you like." Rui bing's voice that brought me back.

"Tell me the address, and we'll get a taxi to come over. You probably have a lot of things to take care of."

The clerk handed me a pencil and a piece of paper. I wrote down Fourth Peoples' Hospital, Xi Dong An Lu, number 501, second floor, special care unit.

In the taxi, I sat numb and speechless next to Wei. He seemed to sense my disappointment and loss. Not only did I fail to carry out my mother's unspoken wish, there would never be the opportunity to speak to Ya Du, between sister and brother.

Quietly Wei put his hand over mine, "You tried everything in your power, Da Ge." He called me Big Brother with the same affection Jen did. Then he gave my hand a squeeze. "*Tian Yi*," he said. The will of Heaven.

I wondered if Ya Du felt it was the will of Heaven when our mother vanished from her life, when she was only three. Did she know what made our mother so determined about leaving her first husband that she was even willing to consent to never contact her first-born child again?

I was not able to tell her that our mother tried to look for her on numerous occasions. At the end of the World War with Japan, when my father went to take over the Manchurian railways, several times she asked him to help find her daughter.

When Nixon reopened the door to China, my mother was among the earliest to revisit Beijing. With the Mainland government trying very hard to ingratiate itself to Overseas Chinese, especially those it thought would be helpful to its mission of gaining inroads locally in the overseas diaspora, the people at their Foreign Office invited my mother to meet with them. She used the opportunity to ask their help in finding her daughter, knowing the government had collected detailed information on everyone. None of her attempts succeeded.

Rui bing was at the hospital entrance when we arrived. He looked as though he had just seen a ghost, even as he tried to maintain his composure.

He held the door of the taxi open for us to get out and tried to pay the driver. But Wei had already given the driver our fare. "They had to move my mother out of the room because they needed to put another person in there," he said apologetically.

I did not want to add more to his distress, I touched him lightly on the back and said, "That's alright. I'll just have to wait for the funeral." Then I said gently, "Let me go to the bank and get you the money."

"There is no need any more, Uncle."

"You must have expenses you have to meet, in addition to the funeral and the burial." I reached for his hand and added, "This will just be something from my heart and something that your grandmother would have wanted to do."

A light snow began to fall. Frozen tears from Heaven, I felt. I remembered my mother had told me Ya Du's birthday was just a few days before mine, and she was ten years older. She would be sixty-three.

Rui bing flagged down a taxi for us. On the return trip, the white flurries enveloped the car and muffled the traffic noise. Wei left me alone, in my own silence.

Late afternoon my nephew called. He had arranged the funeral services for the weekend. How times have changed. My mother used to say the body had to lie in state for forty-nine days to give the soul time to transcend. There was no place for such niceties in Mainland China after Mao.

"You should return to Beijing first. I can handle it alone here." I looked at Wei and thought about the enormous help and support he and Jen have given me.

"It's only two more days. Of course, I'll stay with you. I would not think of doing otherwise." He was sitting on the edge of the bed across from me when I spoke with Rui bing.

I got up and walked over to him. "I think I should just have to accept your kindness again. Once more, among all the things you have done for me." I hugged him close, and he hugged me back.

"I think I'll just order up some soup noodles from room service." I managed to say. "But you should go down to the dining room and have a good meal."

"Soup noodles sound good on a cold night like this. I'll stay up here with you."

He checked the menu. "How about their special, snapping turtle soup with ginseng?"

He handed me the menu, and I noticed the description of the benefits of this special soup, 'Good for regaining Qi and strength. Increases potency.'

The hot soup and noodles were soothing. I looked out the window after we were finished. The garden below us was blanketed in white. My mother used to tell me she could skate on the frozen lakes and ponds in Harbin all winter long. There would be festivals with ice sculptures and whole houses carved out of ice. After she died, I couldn't bear to give away a fur cape of hers, trimmed with a sable collar and brocade that she had kept from her days in Harbin and Russia.

Suddenly a crushing sense of failure and loss hit me as I took in the blanched scene of oncoming northern Manchurian winter. I stumbled toward the bed and crumpled. I felt Wei's touch. He was holding me with both arms.

I broke into an open sob and tried to reach for a piece of tissue to blow my nose.

"You've tried your very best. It's the will of Heaven." I heard him repeating as he put a piece of tissue in my hand.

"I'll help you into bed. You should get some rest."

I let him help me undress and get under the covers. I heard the click of the light switch as he put out the light and got into bed next to me. Then I felt his arm around me.

I shuddered. His gentleness and kindness overwhelmed me. I turned around and held onto him, as if for dear life.

His words still echoed in my head, "It's the will of Heaven."

Detail,
Dream of Constantine,
Piero della Francesca,
1464

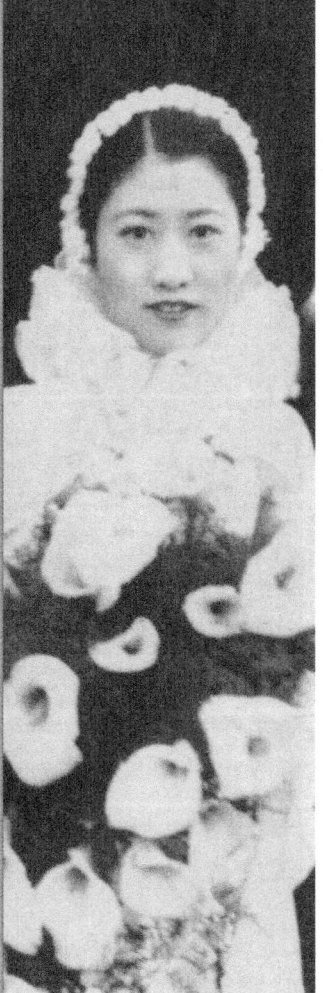

Left top: My father as a student in Japan;

Left bottom: My mother's engagement photo;

Right bottom: My mother's wedding photo.

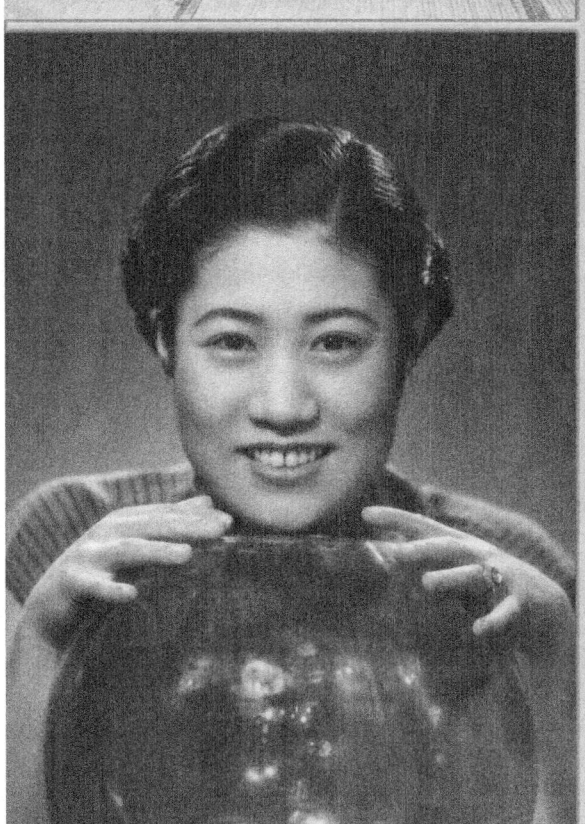

Left: Author with his mother, daughter and son; Right top: Author at four months; Right bottom: Author with father and mother in Shanghai after WWII.

Top: Author and Adele; Below: Adele; Right: Joyce, author's ex and mother of his two children; Bottom Right: Aunt Fu

Daughter's remarriage in Grignols, France. Author, second row, far left. Son, fourth row, far right. Teng, third row far left, behind author. Mark, fourth row, far left, next to Adele.

Along Alien Roads

There is not much that I remember from my high school English class in Tokyo with the exception of the American teacher, a towering woman with messy hair, who read excerpts aloud of Shakespeare's *Tempest*. I can still hear her shrill and booming voice with the line spoken by Antonio: "What's past is prologue; what to come, In yours and my discharge." She was no doubt trying to exhort our young minds to take hold of our future, when most of us had no idea of where we were heading. It has taken me many years to appreciate those words.

By the time I landed on these strange shores at sixteen after a long voyage on the high seas, I did not know what lay ahead of me, even though I was not detained or quarantined on Angel Land for months or years like earlier forebears of mine. I was tossed into the wave of science and engineering students from overseas, a seemingly natural pathway where proficiency in English was not at a high premium.

I had no clue of what I really wanted to become, except a good student and not a disappointment to my parents. It took me four years of trudging through thermodynamics and fluid mechanics, qualitative to quantitative chemistry, and a year in du Pont to realize the brew was not for me.

At the same time, I was now being hit full face in the prevalent college culture of pursuing the opposite sex, while not even aware of the undercurrents of my own sexuality.

Looking back, the two important decisions in my young life I remember making with some forethought were getting into medicine and marrying my medical school classmate. Choosing medical school might be taken as the will of heaven if I conceded the Ouija board to be part of the celestial circle. Several months after I returned to graduate school in chemical engineering, on the eve of a Chinese New Year celebration, I asked a question about my future in the game we were playing for fun. The Ouija Oracle pointed at health care, to my surprise.

I did not know I was going to be committing more than ten years of my life to become a Board-Certified Head and Neck Surgeon. A friend teased me good-naturedly that by the time I got out, I should be old enough for my first heart attack. Along the way, I married my classmate in our shoulder to shoulder long-distance marathon of training, doing so over the strenuous objection of my mother.

The most unexpected storm along this path was my encounter in the freezing men's room of North Station. I was completely unprepared for what happened and even less for how it affected my choices and shoved me in the years ahead.

Outside my marathon of medical training, Martin Luther King, Jr. was marching into Selma; Allen Ginsberg was reading his poem, "Howl" and heralding a generation of people to arrive in San Francisco with flowers in their hair. Paul Mazursky's film where the title, *Bob and Carol and Ted and Alice*, said it all about mate swapping, and retreats in Esalen relaxed our inhibitions. Although I was wearing blinders like a race horse trying to reach the finishing line of my medical training, I could not help noticing the scent of free love in the air.

There was another side to all the fear and revulsion of my first encounter with a man that I could not even admit, much less accept. Even though I had access to the limited information published in journals and texts in the medical library on the cold, clinical subject of homosexuality, there was almost nothing written on what I was feeling. Reasons given for what was then still largely considered an illness and abnormality were simplistic and difficult for me to shoehorn my own experience. Its pull on me was very real and strong as if I had fallen into an opium den of pleasures and lost all will and ability to resist. I found myself in a world more unknown to me than the day I landed in this foreign country. I had at least read and heard about America before coming over, but I knew nothing about the "love that dare not speak its name" as first mentioned in Alfred Douglas's poem celebrated by Oscar Wilde.

When I found a therapist, who was also married with two young children yet accepted his own affinity for men, I grasped onto him like a lifeline.

The Stonewall Riots and the beginning of gay liberation, Nixon's Watergate and Charles Reich's book, *The Greening of America*, opened my eyes and shoved me further along in facing the real world of America. They helped me realize I was not alone in my precarious struggle to reach a safe shore.

After more than ten years of hand-wringing at the therapist's, and hearing others with similar anguish and agony in a men's group, I was able to feel that I could be myself at last. The ground did not cave in under me. I could feel fresh air rush in to fill my lungs and through my whole body. The relief was overwhelming as if I could breathe for the first time without a huge boulder on my chest. It made me realize I would not want to live and deny what I was to myself, ever again.

When I was at the doorstep of adolescence, one of the Chinese classics I was allowed to read was *Shui Hu Zhuan*, a fourteenth-century Chinese epic about Robin Hood-like men bonding in the face of an unjust officialdom. In English, it was translated as *All Men are Brothers* by Pearl Buck. When I was going through my own struggles with feeling like an outcast, the novel had a fresh resonance for me.

The support and camaraderie of the characters in the novel were what I eventually found in the gay men's groups. At that shaky stage of my life past forty, I realized I had found my own "family" where I had no fear of being shamed and turned away. Some of the men became lifelong friends. My children remembered one of them as being the gentlest man they had known.

It was the late seventies, and Gilbert Baker's rainbow flag first flew at the Pride Parades I took my children to watch in the city. To them, it was probably only a fun and colorful event, but for me, the bluebird in the sky seemed within reach.

This new self, coming out of the darkness, made me more open to the people who came to me for help. I felt the dividing line between myself as a physician and my patients, which I had been trained and taught to keep, melted away in the process. I was able to be myself in front of them without the feeling I had to hide a part of myself or might be ridiculed and compromised if they discovered that part of me. They responded to me more as a real person like themselves rather than a distant God-like figure on a pedestal.

In my personal life, I felt I was able to come clean and be open and honest with my wife, even though it meant we were going to head in different directions. But I felt our deep connection, which drew us together in the first place, would survive. For one thing, we would always be parents to our two children. It was not an easy line to tread in the beginning, but eventually, after our children were grown, she even became a friend of Adele. I felt a swell of prayers answered when Adele told me she noticed I was the one to whom my wife came for help and advice.

Thinking about the people who were important along the path I have tread—my wife, my lovers, many intimate friends, and those no longer here, I have the feeling that if we were to sit down for a cup of tea together, warm feelings of mutual affection and care would remain. The differences that once pulled us apart would no longer matter.

I could not say that what came was all mine or in my discharge, as my old English teacher in Tokyo had hoped for her students. But it has been an extended train ride I don't regret, from the time I was taken as an infant in war-torn Hankow to meet my grandmother in the South of China, to the first train ride I can remember with my father when he came back after the War in a red-carpeted private Pullman car, leading to the train that I thought was going to be the end of my life, pulling out of Boston's North Station into the snow.

PART III

Chapter Twenty-One

猴

I was still trying to catch my breath when the conductor started down the aisle, wad of tickets in one hand and ticket puncher in the other. He looked me over through his bifocals. What caught his eye was probably my cheeks drained of color between the collars of my Loden coat, as if I had just stepped out of watching Hitchcocks's *Psycho*, after seeing Tony Perkins stabbing Janet Leigh in the shower scene. But his grandfatherly gaze softened when he noticed the intern's uniform, "You okay?" he asked.

"Much better now," my words stumbled out, "a little too much eggnog." I lied. "Had to throw it all up in the john back there."

It had been a particularly cold December night in Boston's South End. The icepick chill before another blizzard gathered in the air outside. I had downed more beers than I should at the party for surgical interns, relieved after surviving the forty-eight-hour double duty shift in order to get Christmas day off with Joyce, my bride of two years.

"Got to go, before I miss the last train!" From behind the tangle of tinsels and balloons put up by the student nurses, I grabbed the Loden coat left over from college days, wrapped the long, wool muffler knit by my mother around my mouth and neck, and dashed out. A chorus of "Merry Christmas!" from my fellow interns and the nurses followed me down the hallway.

Two long blocks from the hospital to the elevated train stop along the streets still covered with some snow from the last storm and twenty minutes wait on the freezing platform above street level tested the limits of my cold endurance. Tugging my coat close to keep my teeth from chattering, I wished I could be with the crowd of warm, merrymakers in the bar below.

Some black folks in that neighborhood bar had taught us the twist. Joyce and I stopped by on the occasional night out to relax, when we were still in medical school. Great way to let go, after cramming in too many hours of Harrison's bible on Internal Medicine. Joyce was quick to pick up the new dance. The people delighted in taking two newlywed medical students by the hand and loosening us up from our starched white uniforms to show us a good time.

When the train finally pulled in, instead of the warm car I was expecting, its heating system was shut off. The maintenance crew must have taken off early for Christmas, I could only curse under my barely warmed breath behind my muffler.

By the time we pulled into North Station, I found out it would be another twenty minutes before the last train to the North Shore. The waiting room was not any better, damp and cold like a meat storage locker. At one time a grand, chandeliered hall for Bostonian Brahmins heading north for their summer homes, now the three-storied ceiling and fixtures were dimmed by over half century's smoke and soot and years of neglect following waves of Irish, then Italian immigrants. I suspected it was now kept intentionally insufferable to discourage local drunks and vagrants from using it as overnight shelter.

Still, the old wooden benches were nearly full of the same characters I saw in the emergency room, dragged there every Saturday night where they got dumped to dry out from cheap booze or treated for frostbite. Puddles of vomitus and urine filled the corners, from those who couldn't make it to the men's room or simply no longer cared.

A sign, 'Out of Order,' hung askew on a metal stand outside the men's room on the ground floor. I did not think I could hold onto my beer filled bladder till I got on the train. The only other usable facility was on the third level up. When I finally reached it, I could almost follow the scent of stale urine into the men's room.

With great relief, I stood in front of the long, metal trough tucked in the back, beyond the outer room of stained washbasins and mirrors. For several seconds, I sighed silently emptying my full bladder. The mist from my warm breath partly obscured my view, as I lingered for a few more seconds to savor the relief.

Abruptly I was pulled back from that warm feeling. Out of the corner of my eye, I became aware of a pair of eyes like a falcon on a hare, trained on me from the far end of the trough. I was stunned. At the same time, I felt an uncontrollable response pulsing between my fingers, as I tried to shake off the last droplets from my bladder.

I couldn't lift my legs to run from the man's footsteps shuffling toward me. My ears pounded, and my throat constricted as if a massive pair of hands were choking me.

Paralyzed and rooted to the spot, it seemed an hour as I struggled with my shaking hands to zip myself up. I can't remember how I got out of there and fled down the dark caverns of the long terminal corridors. My lips were glued and throat so parched that I could not let out a gasp. Behind me the footsteps stalked. I tried to push my legs forward, but somehow could not gain much distance between us. I clutched the starched cotton of my pants, trying to dry the cold sweat from my palms.

When he caught up with me on the landing of a poorly lit stairwell, my arms and legs were shaking uncontrollably, and I felt they did not belong to me.

He wasted no time to reach under my belt, his large palm branding me like a hot iron when he took hold. I shuddered and exploded.

This was not the first time that someone touched me there. I had chalked those up as kids fooling around, but this time the intensity of my own response was like nothing I had ever felt. I must have realized it deep down, but I was completely incapable of facing what I knew outright. *I had really wanted it to happen.*

A few seconds and it was all over. But his hand held on. I fumbled for my handkerchief to wipe myself, trying to get rid of the evidence I imagined that was soiling my coat and pant legs. A frantic urge to wipe away everything, the sharp stench of the moment and telltale vestiges of whatever was happening to me.

He mumbled something and tried to pull me close. I couldn't hear what he was saying and struggled free, then flew down the stairs. How long I ran, I could not remember. I kept hearing footsteps pounding, but it was my own heartbeat. I ran without daring to look back until suddenly I realized, it was only my own soles slapping the concrete of the train platform.

The platform director was blowing his whistle as I flew into the last car.

"All aboard for Beverly and all points North!" I heard him bellow, then collapsed into the seat closest to the doorway and tried to catch some air.

"Better lairn t' care o'yerself, Doc." The silver-maned conductor alongside me drawled in his Irish brogue, as he shifted his weight to his other foot and waited for me to reach for my ticket. I was too nervous to listen to what he was saying. Trying to remember his face now, he was a man as hearty and kindly as Seamus Heaney at a poetry reading.

I checked my thighs to make sure there were no incriminating stains on my starched pant legs and then tugged at my Loden coat to cover myself. I felt as if the conductor was taking in every gesture I was making under his bifocals. Somehow, I managed to dig into my back pocket for my monthly pass. I sighed, feeling a quiet reprieve when he did not seem to notice anything and believed whatever words came out of my mouth.

"Merry Christmas!" he said and winked at me as he handed the pass back then ambled down the aisle.

A merry Christmas was not going to be. Not as we had planned.

Joyce and I had been wishing for a real Christmas celebration that year. We had been so busy with finishing our medical studies, passing our National Exams to get our medical degrees, and getting internships that we hardly had any real time with each other from the time we married, much less time to bother with Christmas and holidays.

That year we bought our first Christmas tree for the apartment. Joyce had gotten the place as part of her benefits from the hospital where she was an intern. We carried the tree on top of the red beetle; our first car bought together with our first month's salaries and graduation gifts as a down payment.

I put up the tree lights and the few ornaments we could afford, a few days earlier. We were going to surprise each other with the presents we got on Christmas morning. I had to hide the amethyst and gold bracelet I bought from a shop off Beacon Street, and tucked it deep inside the top of the closet, too high for Joyce to reach.

As I finally took my first deep breath after settling into my seat and looked out the train window, the night sky was pitch black, the ground spotted with frozen snow of the last storm. I had always liked train rides, ever since riding with my father when he came into my life after the Second World War. The slow rumbling motion of the car had often put me into a slow lullaby, and I often used it to rest and relax on my way home from the non-stop day and night work schedule at the hospital.

There was no rest for my mind now. The landscape outside looked like Dostoevsky's *Crime and Punishment*. As the train bumped along its tracks, I thought of Tolstoy's *Anna Karenina* and her final moment of desperation. The marital vows I repeated in front of the Justice of Peace rushed back as an indictment.

The sense of betrayal, guilt, and shame was so overwhelming that I didn't know where to turn. I wished I could redeem myself by walking into a confession booth and ask for forgiveness from a priest. I wished I could find a path to forget what had just happened. I could not think my way out. And the more panicked and obsessed in finding a way out I felt, the more it came roaring back in my face. It was like the cursed thing in Dostoevsky's story, the more you tried not to think of it, the more it will come to mind.

I thought Joyce would be able to tell that something was wrong with me, as soon as I walked through the door of our small apartment, and I might find myself spending the night on a frozen snow bank outside, which would be just punishment for what I had done. Even that would be too easy.

That was the Christmas Eve over half a century ago. Some moments in my past stand out starkly, like the ideograms of an old sutra written in blood as an offering to the Qing Emperor and now stored in its own carved box on my bookcase. While others feel as blurry as finding my way home through a blizzard. Along with seeing my mother lying on a bloody hospital bed after she overdosed a few months past my eighth birthday, this was one of those nightmares I will never be able to erase from my memory.

This night awakened something I had not even acknowledged to myself. I thought it changed my life with no return.

Chapter Twenty-Two

雞

My favorite snapshot of Joyce is the one I took the year after our daughter was born, in an antiqued gold frame, the shape of a fish with a circle in the center for the picture. The word fish in Chinese is a homonym for Joyce's name, Yu, given by her father because the character meant happiness. On the left side of the ideogram is the symbol for heart, reminding the Chinese reader where the happiness comes from. The year I moved out, I covered the picture with one of our daughter; her third-grade class picture. She gave it to me the day before I told her I was leaving.

Leah's eyes, a startled fawn blinded by fog light in the dark of night, when she heard my words close to four decades ago, stare at me now even with my own eyes closed and always will. For her nine-year-old heart, the shock was too much, I doubt she heard any word I said after that—that I would always love her.

Joyce was radiant in that snapshot. Too bright eyed and unsuspecting for me to look at after I moved out. I moved her into the background of my new life, yet hoped not to erase all those years we had together. I realize now I was much too simple minded to think that I might even be able to erase the memories of a person who was at the center of my life, from day break to pillow talk for so many years.

In that picture, her long hair, a sheet of black lacquer shimmering to her thighs, was swept up high on her head like a Manchurian tiara. Her eyes, slanted slightly upwards at the corners, rhapsodized as eyes of the mythical phoenix in traditional Chinese novels like the *Dreams of the Red Chamber*, told me how happy she was at that moment of her life.

She had good reasons to be, when the picture was taken. New motherhood, a professional career on the horizon as a medical specialist, and a husband she thought was completely devoted to her. I thought so, too. I was still trying to delude myself, not to think about my own doubts and fears of the part of me, which seemed to have dropped in on me like an unwanted guest who refused to leave from a world unknown to me until that Christmas Eve in North Station of Boston.

Like my parents, Joyce and I were not introduced by a proper matchmaker or even through friends of the family, the custom established by our Chinese ancestors for several millennia. Our families did not exchange carved red cinnabar boxes containing formal envelopes with our *Bazi*, the eight Chinese characters where every two designated the hour, day, month, and year of our births, written on rice paper in classical Chinese calligraphy, to make sure we were harmoniously matched according to the astrological cycles and calculations of the traditional lunar calendar.

My mother did manage, however, to find out Joyce was born the same year as I. Under the sign of an Ox. Sturdy, hardworking, and dependable.

"Better to marry someone born in the year of the Rabbit," she counseled. Two years younger, more easy going, and not as obstinate.

"But I'm an Ox," I protested.

"That's different," she said with an air of firm maternal authority.

She was silent when I enumerated Joyce's academic achievements. Her ivy-covered college was the better known one in Cambridge, and she even had a scholarship in the Medical School where we were now studying together.

Furthermore, I tried to reassure my mother, her parents had the same North-South provincial split like mine. A Cantonese father and mother from Shanghai, but both communicating with each other in Mandarin.

When we compared our early childhoods in Shanghai, I found out Joyce and I even went to the same kindergarten on Avenue Pétain, in the old French Concession. What more could my mother want?

"You'd better get your father's approval." My mother was not one to give in so easily. She trotted out the figure of my father, who was living in Taiwan, an ocean and a continent away from the East Coast, even though she was thinking of a divorce from him at that time.

I sent off a formal, black-and-white studio portrait of Joyce. My father's reply came quickly. "She has full cheeks and a sweet disposition," he observed, adding, "She will give you many children and be a good mother."

Fertility was not prominent in my mind then, if anything I was more concerned about practicing effective birth control. Our knowledge of contraception consisted of rudimentary Russian roulette, even though Joyce and I were both in medical school.

It was the early sixties, before the full blossoming of the flower children. Condoms were not displayed next to candies in drugstores. It would have taken more chutzpah than I had to ask for a package from the pharmacist. But I was happy to get my father's message of tacit approval.

Our first date was a game of ping pong in my student union even though I didn't realize it as such at the time. It was many years before the game was credited as the seed of what was called ping pong diplomacy for the Nixon-Kissinger detente between China and the U.S.

The registrar at the admissions office of the medical school was our matchmaker, the *hong niang* in Chinese novels, such as the *Tale of the Western Chamber*, the young girl with the red silk cord pulling the young couple together. Our *hong niang* was a woman of regal bearing with a Bostonian Brahmin accent, lowered several octaves by years of chain smoking. She was sympathetic when I wrote on my application that I needed help with the tuition. "Call her," she said when she gave me the phone number of this Chinese girl who was good at getting financial assistance.

As a student from another country, financial aid through the regular channels was not available to me. My passport was from the Chinese KMT government, which, at that time, had its tail between its legs in its retreat from the Communist takeover of the Chinese Mainland to the island of Taiwan. The KMT's own fate was as shaky as those of the banana republics of today.

With six hundred dollars in savings from a year's work as an engineer after college graduation, and too proud to burden my parents, I was anxiously looking for ways to pay for my medical education. My mother was already questioning my sanity about giving up chemical engineering, a perfectly good profession she thought, and diving into medicine. Unlike today, it was a field little known to overseas Chinese students in the late fifties.

Joyce and I met over a plate of blintzes with cream cheese and strawberries in the small luncheonette on the street in back of her dormitory. It was a few short blocks from Harvard Square, the busy hub of most student activities in that college town. On the other side of the Square, a young Joan Baez started her career at the Club 47 on Mount Auburn Street, with a voice more pure and heart-wrenching than we had heard before.

We compared the similarities of our backgrounds at that first meeting.

"My mother did not get along with most of my father's relatives from the South." Joyce echoed the standoff between my mother and my father's Cantonese clan, between sips of buttermilk. She was on lunch break, working as a weekend waitress at the coffee house, but she managed to slip me an extra blintz with strawberries.

I was too timid to ask her for details about getting money for medical school at that first meeting, although I found her very easy to be around. It felt quite natural for me to invite her for a game of ping pong across town in my student union that evening. The student union on my campus alongside the Charles River was a relatively new and modern structure as compared with the centuries old ivy-covered brick buildings on Joyce's campus.

Sunday evenings were quiet times at the student union. Students who had partied on Saturday nights were now buckling down for homework due on Monday. When we stepped out of the elevator, the top floor was almost deserted. We didn't have to stand around the ping pong table to wait for our turn.

I picked out a couple of paddles and balls from the cabinet at the end and offered them to Joyce.

"You take the better one," she said.

"You're my guest here." I deferred.

"I'm used to worn out paddles." She held on to the more worn out one.

After a few warm up volleys, I could tell she was an excellent player. With pigtails flying she could spin her return volleys into far corners of the table.

"I see you hold the paddle the Chinese way," she said. "The way my parents do."

I realized she gripped hers with her whole hand like a tennis racket.

"We don't have to keep score. Just play for fun?" I suggested.

"It's more fun though," she answered.

I scored a few shots but found it hard to return her spins. Yet somehow, I managed to win the match in the end.

Many years later, as a married couple, we reminisced about that evening. She told me with a quiet satisfaction that she had let me win deliberately. It would have lessened her chances of being considered as a girlfriend if she had beat me in that first game of ping pong.

I remembered she was a better dancer, but never let me feel I wasn't keeping up with her. She had a way of putting herself down that years later a colleague who didn't know her well said to me, "It's hard to believe she graduated from Radcliffe." And I thought, she also got a fellowship for medical school.

When we started our medical practices in the small community outside of San Francisco, we were strongly advised by my senior partner that we had to invite our colleagues home and regularly entertain in order to promote the business side of our practices. I felt uneasy because it made me feel like a used car salesman.

When I showed surprise at her ease with handling the big gatherings at our home, she said, "Remember I was a cheerleader and student council president of my high school." In those days, she was the only Chinese girl in her high school in Scarsdale, New York.

I realized then she was skilled at taking a step back but keeping an eye at what she wanted to achieve in the end.

Two years ago at Joyce's memorial service, her friends from high school days, her roommate from Radcliffe, and her colleagues came from all over. They remembered her in their tributes.

Our daughter and son had assembled a video clip about her life, from Shanghai to Scarsdale, Radcliffe to our lives together, then her life after I left.

I stood and read a poem I wrote about Joyce and her passion for chocolates.

I think back to the day when I left our home, when our daughter, Leah, was nine; and our son, only seven. How devastated she must have felt, even though she managed to hold back her tears in front of me.

Chapter Twenty-Three

狗

Joyce was not on my mind as another candidate for dating during those early months of our acquaintance. I was at the end of a year-long, off-and-on chaste dance around a gentle and proper young woman of Armenian descent. It was too platonic and proper an affair to have stirred up any hormonal surges, and I was devoting all my attention toward getting into medical school. The wariness of becoming involved with a potential classmate in medical school was subconscious, and the image of someone working across a dissecting table of a human cadaver would not be conducive to developing any romantic feelings.

The summer before we got into medical school, Joyce found work in a bar and restaurant on Cape Cod.

"Come down, and I'll show you around."

The weekend after my exams in biology and botany courses that I needed to make up in order to get into medical school, she invited me for a day on the Cape.

I convinced a friend to lend me his jalopy.

"A hot date?" he smirked. Most of my friends were on the shy side around women. Picnics and hikes occasionally organized by the local Chinese Students' Association were the extent of our contact.

"Just a friend who's going to show me a bit of the Cape."

"Just a friend. If that could be believed!"

"Just a friend, nothing more." I insisted, truly believing the words at that time. Nevertheless, I felt a little flushed.

"Drive carefully, the jalopy can't take it too fast," he cautioned and gave me a wink.

The morning of the trip, I hurried through my work at the hospital. The Brahmin registrar at the medical school was good enough to find me work as a phlebotomist and lab tech in exchange for my room and board.

"You're getting an early start." One of the patients on the surgical floor was surprised to see me so early at her bedside on Saturday.

"Lots to do today," I answered half truthfully.

I pushed the jalopy nearly to its limits and got down to mid Cape Hyannis before noon.

Joyce worked at *Hu-Ke-Lau.* The restaurant was faux Hawaiian, with thatched roof and palms, bright plastic leis and lanterns. Its owner was from the Islands. Mainstays of the Cantonese chef from New York Chinatown were egg foo young, chow mein, chop suey, and heavily cornstarched sweet and sour pork with pineapple and sliced maraschino cherries.

She was expected to wear heels and a Suzy Wong cheongsam with high slits to serve drinks decorated with tiny paper parasols. Her first week was hard. Multisyllabic names of all the tropical drinks she could hardly pronounce. But customers left generous tips, registering her happy smile after hearing she was a college kid trying to earn some money for medical school.

The place was not hard to find at the far end of Main Street. It was just getting ready for luncheon business, but the bar area was still unlit. She told me she had arranged to work late the night before and didn't need to get back to work till seven that evening.

I saw a young Asian man, not looking like a customer, standing near the cash register. I asked him where I could find Joyce.

"You must be Andrew." He sounded very friendly. "She's been waiting for you."

I felt a little awkward because of the implication in his words. Joyce told me there was a young Chinese waiter called Bobby who has been very good to her, showing her the ropes of the place. He came up summers from New York's Chinatown where his family struggled to earn a living; he started working without finishing high school to help.

Bobby was a little shorter than me, with a reassuring smile but lukewarm handshake. "I tell her you're here," he said.

Joyce came out bubbling in baggy shorts and strap sandals, with Bobby a few steps behind.

"No trouble finding the place?"

"Your directions were excellent."

"This is Bobby." She turned to introduce.

"We met already," I said, remembering his handshake but taking note of the smile on his face.

"Bobby is coming with us. He knows all the spots."

I felt a twinge of disappointment but rationalized I was not interested in her as a date anyway.

"Joyce said you drove down with a car." He looked at me, bright front teeth flashing.

I took a closer look. He was clean shaven, with the large eyes of a Cantonese. He could have been on a college campus except his hair was a pomaded, modified Elvis, instead of a buzz cut.

"I borrowed my friend's jalopy," I said.

"I don't own a car neither." I began to feel he was trying too hard to be friendly and detected the slight accent in his English. Not from a Shanghai industrialist family, not from Northern Chinese Mandarins, but Cantonese, a Cantonese not from Hong Kong, but from Chinatown, in his case, New York City.

"Your family from Canton?" I felt pretty sure about his answer, but it made easy conversation.

"You from the North, right?"

"No, I'm also Cantonese." It was not unusual for people to mistake me from the North. "But my mother was from Peking." I usually didn't go into the details about her ancestral home in Suzhou, close to Shanghai, because my mother considered herself closer to a Northerner in temperament and usually spoke Mandarin rather than the Shanghai dialect.

"You speak Cantonese?"

"Yes," I said, feeling a bit put off by his doubting my ability to speak the Southern Chinese dialect after I told him I was also Cantonese. "But I only speak Sam Yep."

In 1954, when my mother and I landed in San Francisco by boat from Yokohama, Japan, friends took us to lunch in Chinatown. I tried my Sam Yep Cantonese on the shopkeepers.

"You no speaking Chinese," the clerk said. Finally, an older man came out from the back of the store and explained they spoke Sei Yep Cantonese or Toisan, while the Cantonese I was speaking was Sam Yep.

Later I found out most of the earlier Chinese immigrants were from villages using Sei Yep. People from the same province but from a village over a hill could speak a different dialect of Cantonese. Sam Yep was the dialect spoken in the provincial capitol and in Hong Kong.

"My family speak Sei Yip, but I can speak Sam Yip, too." I noticed he pronounced the *Yep* as *Yip* in Toisam dialect.

"Joyce's father is Cantonese, too." I saw Joyce looking at the two of us and tried to pull her back into our conversation.

"But I don't speak any Cantonese," Joyce added apologetically. She told me when we first met that she had come over when she was nine. Her Chinese was rusty, and we settled on using English between us.

"That's what we call a *Jook Sing*," Bobby said to me conspiratorially but looked at Joyce to make sure she knew he was teasing. The term was often heard in Chinatown in those days to deride Chinese who were too Americanized and didn't even speak Chinese.

"Okay, you guys," Joyce said good-naturedly. "You will have to use English with me."

The three of us hopped into my borrowed jalopy. Joyce had to be extra cautious in the side seat up front, stretching her legs forward to avoid the big hole in the floor under her feet. Bobby perched on what was left of the back seat where the springs were not showing through the upholstery, and told me where to go.

"Joyce told me you waiting to get in medical school." The breeze stirred his hair as we headed toward Provincetown.

"Yes," I answered, meeting Bobby's large almond-shaped eyes, so large that they were almost round, in the rearview mirror. A look of interest and inquisitiveness. I couldn't be sure which was stronger, couched with an underlying offer of friendship that I found reassuring at the time, but I would have found seductive several years later, after my abrupt introduction into that world at North Station. That summer, I had yet no conscious clue and merely answered him, "I am waiting for the results of my MCATs, too."

Before I could explain that these were the qualifying exams to enter medical school, Joyce chimed in and told him what an ordeal it was for her. I began to see she had a habit of downplaying her own intelligence.

"Then I have to wait for someone to drop out before I can get in."

Bobby nodded in sympathy.

"How long have you been in this country?" I asked.

"I was born in New York." He asked back, "You?"

"1954. From Japan."

"You Joyce?" He turned toward her. "When you come?"

I remembered she told me it was 1946.

"Not long after the War, my father sent for us." Then she added, "From Shanghai."

"You speak Shanghai?" His question made me realize she had not told him much about herself.

"I'm afraid I haven't kept up."

"*Nong haw va?*" Bobby showed off his three words of Shanghai dialect, he learned from a customer.

I began to feel more relaxed with the easy banter he carried on as I drove on that long stretch of Mid Cape Highway with the afternoon sun on our backs.

We passed towns with names ending in *wich* or *mouth*, knocked out by views of the Atlantic when the road got near the coastline. When we came closer to the tip of the Cape, the land narrowed. Water on both sides, sand dunes stretched ahead like a mirage, as far as my eyes could strain to reach.

By the time we got to Provincetown, it was past time for lunch in most restaurants. Bobby suggested something simple along Commercial, Provincetown's main street, lined with shops for tourists and more art galleries than I had ever seen in one place since coming to the U.S.

He led us to a luncheonette, popular with the locals he said. I could tell he enjoyed the role of being our tour guide. I wanted to try the clam chowder, but they said it ran out earlier and settled for the cheeseburger; Bobby was ordering, and Joyce had a hot dog.

We walked along as we ate. Joyce and I exchanged glances, feeling like two country bumpkins in the artsy town. Bobby led us around the enormous boat harbor with a light stride close to a strut, with noticeable proprietary pride.

Back on the streets, I eyed a sign on a small cottage, PROVINCETOWN BOOKSHOP, SINCE 1932. I suggested we take a peek. Joyce was also enthusiastic. Tennessee Williams's *Streetcar* was in the window. I had no idea on that first visit the significance of Williams and his world, or the importance of Provincetown until I became aware of my own attraction to it years later. The shop was well stocked with books bulging into the aisles. Our guide lingered near the front where there were a few magazines and cards.

"We'd better go," Joyce said after browsing in the aisles then looking at her watch.

Bobby said he was going to stop by a Chinese restaurant where he knew some people. "You can walk in the dunes. Pick me up when you're ready." He was looking at Joyce and me, then turning to me, he added, "Joyce knows the way."

I was not sure whether he was being very thoughtful or just being very practical. I even wondered if there was a touch of curiosity in his tone.

"What do you think of Bobby?" Joyce scooted carefully into the side seat as we got back to the car.

"I like him."

"He's really been good to me. Shielding me from the older workers, especially the bartender, the first few weeks."

"He doesn't like the beach?"

"He likes to hang out with his buddies in the other Chinese restaurants and bars. I think he knows most of them and hangs out with all kinds of people."

I felt a bit uneasy with her careful explanations about him and wondered if she was thinking if I might be jealous, which made me feel uneasy. I was not clear about the reasons for my own ambivalence at that time, whether Joyce was a date or just a buddy, and neither one of us said anything further.

"There is a turn toward the dunes on the left. Not too far from the town."

Windows down, the breeze brought the taste of salt to our tongue and the smell of the sea close by. "The turn off is not well marked. It's either the first or second turn out of Town."

I turned down the unmarked sandy road, and we both felt the unevenness. I saw the beach grass through the floor on Joyce's side.

"I hope I can get this jalopy back up."

"I think there is a place to park right after this turn."

She jumped out and ran along the path, carrying a small beach tote with a blue canvas trim, sandals flopping in her hands, then looked back and waved for me to follow. The dunes, miles and miles of them below us, over us, all around us, only the sky above and sea beyond. The road where we came in was out of sight.

An occasional bundle of weeds tumbled in the wind. Otherwise, it felt like nothing much stirred.

I caught up with her. "Isn't this wonderful?" She inhaled, arms stretching out, her exuberance effervescent.

"Never seen anything like this!"

Beaches I remembered: Repulse Bay of Hong Kong, two blocks from our house, sand bucket in one hand amah's hand in another; a doorstep to adolescence was junior high class trip to the beach town, Danshui, near Taipei, or even those by the seaside near Tokyo with my parents when I was in high school. Beautiful but always with other people or crowds around. Never the sense of having a whole world to myself. But now, there was all this sand and sky and sea without end, I was so engulfed by the sheer vastness and solitude that I almost forgot there was anyone else there.

"Let's see what the water is like." Joyce ran down to the edge, dropping her sandals on the blinding white sand. I followed, leaving my shoes and socks next to the sandals and rolled up my pant legs.

Refreshingly cool, the water hit us as we waded in, our toes sinking into the sand. Yet the waves felt almost warm, lapping at our legs.

The next instant a stronger wave hit us from the back and wet my pant legs.

"Should have brought along swimsuits."

"Never turn your back to the sea, they say." Joyce got wet, too, but the waves didn't quite reach her shorts.

"I'm going to get out and dry myself."

"No problem in this sun," she said reassuringly. "But wait, there's a small towel in my beach tote. Let me get it for you."

We picked up our things and found a spot at the bottom of the nearest dune, out of reach by the waves.

I enjoyed her company, infectiously light hearted, more as a friend with no conscious thought of dating, but there must have been some awareness of that possibility. Because the awkwardness of dating someone in the same class in med school resurfaced. Too close, almost incestuous in a way, in the same fish bowl with too many eyes watching each other all the time, in a small group of ninety students crowded together and doing the same thing from day to day. Yet, to be honest, I must have thought about dating her, otherwise, why would I have considered so many aspects.

What drew us together was what we had in common. Cantonese fathers, Shanghai beauties for mothers, never accepted by the family clan. I felt we were buddies. Joyce might have sensed my ambivalence and kept her feelings to herself.

A week after the memorial service for Joyce, Adele was helping me clean out my garage in San Francisco. Inside a dusty bin of old towels and bags, I pulled out the fraying small beach tote. The blue canvas trim on its top and bottom has faded, but I could still make out the print of whimsical different colored small sails in the middle, almost like a mini canvas of Paul Klee, one of the artists we both liked on our first trip together to MOMA in New York. The beach bag was passed down to our children, and they eventually left it in my garage. Seeing its poor condition, Adele

23

狗

threw the tote into the discard pile. I put it back in the keep pile. It was something that survived my separation and divorce from Joyce, as well as our coming together again as friends.

Adele was instrumental in bringing us back full circle to friendship, because of the friendship she developed with Joyce through our daughter. "In the end, Joyce trusted your advice more than anyone else," Adele observed. I think she was happy that she had something to do with bringing Joyce and me together again.

Our children had put together a moving, memorial service for their mother. Her friends from high school to medical school days came from across the country and told stories of their times together. The poem I read was about her love of chocolates and indomitable spirit of never giving up. One of the first things she bought was a chocolate cookbook after we moved into the house we built together. Adele's son who now lives in that house took a video of the whole service for all of us. Our grandchildren asked that Tobler's Swiss chocolate bars, one of Joyce's favorites, be given to all who came.

I thought of that day on the beach over five and a half decades ago, when we talked about what we were going to do after medical studies.

I was going back to China, to help my people, I said, full of youthful bravado. I had no wish to stay on in this country, not after being verbally slapped by the Immigration Officer when I tried to extend my visa to study medicine.

"I know your type. All you want to do is to stay in this country!" I felt blood rise up in my cheeks as if he back handed me across the face. I wished I had the courage to throw my application back in his.

Joyce did not comment on my grand plans of returning to China that summer afternoon. Years later when we settled in Northern California after our medical training, with two kids and a big monthly mortgage on my back, she told me she thought my idea for China sounded a bit naïve and overly idealistic to her, when we sat on the beach that afternoon, ocean breeze brushing our faces.

I had asked her what she wanted to do. Pediatrics, she thought, the field most open to women in those days. She liked children, didn't even mind taking care of her sister who was ten years younger, thoroughly Americanized and hardly spoke any Chinese.

"I thought of obstetrics," she said, "but the field was still pretty much dominated by men." Friends of her mother and even her own friends told her, they would rather have a man take care of them if they were having a baby. The doctor with a white coat on Norman Rockwell posters was a man with gray hair and deep voice, not a young woman. The popular television image was a handsome Dr. Kildare, not a Dr. Susan Rosen, and even more farfetched, Dr. Joyce Liu. A surname they either could not place in their mind or at best, only heard of as a faithful slave girl in a Puccini opera.

"Nice way to end a summer!" I turned to her and wondered whether it might be time to go pick up Bobby at the restaurant where we left him. "Thanks for inviting me." Meaning every word of it.

"Come again."

"Don't think my friend will let me borrow his car again before school starts. Only a few weeks left."

"Heard anything yet?" She asked about my admission to the school.

"Still waiting," I said, "You're pretty much all set."

"I have to worry about the tuition for the second year."

"What about your fellowship?" I was surprised that Joyce still had to worry.

"That's only for one year."

"Can't you ask for renewal next year?"

"I did. They want to spread it around."

"Maybe Mrs. Gowing can find something for you too." I thought of the admission's registrar who had done so much for me already.

"I'm going to save as much as I can with summer jobs. Like working on my days off and double shifts, if I can stand it. Bobby has been really helpful and kind." She added. "He tried to get me double shifts when he knew the work would be easy."

"Your special connection." I needled.

"It's not what you think. He's really a nice guy. Haven't even seen him with any girls. Just wants to help."

"Just teasing," I said. "Should we be picking him up?"

"Right. Didn't realize it's almost five."

He was waiting for us curbside. "Better start going back."

He sounded a little anxious. "Can't tell. Traffic on weekends."

"Got time to pick up something to eat on the way?" I wondered.

"Don't worry. Can always get something from the kitchen."

"Bobby knows the chef," Joyce said.

"Sure, he won't mind about me?" I looked at Bobby in the rearview.

"Don't worry," he said, with a leave-it-to-me expression on his face.

I took another look at him in the mirror. Aside from the easy friendliness, there was something assured, bordering on cockiness, and a hint of toughness from the streets, that made him look more mature and older, by maybe five or ten years than Joyce or I, although I was sure from what Joyce told me about his work experience, he couldn't be more than a couple of years ahead of us in age.

"Like the dunes?" he asked breezily.

"Great! Never seen anything like it." I told him.

"Too quiet for me. Nobody else there." There was no hint of irony or unfriendliness in his comment.

I thought of Coney Island and Jones Beach. Very accessible from Chinatown, New York. Sea of people, Roller Coaster on the Beach. My first and only time there, made my face turned green when I stepped off it.

"This has been a great way to end the summer for me." I shifted my gaze to include Joyce. "Thank you both for showing me around."

"You welcome," he said.

"How long you're staying on the Cape?"

"Hu-Ke-Lau close end of September. No business after Labor Day."

"Back to New York?"

"If I find work," he answered without any hint of worry in his voice.

We were facing the sunset on our way back. I had to concentrate on getting us back on time and didn't continue the banter. Joyce and Bobby didn't say much either. Perhaps we all felt a little sad that summer was coming to an end.

By the time we got back to Hu-Ke-Lau, it was quarter past six. I pulled into the back and Bobby went in ahead of us.

"He says what's on his mind. But he's got a good heart."

"Sure it's okay for me to eat here?"

"Not a problem. Bobby's friends eat here often. Mostly waiters on their day off and the cook doesn't mind.

"Have a seat at the table close to the kitchen. That's where we usually eat before the crowds come in. I've got to go and change." She screwed up her face to tell me how much she hated getting into the cheongsam she had to wear.

Bobby came out with food from the kitchen in his hands and on his arms, carrying the dishes with practiced ease. Chicken wings, fried tofu with mixed vegetables, bok choy, and some ribs. A large bowl the size of a tureen of steamed rice followed. He looked good in his work costume, bright Hawaii shirt and white pants showing off his trim body. The outfit suited his Elvis hair well, handsome like a real swinging Islander.

The other help gathered around the table, and he introduced me as Joyce's friend. They were mostly from Toisam, about his age or younger. Not much was said, as they started into the food. Bobby motioned with his chopsticks for me to join in, like at a family dinner table. His warm gesture and smile touched me.

Joyce came out in a midnight blue cheongsam shimmering with sequins. Some paper flowers and little parasols were stuck into her hair. The first time I saw her with lipstick. Even though she gave me a preview on the phone about her work outfit, this Suzy Wong seemed so different from the braid swinging, cotton skirt flying girl on a bicycle I saw in Cambridge.

Another girl in a red sequined outfit sat down near Joyce. A blond, Bobby called Faan Lui, the Cantonese term for a barbarian girl. It was hard to picture a Suzy Wong with blond hair and blue eyes. She was from Ann Arbor, Michigan and a nursing student at Boston University when I asked.

They all ate quickly, getting ready for work.

I got up when I finished and tried to take my bowl and chopsticks into the kitchen like the others. "Leave it for me," Joyce said.

"Thanks again." I looked at Bobby across the table, who was just getting up.

"You welcome!" He flashed a big smile and headed into the kitchen. My last glimpse of him was a corner of the flowers on his shirt and the back of his tight white pants.

"Hope it's good news," Joyce called to me, as she followed him into the kitchen.

A week before school started, I got the call. I was in.

"Congratulations!" Joyce rushed over and gave me a hug. It was the first day of school when all of us gathered for orientation.

I was really touched by her effusive greeting. She even introduced me to some of her new friends, who lived in the same rooming house close to the school.

Our introduction into the haloed halls of medicine on that first day was a trip down to the Cold Room in the basement. I had a feeling we were descending into the Roman catacombs, but the bodies were more recent, and mostly unclaimed indigents from the part of Boston where the school was located. Our first assignment was to bring up the cadavers for our first class of Gross Anatomy the next morning.

A tall classmate, helping me carry the tarp wrapped body exuding the unforgettable smell of human flesh pickled in formaldehyde, looked a bit pale. He disappeared from the dissection room, after we managed to position the body on the steel, dissecting table with troughs on all sides to catch any residual body fluids. The shriveled face and limbs of the cadaver reminded me of reliquaries of saints often seen in old Italian churches.

I noticed Joyce, two tables away from mine, and I heard one of her tablemates suggesting a name for their cadaver.

"Ichabod."

"How do you know it's not Ursuline?" Joyce said, piping up.

"You find out for us," another guy winked across their table.

I could see Joyce blushing beet red. Her tablemates, all guys, could not stop giggling, while she dashed out of the room.

It was probably one of her last public attempts to stand up for women in the medical school of those days. She needed not put herself in such jeopardy because most of the cadavers were men. Women were rare among the unclaimed dead.

The next day the classmate who turned pale after the cadaver encounter did not show up. He was not the only one. Another student also disappeared after that first day.

"That's the way the school gets rid of those who aren't going to make it." A classmate said. By the time we graduated, fifteen out of ninety on that first day were no longer with us. Some for personal reasons, some failed to pass the numerous exams, tests aimed to eliminate the faint at heart or weak in determination. It was not for lack of intellectual ability, I thought because we had all been through college and MCATs, the national entrance exams before being accepted into medical school.

Those early months after school started, Joyce and I didn't have much time to notice each other. All of us worked on our Ichabods or Ursulines five days a week. As the Indian summer turned the dissecting rooms into saunas under the afternoon sun, odors from the formaldehyde mixed with the slowly melting cadaver adipose layers intensified, then turned rancid, seeping into our lab coats, dissecting manuals, hands and fingers, even our hair and shoes.

Even after showering and shampoo, we couldn't completely rid ourselves of that smell of formaldehyde pickled human flesh made rancid by the Indian summer afternoon sun. Eventually, most of us got rid of all our clothing, shoes, and books from that class. I kept the anatomical atlas I used for the dissections as a *memento mori*. Years later when I was about to perform a difficult surgical procedure on a patient, I would open the manual the night before. The residual stains and smells in the book never failed to pull me back into those afternoons in Gross Anatomy class.

A week before Thanksgiving, we had our last on-site examination of all the body parts we had dissected and tried to memorize. Joyce learned not to blush anymore. Not even when dissection got to the groin of their Ichabod and one of her tablemates inserted a chopstick into the urethra to make his member stand straight up under the tarp after lunch one day.

She and her housemates invited the class to their rooming house for a big celebration.

"Bring Art!" Joyce made a special point to include my roommate.

She recognized the good influence of his steady study habits in order to survive our crushing load of sheer medical information we had to commit to memory, while I was still working to shake off my habit of last minute cramming acquired from my years in engineering school.

A lingering late autumn sunset slowed the pace of the evening. On our way to the rooming house, maple leaves not yet swept up in this seedy part of the city, crackled under our shoes. The air was lighter than that of the Indian summer a month earlier, but the chill of winter had not yet arrived. It was still too early for the regulars to come out from the bar at the corner of the Square, fashionable half a century ago. The Square was actually an oval extending to the front of the hospital. The medical school was only half a block around the corner.

When Art and I pushed open the door to the dark brick row house, we heard Duke Ellington drifting down from its upper floors.

The music led us to the second floor where doors to most of the rooms were open. Familiar faces of classmates and less familiar ones of upper classmen we had seen at the school were jammed into the small spaces.

Most of the rooms were as sparely furnished as a monk's cell, but fairly well organized. A desk with textbooks, a straight-backed wooden chair and a bookcase of more medical texts and references. Occasionally a book of verses or a volume of Stendhal or Dostoyevsky stuck out like a stray daisy in a garden of weeds. One larger room with an armchair, its covering frayed from use, was the envy of the rooming house.

Joyce was the only woman other than the landlady, living in the household. Her room was one of the smallest and did not look any different from the others, except for a brown coffee mug on her desk with a Radcliffe insignia.

"Where's Joycie?" My roommate asked one of the guys hustling some girls up the stairway.

He signaled us to follow, not stopping to talk. His attention more focused on the young nursing students, the principal and most accessible source of feminine contact for most medical students.

Out of a class of about ninety barely a handful were women. Three were already married. The unmarried ones were either considered colleagues and potential competitors rather than candidates for romantic pursuit, women who submerged themselves into a mostly masculine world, making them almost hard to distinguish from the men.

By the end of the school year, several of our classmates became engaged to nursing students.

The landlady lived on the top floor. A frail figure with a thin mist of silvery hair, whose Irish husband had succumbed to cirrhosis many years earlier, she was very tolerant and kind to the students, considered them her charges and sympathizing with their breakneck schedules. On weekends, when not preoccupied with her own whiskey bottle, which she referred to discreetly as her cough medicine but hardly a secret to the medical students, she baked cookies and asked them up for tea in her dining room.

That evening she allowed them to move aside her dining table and use the floor for dancing. Sodas and beer were on the kitchen counters and chips on a small, painted side table, its original blue beginning to peek through the chipped white.

Beers had warmed up the place before we stepped into the room. I picked up a Budweiser and edged closer toward the music.

The dining room light was dimmed with a piece of dark cloth, and someone took time to put up streamers and sparklers. The floor was already crowded. My eyes adjusted slowly to the dim light as I tried to recognize the faces.

The beat to the music picked up, and suddenly I saw a small figure in a black sheath swinging out of a fast jitterbug toward me. Into her dark chignon, she had woven a China red ribbon.

"Join us!" she invited me with a big smile.

I was too shy to cut in. I also realized quickly I wasn't as good a dancer as her partner.

I stood with my Budweiser on the sidelines and watched her swing from one man after another. A lively smile lit up her face as she moved swiftly with the music, enjoying herself as the most popular partner on the floor.

Joyce knew these guys, sitting beside them through lectures on essential amino acids or across the table from dissecting layers of cadaver muscles, from the trapezius to the teres minor. She did not feel she had to compete with the student nurses by acting demure or coquettish.

"Where's Art?" She came over to where I was standing. It was close to midnight.

I told her he had gone ahead back to our room at the hospital. We shared the job drawing bloods and doing labs in the early morning before classes began. It took care of our room and board.

"He has a bad knee," I said, by way of explaining my roommate's earlier departure from the dance floor.

By then the room was beginning to thin out.

"Do you jitterbug?"

I nodded uncertainly.

Before I knew it, she put my empty beer bottle on the windowsill and pulled me onto the floor.

She led effortlessly. When I missed a beat, she'd swing me right back into the rhythm of things. Yet she had an easy and natural way about her, not making me feel intimidated.

When the bright lights of the dining room were turned back on at one, I was surprised we had been on the dance floor together for almost an hour.

We ended the evening slowly walking the half block to the hospital for some fresh air. Then I walked her back to her rooming house.

I held her hand at the bottom of her front steps but did not feel bold enough to kiss her.

She started up the stairs, then turned and waved at me smiling, with what I couldn't be quite sure whether it was a twinkle in her eye.

Years later, after the birth of our daughter, when I was telling friends the story of how we met, Joyce said knowingly, "I knew I got his attention that evening!"

Only then did I realize how naïve I was in that delicate *pas de deux* of courtship.

On graduation day three-and-a-half years later, we were already a married couple. Diplomas in hand, we stood around those who made it through with varying degrees of satisfaction and remembrances. Two of Joyce's tablemates from our first few months in Gross Anatomy came around to ask if she still remembered the day they made her blush with their antics over the male anatomy.

"You're right. I haven't paid you guys back yet." She smiled, confident and demure wearing a pale green and white lace cheongsam under her cap and gown.

Chapter Twenty-Four

豬

"How's Joycie?"

It was the first thing he said.

We were sitting in the lounge, tucked intimately back of the main reception area of the small Stanford Court Hotel. My old roommate was here for the West Coast meeting of the Facial Plastic Surgery Academy.

The subdued lighting in the lounge cast a warm glow on him. But I could see Art was losing most of his hair on top, the way his father had half-a-century ago at the head of the table when Art took me to his family Sunday lunches north of Boston. Still trim under his Armani jacket, and as always, a snappy dresser. His favorite place to shop used to be the bargain basement at Filene's. Once he dragged me with him to their after-Christmas sale, where the salesman knew his family well and set aside the best bargains.

I was touched by Art's concern and a little surprised when he asked about Joyce. Although he was my best man in our small wedding party of four, I had the feeling he was not entirely happy about the idea of Joyce coming into my life. She intruded into the intimacy we had established as roommates.

On an earlier occasion, he had called when he found out I was no longer with Joyce, from the different home addresses we now listed in the alumni class directory.

Art and I hadn't seen much of each other after my internship in Boston. But I learned he went into the same specialty I chose, after first completing five grueling years of training to be a general surgeon.

He was attending another professional meeting, and I took him to lunch in a Chinese restaurant known for its seafood. Afterwards, between cups of Oolong tea, I told him I was dating men, when he asked about my life after Joyce.

He didn't say anything and let my comment pass. I was not sure whether I would hear from him again. I had the experience of telling someone I considered a good friend, who followed me in training as a specialty surgeon, but I never heard from him again. I was deeply moved Art made a point of calling me again on this trip.

After a round of scotch and soda for Art, and my sociable sips of Kir, he told me his only son had taken his life not too long ago.

"Don't bring it up with Ann." From the break in his voice, I could tell the loss was still raw for both of them. I didn't think I would have too many occasions to talk with his wife, but she had answered the phone when I returned his call from Boston. She was not ready yet to travel with him on this trip.

I remembered admiring a lithograph his son had done in high school, hung on the wall outside Art's study in his spacious home just outside of Cambridge, one I had visited while in town for my son's college graduation. Standing beside it, he gave me the feeling he was quite proud of his son's work, but later he let slip he hoped his son, rather than his daughter, would settle down and have a family and follow in the grandfather's footsteps.

"My father was one of the earliest Italian immigrants to become an architect in Massachusetts," Art had told me in passing, after one of our customary three-hour luncheons at his family home. I could see how his mother and older sister doted on his every wish when we were there.

When Art implied his son was never going to give him a grand-child, I could imagine his disappointment. I noticed family ties and tradition were as important to his Italian heritage as they were with my Chinese ancestors. He did not elaborate further about his son on that earlier visit, and I didn't want to pry.

The unspoken gulf between Art and his son reminded me of my own relationship with my father. But in the culture of my Chinese ancestors, it was acceptable not to be interested in sports and muscle building as my father was, as long as I excelled in school; while in Art's Boston, it was probably harder for him to accept a son who was not into high school competitive sports and the culture of pursuing girls in college.

I wanted to say something more to him about his son, having come out to him earlier about myself. Still, I wasn't sure how he would take it, and his request of not mentioning anything about his son to his wife made me wonder whether he was ready to talk about his son himself. Much to my chagrin, there did not seem to be a way for me to comfort my old roommate, someone with whom I had been very close and shared a crucial part of my life.

Unlike me, Art prepared himself well for his medical school studies. Years of rigorous academic work at Boston Latin led him naturally into Harvard. He took courses in comparative anatomy and embryology, while I was still muddling around in thermody-namics and fluid mechanics in engineering school.

He was my guide around the hospital where the Registrar at the Admissions Office of the Medical School had gotten me the job to pay for my room and board. I was put into the same room he had on the fourth floor of the six-floor old brick building where the surgeons and doctors in training, called House Officers in the hospital, stayed when they were on call.

When I showed up, Art had already settled into the room a week earlier and took the bottom bunk. I was just happy to get the free room and board. He led me around the subterranean puddles in the hospital basement to the laundry room to pick up our uniforms and bed linens and showed me where to get our meal tickets for the cafeteria.

A year or two later this hospital got some unsolicited attention in a major magazine exposé, pointing out the roaches in the kitchen and rats in the basement corridors of this old Bostonian edifice, an article which was probably meant to be part of the Institution's centennial celebration.

The morning after I arrived Art walked me through my job, how to get the blood samples from the patients for tests (that the young doctors in training ordered the night before), where to place the tourniquet, how tight to pull the cinch, how to pick the most robust vein.

"If there are none on one side, try the other arm. And if that still doesn't work, head for the foot," he explained patiently. "Many patients had been here for a long time, and their veins were more often than not collapsed by all the damn blood tests the doctors order."

This was going to be the first time for me to touch a patient, and I had not even gotten my foot into the door of medical school, which was to begin in two weeks. Art's twenty-second rundown and a quick demonstration on one patient were all the instructions I got. Nowadays there are schools for lab techs and venipuncturists.

But he had me put on a white lab coat like his, and when he took me to the floor where the patients were, I was secretly excited that I was on my way of becoming a doctor. Our first stop was the work room just outside of the patients' ward.

The hospital was founded for indigents and people who could not pay much for their medical care. They were being treated in big open rooms, like a dormitory with many beds. A couple of small sickrooms were reserved for patients who needed to be isolated because of a contagious infection or other special needs.

When we stepped into the work room, Art was all speed and efficiency, pointing out the profusion of tubes with differently colored rubber stoppers used according to the tests ordered. Each tube had to be properly marked with the patients' name, location, and date of the sample. Before going to the patients, all the tubes had to be sorted and readied so there would be no confusion or mistakes when the blood samples were taken.

I had worked in chemistry labs as a chemical engineer, but this was different. I was going to be working on patients, real people, ones who were suffering. That realization and the sheer amount of information to quickly commit to memory began to feel daunting at first encounter.

Then he showed me what to do with the counter full of urine bottles in a smaller side room. Paper strips for sugar and acetone for the diabetics, the centrifuge to spin down the samples, and the microscope to look for bacteria, blood, and other abnormalities.

He saved the stacked, round cardboard boxes for the last. He noticed I was trying to hold my breath when we got close.

"Try to get the stools out for testing as quickly as possible, before the stench kills you." The look he gave me said, better get used to it. The stool sample had to be tested for guaiac or blood and if necessary for additional special testing in the bacteriology lab.

Art stood by me for my first try of getting a patient's blood sample.

"You were a bit too tentative," he said afterwards. "Choose your vein carefully, then go in with the needle quickly. It hurts more if you're too slow and too hesitant."

That was the first inkling I got that there was a delicate balance between being too afraid of hurting a patient and thus actually causing more pain, and recognizing a patient's suffering, then doing something that needed to be done and doing it well and efficiently so that there was as little pain as possible.

I followed Art around like a sorcerer's apprentice those first two days, feeling very grateful as he tried to quickly turn me into a venipuncturist and lab technician. Later I realized, the faster he trained the apprentice, the less he had to do himself because we shared all the work that had to be done.

A week later school started. Gross anatomy, pharmacology, and biochemistry hit me like triple tornados. Art sat at his desk making flash cards and other memory devices for the endless lists of things we had to force feed into the bulging matrix of our brain. At any moment, I felt it was on the verge of burn out.

When some classmates asked me to join them for beer sessions after dinner, I found it hard to refuse at first, trying to be polite and afraid to offend. I thought I could rely on my old ways of cramming before exams. Our first examination two weeks later gave me a rude awakening.

"Got to get yourself organized." My steadily working roommate threw me a lifesaver. He could have let me wallow in failure like what happened to a fellow classmate who had urged me to go drinking at the bar and didn't make it past midterm.

Though the words sounded harsh, and I was too young to recognize its underlying feelings of care, I must have taken his comments seriously. I started to buckle down. Every day after classes and before dinner, we sat across from each other at the old walnut tables in the Medical Library. Classmates got so accustomed to seeing us coming and going, they started calling us the Bobbsey Twins. As the weather turn cold, they could see Art with his long wool scarf wound around his neck, rimless glasses, and skull cap on his head; and I in my old Loden coat trailing a step behind.

Looking back now, I can see why our classmates pegged our closeness. Aside from the heavy load of medical information doled out to us daily, like feeding a goose for foie gras or a duck in Peking for roasting, our work schedule at the hospital and our rooming together forced us into almost identical molds.

Art took the role of big brother at first because he was already familiar with the routine. He knew the best time to get our food in the hospital cafeteria or when the uniforms and laundry would be delivered and collected so that we didn't miss out.

If he saw the oatmeal running low when we hurried in to catch breakfast after getting our blood, urine and stool samples done, he picked up an extra bowl for me if I were a few minutes behind him. We began to look out for each other naturally.

Sunday was our only free day. But we had to finish our work with the bloods, the urines, and the stools at the hospital before we got into Art's black Beetle to head for his family home for lunch.

They lived in a small town north of Boston where many Italian immigrants settled shortly after the turn of the century. Theirs was a large, New England-style house, painted white. I can still see it, on that first Sunday he took me there, near the water's edge, two blocks down between the shadows of the elms.

His older sister greeted us at the door, just beyond a wide front porch.

She was a short, stout woman who had lost her waistline after two kids. Their mother followed a few sturdy steps behind, a small woman used to managing the household. She took my hands into hers after I stepped through the doorway and held me with her dark piercing gaze, just like her son's, to see if I was appropriate company for her only son before she pointed the way into the living room to meet Art's father.

The room felt cavernous with its dark batten paneling around a fireplace in the middle. An oil of ships in the harbor hung above the mantel. The family patriarch acknowledged us from a large, leather armchair on the far side of the fireplace, which made him look even shorter than he was, an aged, male version of his daughter, whose husband slipped in quietly from the dark to shake my hand, but was clearly overshadowed by this tight family circle.

Through a large open archway, I could see into the formal dining room at the far side, a long dinner table, set and waiting, brightened by the white damask table linens and family silver for their weekly family luncheon.

His father sat at the head of the table, smiling contently at his son through his rimless eyeglasses like his son's, more like a Happy Laughing Buddha than a Godfather. His mother and older sister disappeared into the kitchen, only to show up with plate after plate of food for the table. The meal took most of the afternoon, from antipasti to pasta; then the main course, fish to desserts.

On that first Sunday, I thought the meal would be over after the pasta, so I accepted another helping of the spaghetti with a delicious sauce of eggs, bacon, cheese, and black pepper. Then came the grilled meat and chicken. I was too polite and embarrassed to refuse the helpings they put on my plate. By the time the fish came, I felt I could hardly have another mouthful.

Art led the conversation at the table as if he was already head of the household. Occasionally his father mumbled consent. From his brother-in-law hardly a sound.

"Just sit and keep us company!" Art told me to stop when I tried to get up and help clear the dishes that first time I visited, between the seemingly endless stream of food from the kitchen.

When I was growing up, I was not allowed into the kitchen either. I remembered my father's stern words, very rare for him, when he caught me hovering at the kitchen door as my mother was showing the Japanese cook how to prepare Chinese dishes for my grandmother.

"A boy's place is not in the kitchen!"

But my mother said she wanted to prepare me for America, where everybody pitched in.

Along with that admonition, earlier words of my father echoed in my ears again. "A boy needs to get more involved in sports." Good at boxing in school, he liked to challenge me in arm wrestling at the dinner table. My barely developing biceps at the doorstep of adolescence were no match for the hard, muscular bulges of my father's upper arms.

By the time Art and I arrived for my mother's dinner on Sunday evenings, one that became routine for us, I could hardly eat. In time, I learned to moderate what I ate through those long Italian luncheons.

When I told my mother that I was giving up my graduate work at one of the best-known engineering schools in the country to study medicine, she decided to take a leave of absence from her job in the New York City public schools and move up to Boston to keep a closer eye on her only son. She was afraid I might have gone seriously astray.

By feeding us every Sunday evening, she not only kept tabs on me but also got to see what my roommate was like.

Art had an instant affinity for my mother's food. One week it was large meatballs Shanghai style, a dish called lion's head in Chinese with shiitake mushrooms and Chinese cabbage; the next week it was eggplant and sweet peppers in a Suzhou sauce; or if Indian summer was hitting Fenway Park where she had an apartment, there was my favorite, chilled daikon julienne with sautéed, diced spring scallions and sesame oil.

Art told my mother her food was the best Chinese dishes he'd ever tasted. I was always surprised at the amount he could put down following a whole afternoon's feasting at his home. I had to try to taste something of every dish my mother made so that I didn't hurt her feelings, but my roommate wolfed down everything my mother piled onto his plate.

"I always have a place in my stomach for your dishes, Mrs. Chen!"

24
豬

My mother beamed at his compliments, then turned to me worriedly, "You need to eat like Art to keep up your weight!" I had told her how busy I was with first year medical school and my various jobs. Seeing her once a week was already making it difficult on my schedule.

"Art has such rosy cheeks!" she continued, "and yours are so pasty. Terribly pale! Not enough blood in you!" Plump like a fat laughing Buddha was considered good health to the Chinese. Although my mother thought of herself as a thoroughly modern and Westernized Chinese woman, she liked to stick to old Chinese traditions, particularly when they suited her purposes.

Art just smiled and continued munching, while I arched my eyebrows in protest behind my mother's back.

"You just watch what Art is doing." She couldn't stop repeating her mantra.

Turning to him, she said, "Come for dinner anytime you like." I could see what she was doing. If she could entice Art to visit more often, she would get me in the bargain.

I wanted to punch Art on his stuffed face as we made our drive back to the hospital.

"But I really like your mother's food." He smiled in retort.

With time, I think they developed a genuine fondness for each other.

Even when we sat down together years later, Art still praised my mother and her food.

"Could you stay over at your mother's this Saturday night?" Art asked me after our midterm exams.

He told me he was seeing an old girlfriend from graduate school. They had worked together in the lab doing embryology at Brandeis.

"Just make sure you don't soil my sheets," I answered back half seriously.

"Yeah, yeah."

The rest of our first semester together, this almost became a monthly routine, depending on how busy we were and his girlfriend's schedule. I hated my mother's questions the first time I had to stay with her, but then she stopped asking and was just happy to have me and watch me stuff my face.

Art was pretty good in cleaning up afterwards. Only once had I picked up a used rubber that he forgot to flush down the toilet.

One afternoon during our second semester, unexpectedly we found ourselves finished with our school work earlier than usual. "Let's go and check out the pool." My roommate suggested.

We heard about an old indoor pool built years ago by some Bostonian Brahmin family who wanted the young doctors training at the Hospital to have an exercise facility.

"I don't have my swim trunks here."

"We don't need them." Art said. When he saw my hesitation. "It's just like the pool at the Y," he added.

A heavy scent of chlorine from the pool filled the locker room. It had two old wooden benches and a side table, on which was a pile of white towels. Both the benches and the table were once painted white, but now had the weathered look of furniture left out on some deserted beach with little of the paint remaining. We picked up some clean towels from the pile.

Art took off his eyeglasses and placed them carefully on his towel. I did the same with mine.

Without his glasses, he was better looking and ten years younger. The bookish eyeglasses masked the boyishness of his rosy cheeks. They had a softness I hadn't noticed before.

We undressed, Art much faster than I. He had always been very much at ease walking around without clothing after undressing in our room, which made me more relaxed undressing in front of him.

It took us a few seconds to see through the heat rising from the pool surface. The place was deserted. The doctors were still busy on the floors with their patients. We had the place all to ourselves.

"I'll race you," he said, diving in.

His freestyle was much faster than my breaststrokes. I gave up and decided to just go at my own pace.

He was sitting on the edge at the shallow end when he'd finished his laps. I pulled up out of the water a minute later and sat beside him.

"Not too bad for an old man." He tapped me on the back.

"Old man yourself," I replied. "I wasn't keeping time anymore."

"How about ten more laps?" He slid back into the water. "No race."

I decided I wasn't going to let him win again, so I tried my hardest to keep pace with him.

By the time we got out of the pool, I felt I had it for the day.

"Come and get a hot shower. Nothing like a long hot shower after a good workout."

I followed him into the shower room and turned the water all the way up.

The hot water felt like a deep massage. I lathered and covered myself with suds, warm and relaxed, almost forgetting where we were.

"You shit!" I was startled by the sharpness of the cold water against my back.

Instinctively, I splashed him back, annoyed that he was giggling at the shock he got out of me.

He tried to grab my arm to pull my hand away from the shower knobs. He slipped but pulled me down with him. We slid against the tiled wall onto the shower floor.

The hard tile hurt when I hit ground. I was pissed and pushed hard to struggle free. The harder I bucked, the firmer he tightened his hold. I was surprised how strong his arm muscles were. For an instant Art became my father, arm wrestling me when I was ten. No matter how hard I tried, my father's arm had pushed mine down. We were both panting by now. I could feel him breathing hard on my back, and his legs pressed me against the floor.

Everything I had bottled up churned to the surface, like inside the earthen pot of bitter herbs my mother used to brew, then forced me to drink as a child, —his tight hold of me on the ground, the way he has been acting like a big brother all the time, his better preparation for the crushing medical curriculum.

My mother's holding him up like a model son against her perception of my lack of direction didn't help. In some primitive way that I couldn't even explain, I also resented him for getting his needs met with his girlfriend. Before I knew it, my hands reached under and tugged hard between his legs.

"You son of a gun!"

I slipped out of his grip and tried to get up. There was a residual tingle on my wrist from contact with his legs. The kind of tingling I imagined my father might have felt during his student days in the samurai culture of Japan, where near nude wrestling and nudity in communal baths were common practice.

Flushed and trying to catch our breaths, we squinted at each other for what only seemed like a split second. Something made us both back off. We couldn't acknowledge it then to each other. But there must have been a moment of recognition for both of us, we were treading dangerously close to taboo territory. The moment when we realized, facing each other, sweat and water droplets down our faces, breathing was not the only thing hard on both of us.

We never talked about what happened that afternoon. It got shoved quickly and deeply underground into my memory. I didn't even think about it until three years later, shivering when I finally slipped into my seat on the train, after my encounter outside the men's room of North Station, close to midnight on Christmas Eve.

When I thought of that moment between Art and me, now decades later, I wanted to ask myself whether it had indeed occurred or whether it was just part of a forgotten mirage in that jumbled room of memories.

With him a breath away from me in that quiet lounge of the Stanford Court Hotel, time slowed down for us. Though his eyes held me with the same intensity as they did when we first met, as if they wanted to say, I want to be your friend.

There was a bond between us. It had been there through all those years, from my finally admitting to myself that I had an attraction to men, to having children then separation from Joyce, through his marriage to Ann and the death of my mother (whose cooking he never stopped talking about), to the recent suicide of his son, a son he could still hardly admit was probably gay.

Now with Art balding like his father, and my hair frosted with gray, we were facing each other again, husks of our earlier selves.

"How is your mother?" I managed to bring our conversation back to the present.

"She hardly recognizes me when I stop by." There was a twinge of hoarseness to his voice, and I was not sure if my asking about his mother brought him back to the time when we were stuffing ourselves with everything that came out of her kitchen.

I wanted to say that I hoped to be remembered to her, for those many hours spent at her long white damask-covered table, those days when my life was so closely connected to her son's, before Joyce came between us.

But all that came out of my mouth was, "I am sorry."

Chapter Twenty-Five

鼠

We called it *Yu Yuan*, the Garden of Joy. The first home Joyce and I could really afford to call our own. *Yu* was the word for joy and happiness, as well as Joyce's given name in Chinese. I chose it because I thought it would bring happiness, and it symbolized the state of our little family in the house we built together. Indeed, we looked like a perfect success story to our friends. Two young doctors, starting their practices in medical specialties, one after the other, with two cute and adorable toddlers, like little angels.

Several years ago, following a divorce from the man she married after me, Joyce sold the house to Adele's son. She could no longer maintain the large sprawling home and grounds on her own, as severe arthritis continued to take its toll.

When Adele and I go down to visit her son's family on weekends now, I get to see the full-grown trees and bushes I planted over four decades ago. The redwoods in the back have become the tallest trees in the neighborhood. The wooden plaque, which used to hang alongside the front door, bearing the name *Yu Yuan* in carved Chinese calligraphy, now is in my storage as Joyce had no desire to keep it.

On my mother's first visit to *Yu Yuan*, carrying a pot of evergreens in her hand, a traditional house-warming gift of well-wishing for good fortune and longevity for the household, she was taken aback by the red brick chimney, facing the main driveway leading up to the front entrance.

"Too much like a tall tombstone!" She shook her head, "You must cover it quickly."

I wonder, if we had been quick enough to follow her advice on *Feng Shui*, would things have turned out differently? The bright magenta bougainvillea covers the chimney now, too late for me.

The house was only to be my home for five years. An epitaph and swan song to my life with Joyce.

We fell in love with the piece of land, tucked behind a bunch of tract homes, forgotten by the developer. It was a flag lot, I thought of it as swan shaped. Its neck, a long driveway, opened onto a large body, which then tapered into its tail at the other end. We had thirteen neighbors from front to back, a configuration not appealing to most tract home owners.

Yet I liked the sequestered feeling, tucked away from the homes out front, which were too exposed to foot traffic and curiosity seekers for my liking and comfort. Wild mustard and rye grass almost two feet tall covered the ground when the realtor took us there the first time. A small grove of neglected, tired looking apricot trees was the last reminder to what was once part of a large fruit ranch.

The only neighbor in the back, with whom we shared a long stretch of common border with no fence between us, was a mature couple whose house was hidden behind four acres with huge avocado and fig trees.

The man met me with a warm, bear hug and handshake.

"Bob's the name," he said. "Would be happy to help you with a privacy fence between us," he added, after hearing my fondness for seclusion.

I suspected he was also thinking about his own serenity and sanity, seeing our two toddlers scurrying wildly from one end of the land to the other. But looking back, it was more likely he was more concerned that my children might fall into his swimming pool and give him grief.

His wife was a retired, schoolteacher with an affinity for abstract and Asian art. Pamela was serious about the arts and culture and most things in general, while Bob seemed more inclined to take his time and disarm you with his broad, ready smile.

He became my foreman when we decided on a common fence between his well-kept avocado orchard and my wild grassland. Pamela helped us choose a pattern from her book on Japanese country gardens, one that looked equally attractive on both sides of the fence.

"I'll get us started, and you can join me when you get off from your work saving lives." Bob offered in his good-natured banter after he found out about what I did.

He provided all the tools and was naturally handy while I could hardly pound in a nail straight. We split the cost of the redwood grape stakes and posts he ordered.

He even brought me a workman's apron and gloves. "Must protect those fine surgeon's hands!" He said with a wink.

On weekdays, I put in an hour or two on the fence line before the summer sunset, after my office hours and work rounds at the hospital. Bob was a good foreman, showing me how to use a post-hole digger, checking the level for the fence posts, and the way to soften the sunbaked, hard adobe soil with water by prolonged pre-soaking with a slowly dripping hose line.

"Tap in the nail gently first, so you don't split the grape stake." He demonstrated with great patience and expertise after I wasted the first two.

One afternoon I had to spend extra time with my last patient. I didn't get a chance to change into my work shirt and jeans when I arrived at our job site.

"Look at the plastic surgeon in all his finery!" Bob chuckled.

When I explained the reason for my delay, he offered, "Come to my work room. I've got some old work clothes that might fit you. Used to be slimmer, like you."

His house was an adobe hacienda with old, Spanish roof tiles. I could see the edge of an irregular shaped pool peeking out from the far side. He led me around to the back, his work room was neatly hidden out of view from the front garden.

He stood alongside me in his workroom and continued his carefree chatter, as I took off my shirt and tie.

"Let me get you a hanger for those smart, professional trousers."

"Don't trouble, Bob," I said, a little uneasy in my briefs. "I can just hang them up on the hook here."

"Can tell, you don't spend much time in the sun." He looked at my pale chest and legs. "Not like me, close to someone from across the border."

I noticed his thick, bronzed arms and neck.

"By the time we get the fence built, you'll be dark like me!" he said when he saw me checking him out.

It took about two months before we neared the end of our joint project. The work under the midsummer sun gave my arms and shoulders better color, and maybe even a firmer look.

We also found out more about each other.

He was from the southern part of the state, over the mountain from Palm Springs, brought up on a farm, although his mother taught school locally. His father came from Massachusetts, groomed to become a college professor but got a lung infection and decided to move to the desert for health.

Bob loved the desert of his childhood, disappointing his parents who had hoped he would go to college in the East. He dabbled in business and real estate and made good with his easy smile.

He was going to get himself a farm in Steinbeck country when he met Pamela who had just graduated from a woman's college in the East Bay.

She rekindled his interest in books and introduced him to her world of art and design, then convinced him to settle in an area by the Bay, which still had the feel of ranches and farms, but accessible to some of her big city interests.

"I was an only child, too," he said when I responded to his questions about family and siblings.

"As far as I know," I added. "My mother always implied my father had a woman at very port."

We also found out we shared the discomfort of having no brothers or sisters. He decided to reach out and hug the world, while I saw myself holding back until I could see an extended hand.

I began to look forward to our late afternoons and was sorry that our job was close to the finishing line, foretelling the end of our fence-building camaraderie.

One early Saturday afternoon Joyce took the children to the zoo in the City to give me some extra time for working on the fence. Only a small section was left to be done.

"We should save this section of the fence for a gate, so we can visit back and forth." Bob looked at me. "What do you think, buddy?"

"Great idea!" I concurred.

It meant a little extra work, but seemed like the perfect suggestion, echoing the beginnings of our friendship.

He went back to his workshop and brought back the post-hole digger.

We sweated for over an hour, digging into the hardened adobe soil for two more holes because we had not prepared the ground.

When we finally poured in the concrete around the posts, Bob wiped his forehead with his red kerchief and broke into a big smile.

"How about a break with a swim to cool off?"

"You'd have to lend me some swim trunks," I said.

"I'll see if I have any old ones. Like I said, I used to be thinner like you." He winked at me and started back toward his house.

I followed him across the grove of avocados and figs.

"Come on in," he waved when he saw me stopping at the front door. "The house's a bit messy today, Pam went to visit her sister up in the wine country. I usually wait for the last day before she gets back to straighten things up."

Their living room had a relaxed, but well put-together feel. Rattan sofas and armchairs with oatmeal-colored duck fabric cushions. The Mexican floor tiles were covered with a grass mat in the middle. An oil painting of a young woman was hung off to the side. I could detect the resemblance to Pamela. The same pageboy cut she had now.

"That was a birthday present from her father when she graduated from college," he explained when he came back into the room and saw me studying the portrait. "Sorry, buddy. Don't know where the old swim trunks got packed into." Then he looked at me and added, "Pam won't be back for another couple of days, and nobody will see us from a mile away anyway. We're so well hidden behind all these trees here."

I hesitated, feeling a little awkward.

"I'll join you skinny dipping if it makes you more comfortable."

"That's okay. I'll just wear my briefs," I said.

He went into the back hallway and came out with two bath towels, "You can change in the guest room there, and I'll join you in a minute by the pool."

The room was sparsely furnished. A single bed was covered with a chenille spread. A campaign chest of drawers, and a chair and a matching writing desk gave the room an uncluttered look. An abstract oil hung above the bed facing a mirror across the room.

I saw myself in the mirror after I folded my clothes on the chair.

My face and arms were tanned by our afternoons in the sun, but my legs and thighs were still sallow and pale. Quickly I wrapped the towel around myself and walked out to the pool.

Bob was already in the water. "What took you so long?" he quipped.

"I was admiring the painting over the bed. Is it Pamela's work?"

"It's one of her earlier works which she's shy about presenting to the public. But I like it."

"You've got good taste!"

"Naw, I'm just a country boy. What do I know?" He smiled. "Now come on in." He waved his hand out of the water and made it splash on the surface.

I dropped my towel, laid my glasses on it and quickly got in the shallow end, all the while feeling a little self-conscious as if his gaze were following me.

The water felt warm but refreshing. A whole summer of sun had warmed it, reminding me of the semi-tropical beaches of Taiwan, when I was on junior high field trips.

Moving in that water was like a slow massage after the hard work. After several laps, I noticed Bob was resting on the edge of the pool at the shallow end. I breast stroked toward him. As I got closer, lifting my head out of the water, I realized he was not wearing any swim trunks.

"Ever go skinny dipping?" He saw I had noticed.

"Don't think I ever have." I lied, at the same time remembering swimming in the pool at the Y when I was in college. But I always associated skinny dipping with a lake or by the river in the countryside.

"You should try it. Makes your whole body feel liberated."

"I can see what you mean."

"I used to go skinny dipping with my friends when I was growing up. Always felt great! Believe me!" he said emphatically while slipping into the water.

Any further refusal felt awkward, so I slipped off my briefs underwater and saw him close up in the water.

I felt my heart starting to pound. It was hard for me to breathe, the same feeling of fear and excitement in the men's room in Boston's North Station. Not wanting Bob to notice, I submerged myself and swam toward the deep end of the pool.

I kept up a faster pace for several laps, trying to avoid getting too close to him. Aside from my heartbeat, I was beginning to feel the smooth lapping of the water against every part of me. I began to relax and enjoy the feel of it.

I reached the deep end and held onto the ledge, relieved by the feeling of finally having regained my composure.

Suddenly I felt him grab me from behind and gave me a hard squeeze.

I squirmed under the grip, then panicked, feeling myself aroused.

The warm water was a natural lubricant. It wasn't too long before I noticed pearly strands streaming under the water surface in front of me.

We didn't talk to each other when we got out of the pool. I couldn't find the right words for anything to say and avoided eye contact with him.

Bob sensed my discomfort and didn't try to break the silence until we got inside.

"You can use the guest room shower to rinse off if you like." He offered as if nothing unusual had happened at all.

"Oh, thanks. Thanks a lot" I managed to say, a little stiffly.

We finished the fence over the following week. Bob was his old friendly, jovial self, greeting me with a twinkle in his eye when Joyce came along to admire the work on the fence.

The contractor handed us the key to our first home the following spring. By then, I had put in the ground plants, bushes, and trees, recommended by the *Western Garden Book* and a woman who knew a great deal about good natives for our area. Agapanthus for color and architecture along the driveway, pittisporum nigri for screening density, and redwoods for height and shade.

Joyce and I were a bit sorry that we did not have a view from the house, having come to the West Coast, we had dreamt of the open seas. In its stead, the architect gave us an atrium in the middle of the house where we could create a view of our own, like the homes where I had lived in Japan.

In the pile of left over building material, I found a piece of redwood, used on the house. It was the right size and weight to use as a plaque for me to carve the Chinese name we had chosen for our house.

Yu Yuan, the garden of happiness.

Chapter Twenty-Six

牛

The return address on the envelope was the Buddhist Center in the mid-peninsula city where I used to work as a doctor for over twenty years. A part of my life I had put to rest in the several years since my retirement. The letter was forwarded from the hospital to my home address in San Francisco.

The handwriting was familiar. It had been a long time since I had last seen it, thus couldn't be sure, until I opened the envelope. An invitation to attend the celebration of his new life in a Buddhist monastery.

Jimmie and I met thirty years ago. I can't remember who brought him to my home next to the hilly county park overlooking the town where I worked, the home I had finally settled into after moving out of *Yu Yuan*.

Our group met once a month in different people's homes on Friday nights after work. What brought the group together, aside from the spirit of the Stonewall Riots, was either our work or home was in the mid-peninsula of San Francisco Bay.

Those riots in New York, barely ten years away, in the gay bar called Stonewall Inn on Sheridan Square, were still fresh in our minds. Yet when the group met, it was mainly to network with our own kind in the area.

Between ten to fifteen men came. Marty was a travel agent

and his boyfriend Jon, a social worker. Rob worked for a company in Silicon Valley, and Reed ran his own lawyer's office near Stanford. Keith was a therapist practicing in the area, and Chuck sold real estate.

Marty and Jon became early casualties of AIDS, several years before President Reagan even mentioned it nationally. Jimmie must have gone to Marty for advice on travel and heard about the group.

He brought some chow mein with *chia siu* in take-out boxes and set them on my kitchen counter. The savory bits of barbecued pork with the Chinese noodles made a good compliment to the pizza, chips, and cookies brought by the others. We were the only Asians there. He was a head shorter than most of the men. His full cheeks looked as if he had not lost all his baby fat, but his full upper arms and sturdy thighs gave me the feeling he came from folks who worked closely to the good earth.

Being basically shy and not used to speaking out, we didn't say much to each other when in the group. But after the others left, Jimmie lingered to offer help in cleaning up. I felt a mutual interest in finding out more about each other, but also sensed the beginning of a dating dance, possibly leading to something further. The easiest common ground for conversation starters was our ancestry.

"You're Cantonese, right?" It was a pretty sure guess for me. I knew he was American born from his English. Cantonese were the earliest Chinese immigrants to California.

"You're probably from the North, judging from your height," he replied.

I was not sure how I felt about his comment at first. Tall was a compliment, but I wanted him to acknowledge my father's Cantonese heritage. Later when we got to know each other better, he told me he meant the comment to be complimentary—my height was something he liked.

He next told me his parents had a farm in the South Bay growing chrysanthemums.

"Do they still live there?" I asked.

"No. They eventually sold to track home developers. It was too much for them when the kids grew up and left." His Cupid's bow darted upward when he pronounced the word *grew*.

"Me and my brothers and sisters had to water the plants every morning before we went to school, and when we got back from school, we had to haul fertilizer bags for my dad. He had a bad back from his years working as a houseboy when he first came over." I was right in my guess about his roots, when I had noticed his sturdy body earlier.

"You probably never had to do much physical labor," he added.

The way he said it did not make me feel it was meant as a put down. His whole face lit up when he spoke, the way he pronounced the word school as if there were quadruple o's—his full lips protruding, almost an invitation to a kiss.

The earliest immigrants from China were coolies. The word in Chinese literally meant bitterness and strength; they used their muscles and sweat, and in this country, sometimes their lives, to earn what they could. They looked up to those who came to study and get degrees and become professionals, which they hoped their children or grandchildren would be some day.

I wanted to tell Jimmie about my own experience in the New World. What I suffered at the hands of the immigration officer in Boston and the difficulties I had trying to pay for my own medical education. I had to admit I didn't do much physical labor, although some of my fellow students worked on farms and boats during summer vacations.

"My father was a Paper Son," he said, as we continued the cleanup. He was fast at washing the forks and plates while I dried them with a dish towel. He explained his father's family had bought papers from an Overseas Chinese man, one who had a son on a home visit to his village in Canton. That son would be documented with the American authorities. Someone could then buy that document and use it to send his own son to the U.S.

When his boat came through the Golden Gateway of San Francisco, Jimmie's father assumed the family name of the son on the bought papers, and he had to memorize all the relatives and facts of his paper family. Then there were months of waiting anxiously at the detention barracks on Angel Island, hoping that he had passed the interrogations and investigations instead of being put on a boat back to China.

"My father was lucky," he said. "He met people on the Island who were held there for many years."

"And your mother?" I asked.

"She was a picture bride." He shrugged and smiled when he realized this sounded so much like stories we'd read. His father was sent a photograph of the girl his real family had chosen for him, after he had saved enough money ten years later from his wages working as a houseboy. "My mother's family was from a village next to my father's."

"I get my height from my mother's side, who's from the North. But my father's Cantonese," I said when I told Jimmie about myself.

He was fascinated by my parents' different backgrounds.

I told him my father only visited the U.S. a couple of times after my mother and I came over. He never considered settling in America. My mother did not want to go back to Taiwan with him, and they divorced thirteen years later.

"I can tell your mother must be a very independent and smart woman, to be starting a life on her own in this country."

"Yes. She was already forty-six but only knew three words of English when she went back to school to get her teaching certificate." It made me realize what a difference there was between my mother and a woman chosen as a picture bride.

Despite these differences in our families, and the gap between our age of more than ten years, we had an immediate and mutual sense of kinship. It was a feeling not articulated but somehow reinforced when I noticed he paid particular attention to the Chinese scrolls on the adobe walls of my house and the porcelains on the carved cedar chest. This feeling also made it easier to hug each other after we finished the cleanup, which led to his spending the night.

I could sense there was something strongly emotional for him when we came together. For me, it was as if I was holding a younger brother, a brother whose family was from the same area as my father's and the brother I always wanted but couldn't have.

As he started to fall asleep, I thought of the first night I spent in Joyce's room. I had to initiate everything with her, even though she did not put up too much resistance until I tried to pull down her undies. This was followed by alarm and panic when she felt me soften and relax, then realized I had come between her thighs.

Even though we were both medical students, we were still naïve and afraid she could become pregnant just from that close contact of body fluids. We waited anxiously, worrying a baby would put an end to our studies and future plans in medicine, until she finally had her period several weeks later.

Jimmie was not shy once we got to my bedroom. Our clothes dropped to the floor without much hesitation, even though he said he was inexperienced and just coming out.

Although I had been to the gay baths, this was the first time for me with someone in my home. It added to the intensity and hunger to explore each other's bodies with none of the concern and apprehension of having other people close by. The only sound outside my bedroom of the old adobe house was from the water trickling into the fishpond. Jimmie responded to my moves with equal intensity, given the differences of our body builds. His was firm and muscular with a chest and abdomen like those I had ogled in the gym, while mine was at best a slim swimmer's build. There was none of the holding back when I was with Joyce the first time, nor the alarm and apprehension afterwards, now it was the culmination of an encounter both Jimmie and I wanted to happen mutually. With Joyce, we began to fret about unwanted pregnancy afterward and hardly slept the rest of the night, then I had to hurry out of her room before dawn to avoid detection by other doctors and staff arriving in the morning. With Jimmie, we collapsed into each other's bodies, completely fulfilled.

26

牛

The next weekend was my turn with the children.

"Want to go with me to pick up the kids?" I dialed him from my office, closing the door behind me. I didn't think of myself as closeted, after years of paying my dues sitting across the therapist's chair, but I wasn't going to wear a badge on my doctor's coat in white.

"Sure," he said quietly, making the word sound like several syllables as if he was measuring his response, but in his voice, I could detect there was an unspoken eagerness.

"I would love to meet them," he added.

From the time we spent together that first weekend and our calls during the week, I learned there was something timid about him, preventing him from fully expressing himself. Yet behind that bashful surface, I also felt he knew what he wanted and would not be pushed into doing anything he didn't want to do.

On our way to the house that I built with Joyce where she still lived with our children, Jimmie told me his family's flower farm was in the small town just south of it. He said the whole area used to be filled with apricot orchards owned by early Portuguese settlers, save a few flower farms by the Japanese and rarer still, the Chinese.

As we drove into the driveway, he noticed the sign *Yu Yuan* by the front entrance and quickly ducked his head below the dashboard. I pinched him in the thigh and told him Joyce was not going to report him to the police. He was so nervous that I let it drop.

He told me later when he saw the Chinese characters *Yu Yuan,* he just couldn't face being seen by my wife. I began to understand how much burden he was carrying for having Chinese parents, a firstborn son of parents from Canton and what he felt was expected of him. Those Chinese characters and the prospect of seeing Joyce, a fellow Chinese, brought out too much of the cultural censure for him to face. Confucius taught that one of the foremost duties of a son was to have children to carry on the family name. Having children as a gay man three decades ago, was not yet something he could hope for. It was easy for me, he told me later, because I already had two children. This desire and pressure he felt from his parents to have children of his own to fulfill his duties to them became the main reason he decided to get married to a woman several years later.

"Hi, I'm Jimmie." He seemed to have lost all his discomfort when my kids got into the car, and we drove away from the house. I asked them where they wanted to go for dinner. He seemed very happy when they chose MacDonald's, while I grumbled but thought at least it was not an expensive restaurant. That night, he insisted on sleeping in the living room, while the kids slept in the guest room but climbed into my bed in the morning.

He helped us make breakfast. Pancakes for the kids. Toast and fruit for me. He sided with them when I tried to coax some fruit before the pancakes. We compromised by having the fruit on the pancakes.

My children picked up on his ease and rapport with them right away. They were soon talking to one another as if they were three kids getting together. My daughter was ten and watchful like a grown-up, my son, still a carefree seven, and Jimmie acted younger than his twenty-nine years when he talked to them.

Sunday was warm. The three of them overruled me when I suggested Golden Gate Park, hoping we would get a peek into the museum. The consensus was going to the beach in Carmel.

Jimmie threw Frisbees with them on the sand as I sneaked moments to check the headlines of the *Sunday Times* I had brought along. Then they decided to include me in their play by burying me up to my neck in the sand.

"They're fun to be with," he said after we dropped them off that evening. He pushed me away when I tried to hug him in the car, but he was more relaxed when we got back to my place.

On the weekends when my children were with Joyce, we went into the City. AIDS had not yet surfaced in the Castro and buffed, male bodies of all ages were rubbing against one another without much restraint. When we were walking amongst them, Jimmie let me hold his hand, but as soon as we were away from the area, he was quick to put his hand back into his pocket.

For me, being next to Jimmie in the crowded Castro was an additional affirmation. It was more common to see Asian men with a white man, in spite of the Asians being called potato queens. I even heard an Asian man asking how could he be expected to date another Asian, it would be like two women rubbing against each other. I was too polite to point out that he could find himself thrown out of a gathering with our lesbian sisters present. My therapist friend was also careful to point out if we didn't like what we saw in the mirror, there was some profound self-hate involved, a point well taken in the case of J. Edgar Hoover who had lived with his longtime partner but had viciously hunted down homosexuals for persecution.

I was surprised Jimmie did not back out when I told him my mother asked us to stop over for dinner in her apartment.

I was anxious myself when I first told my mother after I moved out of Yu Yuan. It took years of talking to my therapist about my fears of being a disgrace and disowned by the family, then months of rehearsals of what and how I was going to tell my mother, still one of the most important persons in my life, before I could tell her the truth.

She didn't bat an eye when she heard me say I was seeing men and asked me if I remembered the large house in Beijing where she took me to meet the brother of a past Prime Minister. I was nine, and the man received us in a long, flowing kimono. He was a *tuzi*, she said, a bunny, the mandarin slang for my kind. Then, in the end, there was the surprise when my mother implied my father had visited male bordellos in Peking.

But when the elevator doors opened onto the paneled Japanese silk screens facing us on my mother's floor, I could feel Jimmie stiffening.

"Mrs. Chen, thank you for inviting me," he said formally when he followed me pass the entrance hallway and met my mother.

It did not take more than a few questions for my mother to size him up. I was familiar with her skills in getting information out of my friends and people in general.

He was an ABC, American-born Chinese, because he did not address her as Auntie Chen. A FOB, or fresh off the boat, would have used the more honorific term, although it had nothing to do with being related by blood.

She was very polite and solicitous, almost to a fault, urging her food on him. Knowing my mother, she had quickly figured out what was going on between him and me. She would not even have minded if I held his hand at dinner. I remembered how accepting she was when I told her about myself. She used to say, even a son with scabies on his scalp was still a good son to his mother, but I knew Jimmie would have crawled under the table if I did.

"It's nice you are so open with your family," he said when we got back to my place. My bedroom had no curtains because the garden backed into the County Park and Nature Preserve. He peeked out of the windows into the darkness of the woods beyond the old oak trees.

"Nobody can see us," I said, remembering when he withdrew his hand from me when we moved out of the safety of Castro street.

"It's taken me quite a few years," I told him more about myself, as I propped my head up with my elbow facing him. I could tell he was not ready to call it a night.

There was the shock of my first encounter with a man in that freezing men's room in Boston. The years of denial and refusal to believe that I was really doing it with men leading to a double life of despair, self-doubt, and shame. How I was afraid my career as a doctor would come to an end, and I would lose everything I had and worked for.

How living under such constant fear and anxiety became so unbearable it drove me to the couch of a therapist. Week after agonizing week spent in his office, where he also gave me books from his large library to read for validation that I was not a freak, then putting me into a group of men who were also trying to find acceptance. From the books, I found out there were men in history I admired, like Leonardo da Vinci, Michelangelo, Alexander the Great, and many others were in my company. Over the years, beam by beam, I eventually reframed the new home of my own self, a person freed from most of the guilt and shame. Once I was able to admit who I really was to myself, my family, then close friends, I felt I could finally breathe again, lifting a boulder that had been crushing my chest. I was telling Jimmie my whole story.

He looked at me with an intensity that told me this was a world he was still looking at from the outside, not sure of the landscape where it would lead him, yet I felt myself yawning and looking at the clock on the side table. In retelling my own trials and troubles, I was really hoping it might help my young friend.

"One thing I am certain. I don't ever want that double life in the closet again." I thought of the two sides of the character Dimitri Gurov described by Chekhov, "*One, open and known by all who cared to know… and another life running its course in secret, where everything that was essential, of interest and of value to him…everything that made the kernel of his life, was hidden from other people.*"

I gave Jimmie's bare arm a reassuring squeeze. He kept his T-shirt on. I kidded him the first night we were together that he must have some Mormon blood.

"I don't know," he said and moved into my arms.

I knew his words were his way of saying he was not yet ready to come out of the closet.

"I'd like that," he said. It was not usual for him to be so excited at something I suggested, now that we have been together for a few months. He could still get very upset when I tried to touch him affectionately when we were seated in a booth for lunch in a South Bay Chinese restaurant.

But his face could open up when he was happy like the first blossom of quince in spring. And his eyes and eyebrows danced up and down on his baby face like a child discovering a whole other world with a new plaything. Even his fingers joined in the dance to help him say how delighted he was. His bright smile now told me he'd really love to go on a trip to Boston and the Cape together.

On our flight over to Boston, I couldn't help but feel his tension, sitting next to me. He seemed to shrivel every time a flight attendant walked by us as if he thought people could tell what we were to each other. For him, it was still a love that could not be named. But he finally relaxed after we got into our rented car and drove away from Logan Airport.

I booked us into a Bed and Breakfast run by a gay couple just outside of the city. On the way over, we got close to the medical school where Joyce and I studied. I saw the differences a quarter of a century made. The complex of buildings loomed much larger than I remembered, with more of blanched concrete and polished steel, instead of old bricks and grace. It did not make me want to see the school again.

This was the place where Joyce and I had first fallen in love. I wondered while I was driving past, if the old building was still there, hidden in the massive complex, where for the first time I spent the night in Joyce's room when we both had summer jobs at the hospital.

For Jimmie's first full day in Boston, I showed him the Public Garden and Commons.

We splurged on afternoon tea at the Ritz, a taste of another world I could not afford when I was a medical student. It would be a treat for Jimmie to remember, to sip tea and sample sweets while enjoying the view of the Garden, the part of the city I had always cherished.

From the Ritz, it was a short walk for us to Faneuil Hall and Quincy Market, quite a different world, full of its history of the early settlers from another part of the world, far apart from where our common Asian ancestors came.

The market place was now a large, open space crisscrossed by upscale shops and eateries. I found Durgin Park, the old restaurant, which used to offer a huge slab of roast beef on their oversized oval plates, for $4.95 when I was an undergraduate on the other side of the river Charles. The price was now more than triple, and I wondered if it was still popular with hungry students.

"Can we see Chinatown?" Jimmie's only request.

"It's much smaller than the one in San Francisco," I said, remembering he told me once that he still had relatives living there. "We're only a few blocks away."

It was just a couple of streets and alleys with shops when Joyce and I were in medical school. Ten minutes by foot from our fifth-floor attic walk up by the school, our first home after we got married. We used to walk there occasionally when we felt like some exercise and Chinese groceries if we had a little free time.

The area now looked more spread out. Jimmie pulled us into a grocery store with Chinese vegetables and canned goods. Large strips of red paper with Chinese calligraphy auguring good earnings and prosperity were pasted on the walls. A blue porcelain jardinière held a kumquat tree, which came up to my knees and still had the ribbons of congratulations from the store opening. Once bright red, now a dusty rose.

The shopkeeper in back of the counter looked up at us from behind his reading glasses and Chinese paper. Jimmie engaged him with a few words of Toisan, the dialect most commonly spoken in Chinatowns in those days and where his father came from.

The old man seemed amused by Jimmie's attempt in speaking Toisan, but was very friendly to us when he heard that we were visiting from San Francisco, and I had studied in Boston.

"Your Cantonese is pretty fluent," Jimmie once said to me. I thought my Cantonese was more fluent than his, although my dialect was not Toisan, but the shopkeeper understood me well. I tried to give Jimmie's hand a squeeze, but he ducked and gave me a dirty look.

He smiled at me after we walked out of the shop, carrying a sack of tangerines, which I thought we should buy after engaging the friendly man in conversation. In back of my mind, I thought tangerines and oranges were also for good luck.

"You want to take in a museum?" Without waiting for his answer, I added, "It's on our way back." Looking at my watch, we still had over an hour before closing time.

When we got to the garden court of the museum on the Fenway, I saw wonderment sparkle in Jimmie's eyes. A friend of mine proposed to his wife in front of the grand staircase. The Venetian Palazzo, built by Isabella Stewart Gardner for the art works and paintings she brought home to educate the New Englanders in the culture of the old world, looked just as spectacular as it did during my first visit as a college student.

Playing tour guide now, I took Jimmie to the paintings of Gardner by Sargent and Whistler. I pointed out the stunning portrait of a woman who was not beautiful but made to look like a Madonna with a halo around her head, and the almost unearthly lighting from the left on the three figures in the Vermeer and the rare Rembrandt depicting a storm at sea. The place was not crowded, and the guards stood discreetly at a distance, making us feel as if we were at some private viewing.

Jimmie was rapt and awestruck seeing these masterpieces and listening to whatever I had to say about them, a feeling I could remember having when I first saw Monet's *Water Lilies* at the MOMA in New York. I was happy in showing off a bit of what I knew, especially thinking back now, some of those priceless paintings were stolen a few years later and have never been found again. But I also began to recognize he was indeed so much younger than I was.

In my mind, I had always looked for someone who was a peer and could share things in my life. I did not see myself playing a role as Henry Higgins, notwithstanding our common ancestry being the glue that pulled us together.

Early next morning I took him to Rockport on Cape Ann, the village where I spent my honeymoon with Joyce. I remembered she was too excited to fall asleep. We got up and combed the rocky beach under the moonlight and stars, finally ended up on the wharf, waiting around for the food concessions to open.

On our honeymoon, signs had advertised three dollars for all the lobster you can eat.

Jimmie and I got to the short boardwalk before lunch, and I picked a table at a lobster joint midway down the wharf, close to where I went with Joyce, but I could not be certain. The whole wharf looked more tidied up, and the places looked more upscale.

Jimmie finished his lobster and did not want another one.

"Even Joyce had a second one." I nudged him.

"Please don't compare me with your wife!" I realized I had clearly pushed him over the edge with what I thought was a little gentle teasing. I had seen his anger flash, like the time he thought I was too demonstrative in the booth of the Chinese restaurant not far from the Castro.

Still, I was surprised by his intensity, I touched his knee under the counter. "I was only kidding," I said.

"I don't like it!" He pulled away from me. "I am not your wife!"

We paid the bill and walked down the wharf in silence.

"You have a temper just like her." Were words on my lips, but I decided to hold my tongue and not kid him any further. It was his first big blow up at me.

We didn't talk about it afterwards between us. But I should have known being reminded about Joyce really bothered him, even the first time when he was with me to get the children, he ducked so fast under the dashboard when he thought he was going to be facing her. Decades and several more partners later, I realized it would never be a wise thing to make comparisons with an earlier loved one.

A color photo taken later that afternoon by a kindly passerby showed us side by side in Greek sailors' caps we had bought on the wharf. He looked serious, buttoned up in his navy pea coat. I, a head taller, had on a smile and a tweed sports jacket. We must have made up by midafternoon before we left to drive back to Boston.

By the time I arrived for his Buddhist ceremony at the monastery, the place was already filled with people I did not know.

There was a small rock garden in front. I could see an attempt at building something like the famous Zen garden in Kyoto.

I looked around for someone familiar in the crowd. An equal mix of Asians and Westerners, friends and others who were also beginning their lives in the monastery, I suspected. A few were dressed in monks' robes for the ceremony.

I spotted him in a far corner near a small bamboo grove. His son and daughter were among the people around him. I felt I knew his children, from the pictures he sent. Each one as they arrived, a year, then three years after his marriage.

His son was good looking, sensitive with full cheeks and square jaw, a younger version of Jimmie when we first met.

I remembered how much he envied me having children, and how he really enjoyed being with mine.

I caught his eye, and he waved me over.

"You remember Dr. Chen." He turned to his son. I had been invited to his violin recital when he was in the third grade.

The young man held out his hand. "Call me Andrew," I said.

His daughter reminded me of his wife. Petite, small pointed face and almond like eyes. I was a guest at their wedding.

His wife was not there, and I didn't ask.

"Thanks for coming." He was smiling, but I could tell it was a little forced, and he was trying to hide his nervousness. There was the same warmth in his eyes that I remembered which always made me feel it came up from his heart. A touch of gray at his temples and his hairline was beginning to recede. A little heavier, I thought, but couldn't be sure with the robe he was wearing. Otherwise, he hadn't changed much.

He led me to his sisters and brothers. I remembered them from his wedding, along with his parents.

"Your parents well?" I tried to make conversation with one of his sisters.

"They both passed away," she said. "They'd be here, otherwise."

At the wedding, his mother had on a brocaded Chinese dress and, what I imagined, all of her jade and gold jewelry. The deep maroon gown and the bright green jade made me think it was Christmas Day at the reception. I saw Jimmie's face in her. His father was already a little bent over. I remembered his bad back from his earlier work.

They were both beaming at the sight of their eldest son marrying a pretty Chinese girl who had just come over from Southeast Asia.

Jimmie was fulfilling his duties to his parents and to his family. It played a big part in his decision to stop seeing me not too long after our trip together.

A mutual friend, Ernie, told me they were seeing each other for a while afterwards. In the end, he succumbed to his ingrained duty as the oldest son to carry on the family name by having children. Even though it was a name from the paper, one his grandfather had bought. It was a name the family had lived with for more than half a century.

After the Buddhist ceremony and ritual sutra chanting, I stayed around to congratulate him.

I shook his hand and offered the Buddhist blessing holding my palms together. "I hope that's the right gesture for the occasion."

"Anything." His voice sounded a little subdued, the way he was when he felt awkward.

"I hope you will be very happy." Then I added, "And fulfilled."

"I am trying." I detected a relaxation of his initial awkwardness with me. "The sutras have helped."

The time of our first encounter at my home in the hills came back to me. The initial dance between us that evening, after the other people had gone, the passion of our first night together. Some thirty years ago.

"I'm trying." he repeated now in front of me.

I saw the silent words on his lips, "And, how are you?"

Over these past three decades, I had tried to encourage him to accept himself. When his wife left him after fifteen years of marriage, he was devastated, and his children blamed their mother for leaving. He came to see me, and I told him this would be a good time to tell his kids the truth, that he had neglected his wife, and could barely stand to continue marital relations with her.

Instead, he has persisted in keeping the myth. He could not bring himself to face his children and tell them the truth about himself. A couple of years later he told me he was volunteering at the Buddhist Temple and going to the lectures. Jimmie was never a brave man, I thought. He could not face seeing Ernie, even when Ernie was dying from AIDS. He confided he was still going to the gay baths sometimes.

I wanted to tell him about Adele, that it was not what I had expected. I had to go back to my therapist when I discovered I was in love with a woman again. I learned to accept myself and the changes that happened in my life as it evolved. I wanted to tell him that I hoped he would have a chance to meet her someday.

But his son and daughter came over to ask him to join them for some family pictures of the occasion.

Chapter Twenty-Seven

虎

I was only aware of him, next to me on our large, yellow beach towel. The fine hairs around his temples and on his torso sparkled like gold dust under the afternoon sun over the Pacific.

His eyes pulled me in, smiling, their blue blending into the horizon in front of us, as if he was saying everything was all right.

Earlier Ernie had explained, "They are from Mexico." He had unfolded the small paper packet with what looked like clumps of shriveled shiitake mushrooms.

"Trust me," he said, voice gentle as the breeze from the Monterey cypresses on the bluff, as he put some pieces into my mouth. No reason not to.

"Yes, I've just about tried them all," he added.

He didn't forget anything, even the massage oil tasting like warm almond milk on my tongue later.

Face down, first my back and shoulders, then my waist, and onward down he kneaded the oil, all the way to my toes, fingering each one. Then my arms and fingers, making them tingle under his soft, confident touch.

"Turn on over," he whispered into my ear.

"You're so smooth." His palms barely brushed against me. "Just what turns me on." Teasingly, he pulled on the lone hair around my left areola.

Just then I squinted and saw the rainbows of butterflies fluttering, wave after wave of them across the window pane above the sun deck wrapped around the bedroom.

I had not been reading Zhuang Zi. The Chinese Daoist sage and his butterfly dream could not have been further from my mind on that sunstruck afternoon.

Nor was I remembering our Japanese garden, springtime in Taipei when I was eleven, flocks of them painted with kingfisher blue flitting from azalea to azalea by the arabesque of the fishpond.

But when I think of him now and our times together, I cannot help being reminded of the philosopher's dream of becoming a butterfly, two and a half millennia ago.

Ernie had a way of suggesting things, as light as butterfly wings, never making me feel confined or forced into anything. As if I could always float out, just as I floated into his life.

He seemed preternaturally calm and gifted in making me relax around him, from the first day we were together.

It was a weekend Men's Group on the street above Castro, where we met. The Castro was still at its prime, the days of Harvey Milk, the first gay supervisor elected in San Francisco, still fresh in our minds and the plague only a phantom waiting in the wings. I was footloose after Jimmie imperceptibly receded from my life.

"Feel like a drive to the beach?" Ernie suggested as if it was the most natural thing when the Group broke for lunch. We ended up with a picnic under the cypress groves in Lands End with a view of the Golden Gateway.

Between bites of pastrami on rye, he told me he had been to Vietnam and survived. But he left his heart in Asia, he added with a smile and twinkle in his eyes, which made me notice for the first time the clear aquamarine of his eyes.

He was good at filling me in quickly about his life. It was what happened a lot between many of us those days. After years of being in the closet, hiding our personal lives, ourselves, what we really felt, so that we nearly burst out telling one another whenever there was an opportunity. And with Ernie, words flowed like ribbons of silk out of his lips.

"After having survived the Korean War, I got out and took advantage of the G.I. Bill."

I figured it was the year before I arrived in San Francisco with my mother.

"When I finished my studies and training, it was about the time of the flower children in the Bay Area," he continued.

I told him that for me it was like being a race horse with blinders on, so completely immersed in my training to become a surgeon, that I missed the direct impact of that period of blossoming at its height. But I remembered the lyrics of the Mamas and the Papas song, *If you come to San Francisco, be sure to wear some flowers in your hair.*

"I let down my hair and married the first woman who came along. She was French." I could fairly see Ernie with golden locks down to his shoulders doing Gene Kelly's *An American in Paris,* in reverse.

Three children later, he was out. With his degree in psychology, helped organize the first gay chatlines in the Bay Area.

The sun came through the feathery cypresses, coloring his cheeks with a blush of pink when we finished our sandwiches. I felt he could have floated in and out with the occasional monarch butterfly at a distance as we were sipping tea in Lewis Carroll's Garden for Alice.

He phoned that evening. "I've got an extra ticket to the Symphony tomorrow evening. They'll be playing Mahler's Fifth. Are you free?"

Being almost tone deaf and barely conversant about music, I hesitated for a moment.

"No pressure. But I think you might enjoy it. You'll be my guest."

I accepted and enjoyed being with him again, touching each other from time to time during the lingering adagietto.

The following weekend I invited him to Ibsen's *A Doll House*. Plays, particularly tragedies, were my preference. Ernie said he liked musicals but took in some local playhouse productions from time to time.

By then, we had already spent nights together and found out more about each other.

Between us, there was no feeling of pressure or obligation on either side. It soon became our world, so different from my world before him and even my world now, three decades later.

I thought it was the best possible place to be. No commitments were necessary. The wish when we woke up each morning with the feeling of being beholden to one another was all we needed, so we both thought.

I did not need to tell him what I was going to do the next day. It seemed so easy. Unlike the world of commitments and promises, in my marriage earlier, sanctified by a legal certificate and even unlike the one I live in today.

For the last two decades, Adele and I have made a life together. Two years ago, we decided on a place together in the columbarium, the same cemetery where my mother has been for the last quarter of a century and where my father's ashes are reinterred. But, Adele still made me feel she wanted to know what I did with nearly every minute of my time.

"How long are you going to be at the Y? Come back soon!" I felt it was the only time I had by myself. If I pushed back, she told me I spent all my time reading, even though I was at home with her. Or worse, in front of the computer. Not her.

The best moments were when I climbed into bed, and she was already purring softly, fast asleep. I could relive the tenderness and love we felt for each other in the years we have shared together, and not the strains of day to day.

The year and a half we were together, Ernie and I did not seem to need cords to bind us.

But in the end, we were fooled. At least I was. Things seemed to have happened without either one of us paying much attention at the time. It felt so good to be free. It would have felt unnatural for me to question if we needed any glue to keep us together. Looking back, Ernie probably felt it later, too.

José from my weekly Men's Group knew books and Buddhism were both close to my heart. He asked me to dinner to meet his friend who had a bookshop and was an early disciple of Suzuki Roshi, the founder of the San Francisco Zen Center. Ernie had late appointments with his clients that night, and I went to the dinner alone.

That evening Charles and I talked about the books we liked, from Shakespeare's sonnets to Basho's haikus. He told me about his bookshop, named after Walt Whitman. It had most of the authors I wanted to read. With the stir of Stonewall tingling around us, I wanted to catch up on all the gay authors I had missed. Our friend José faded into the background like the perfect host.

An invitation to visit the bookshop ended up with me spending the night in the backroom of his bookshop.

Ernie did not ask me what I did that night, although he said he tried to call me after work. I told him later about meeting Charles and the bookstore.

"I know him. Often, I'd drop in his bookshop at lunchtime. It's not far from my office." Ernie said. "It's got the best stock for gay reading in the Bay Area," he added, without any sign of concern.

At that time, Oscar Wilde and Whitman were the only gay authors I knew. I hadn't heard about Isherwood's *A Single Man* or E.M. Forster's *Maurice*. Charles opened my eyes to his world of C. S. Cavafy, J. R. Ackerley and even Ronald Firbank and John Addington Symonds. I could pick out any book from his loaded shelves, and he could tell me about the book and its author.

"Did you tell Ernie about our night together?" Charles wanted to know right away when I saw him again.

"He didn't ask for details."

"We could be a threesome," Charles proposed. "I know him anyway. He comes by the bookshop often."

I consented when he said he was going to talk to Ernie. I was a little uneasy but not enough to object and admittedly, also touched by the intensity Charles showered on me. In equal measure, I was impressed by his knowledge of all the books by gay authors I never knew existed.

A few weeks later Ernie asked me to have dinner and talk. His tone was even and congenial as I imagined him talking to one of his clients in his clinical psychology office.

"I'm not saying that you shouldn't see Charles," he said after we put in our orders in the Japanese restaurant we liked. I did not detect any anger, and he even looked sweetly at me from his azure blue eyes.

"Charles talked to me." He took a sip of the warm sake he ordered and held my hand. "But I'm just not attracted to him."

"Can we still see each other?" It was my way of saying I still cared about him and didn't want our feelings for each other to end.

"Sure," he said. "We can see what happens."

That was the last night we spent together. We hugged each other. I was trying to find some way to hold on to what we had for each other, with a different level of intimacy. But we both knew the ground between us had shifted.

I did not realize I had to make a choice at that time. Ernie and I had no commitments. From the beginning, we thought we could look into each other's eyes and be happy together from day to day.

Charles roared into this space like a whirlwind. He invited me to Green's. In those days, it took a month or two to get a table at that flagship vegetarian restaurant in Fort Mason, but he knew the people at the Zen Center because of his earlier involvement with Roshi Suzuki. He had tickets to the Symphony, he wanted me to meet his old friends.

On the weekend, he asked if he could bring a picnic lunch to my garden, where we read aloud some of Shakespeare's love sonnets. He even invited me to zazen at the Zen Center on Page and Laguna.

I ended up doing more with Charles in two weeks than Ernie and I were doing in a month.

"I am also seeing Chris." Ernie let me know on the phone when we spoke the following month. But I had already heard that from friends.

We saw less of one another but remained friends. The change seemed as easy and natural as those butterflies in flight on the sun deck that afternoon by the sea after we first met. There was no feeling of being hurt, I thought, from either side.

"Have you heard that Ernie came down with it?" It was Jimmie on the line six months later. I heard they've been seeing each other. It didn't surprise me because I knew about Ernie's special fondness for Asians. They had met when Ernie and I were together. Before me, Ernie lived with a Nisei for a number of years. Many things in his home, reminded me of this earlier boyfriend. Obis, kimonos, imari porcelains.

"Are you sure he has it?" I didn't want to believe that Ernie was coming down with the most feared diagnosis of that time.

I was beginning to hear about Kaposi's sarcoma, a rare skin cancer described in medical textbooks, until then, only found in certain aging Mediterraneans, was now showing up in gay men.

Medical experts couldn't tell us how people came down with it. It seemed to be only happening in the gay community. A prominent man of the cloth preached from his pulpit we had it coming to us. A well-known commentator suggested we should all be tattooed like those in Auschwitz and Buchenwald. I had read people like us were herded into those camps along with the Jews and Gypsies.

It didn't occur to me then to be worried that Ernie and I were together for more than a year. Even if I wanted to find out whether I also had the disease, there was no official test available at the time.

I remember that period when we were living in the darkness of fear and the unknown. I also remember the feeling of a death sentence for those who found out they were positive when the test became available several years later. I was with Gene by then.

We had been together for almost a year, and I suggested we should both check again, even though Gene told me his doctor at U.C. reassured him he was fine when we first met.

When he came back from his doctor's office, he was ashen.

"He told me I was fine!" Tears filled his eyes, turning his face usually filled with compassion for others into that of a frightened child. His lips quivered in agony and confusion, when he finally got his words out. "He now says I was positive several years ago." His doctor had only wanted to assure him his health was still all right. There was no proven treatment anyway.

27
虎

This was followed by horrible fear surging through his teary eyes. "What if I passed it onto you?" I had to reassure him I tested negative, but also felt guilty that I was the one who was spared.

Even when we went to see my friend the HIV specialist, and he explained to us how we could live safely as a couple, Gene was not reassured. When I tried to hug him later, he pushed me away. He felt like a leper, he said.

I was hurt that he was pushing me away because I thought whatever sickness and hell he was going to go through, I wanted to go through with him. I was prepared to be with him till the end.

I thought about love and commitment differently from the time I was with Ernie. Charles had wanted commitment, and I still thought love should be from day to day, the way it was with Ernie and me.

When Gene came up to hug me at the end of the memorial service for Charles I had arranged, both Ernie and Charles were no longer, all within a few years. Something inside of me was changing, ready for a firmer bond with someone I loved. And Gene was the gentlest and kindest person I had ever come across. I could see his pain when he saw a cricket die on the grass in the park. Even my children remembered him that way. I treasured the first record he gave me, *Lady Day Blues* by Billie Holliday. And the album that became our song, Whitney Houston's "Didn't We Almost Have It All?" It was emblematic of what we felt when we had each other.

But in the end, I didn't stay with him. After being with him yet not really being with him because he withdrew himself from us, from what we had as a couple. He would not even let me touch him because he was afraid it could lead to intimacy. I told Gene I could not bear it any longer to continue like that.

Looking back, I feel I should have stayed. Even though I rushed to his side when his old friend called me, Gene was down with full blown AIDS. I knew in my heart, were the words of a later song by Whitney Huston, "I Will Always Love You."

When Jimmie continued on the phone about Ernie, his words hit me like knockout punches to my head. "Conant was the one who did the biopsy." Jimmie's words when I asked him if he was sure about Ernie's diagnosis. I knew Ernie worked closely with Dr. Conant as the psychologist in that clinic at the forefront for treating a lot of gay men coming in with the disease.

"Jimmie must have told you," Ernie answered when I got on the phone.

"Can we have dinner or tea sometime?" I wasn't sure how he would feel talking to me about it on the phone.

"Sure." He sounded as if we had been in touch all along.

He chose a Japanese restaurant within walking distance to the Castro, the one we used to go to when we were together.

He looked as cheerful as he always seemed to be. A blush of pink still on his cheeks, blue eyes clear and smiling.

He told me he was not too worried. He showed me the area around his left ankle, where Conant had cut out the lesion. It looked no different from those on my patients' skin after I had cut out something cancerous.

"I survived the bullets and killings of the war in Korea. And Conant is on the frontline for the latest treatments." Ernie sounded reassured and confident.

But the black pox, as the Kaposi's sarcoma came to be known in the community, started to show up on his face. At first, a few, then too many and faster than Conant could cut out. He started Ernie on a new medication that came out. It helped about half of those treated, Ernie said.

I checked in with him every couple of weeks, treading the fine line of not wanting him to feel that I was treating him like a doomed man, but wanting to let him know that I still cared about him.

He had some bad reactions to the new medication, and the dose had to be reduced.

"I decided to stop working at the clinic." He told me on the phone six weeks later. "It was causing more concern and anxiety in my clients to see me like that."

But he continued to do his own shopping for groceries in the stores as if the stares from people didn't bother him.

When I hugged him on my visits, he hugged me back, just as he had before this happened. I did not detect any sense of despair or feeling of helplessness. At the same time, he told me he had sold his share in the building he owned.

He began talking about his children. "Kim will be fine. She can always take care of herself." His eldest was at the peak of her adolescence and was becoming a beautiful young woman. "She knows how to get what she wants from a man." I felt uneasy the way Ernie seemed to be putting her on the block for sale. But I didn't think it was the time for me to tell him how to bring up his children.

Marty could enlist in the Air Force and get himself a good education. He was a strapping boy when I last saw him and the middle one of Ernie's three children.

"Erin is the smartest of my kids. She will get her Ph.D. someday." He caught himself for a moment, as if he couldn't bear to hear what he was going to say, then went on, "Don't think what she'll get from me can support her all the way." He was thinking about what he could provide for his kids. The customarily confident tone in his voice wavered to barely audible.

That was the only trace Ernie let show, in facing his own mortality. His attention was always focused on ridding himself of the disease.

He heard of some doctors south of the borders treating patients with amygdalin, the apricot seed, which was supposed to help. He got the name of a clinic and flew down for a course of treatment.

"I feel much better." He told me when he came back. But I couldn't see much difference on his face when I saw him.

Actually, I noticed his cheeks were getting hollowed out, and his clothes were hanging loose on him. Ernie always paid close attention to his clothes and how he looked in them.

A month before Christmas he told me he bought a ticket for himself and a young man to accompany him to the Philippines. There was a doctor who could remove tumors from patients without using a knife. "I saw him demonstrate on Filipino television," Ernie said, full of hope again, and I thought the significance of Christmas might also be on his mind.

I decided my best way to be supportive was not to question the efficacy of these treatments. Nothing was proving out to be effective officially, as far as I could find out. He tried a macrobiotic regimen for a month, then beet juice and garlic, even coffee enemas. Nothing did much to change his steady downhill course, but Ernie never seemed to have given up hope.

"Remember the house we looked at on Liberty?" he said on one of my last visits. It was a storybook like house perched on top of the hill with a manicured garden and blue and white fence in front. When we were a couple we used to drive by and say if we just had enough money between us, we should buy it together for our old age.

We talked about sitting on its porch in rocking chairs facing one another and enjoying the view of downtown, when we grew old.

I almost choked at the memory, but managed to give him a little affirmative smile back as I sat next to his bed.

"I picked up a used copy of Zhuang Zi the other day," he pointed to a paperback by his bedside.

"The stuff of feeling like a butterfly sounds pretty good," he continued.

I wondered what made him look into these ancient Daoist's writings. Was it the philosopher's espousal of escape from the pressures of society into an individual path of freedom? The opposite of the conforming rigidity of Confucius.

"Remember I told you about the rainbows and butterflies when we were on the deck in Bolinas by the Sea?

"And I said I felt I was being tickled by ten thousand peacock feathers all over my body," he answered without missing a beat.

Then I remembered how carefully he tried to explain to me we each could have our own trip with the stuff he brought along that weekend.

Years later when we were reminiscing, I asked Jimmie if he saw Ernie at the end.

"No." His hushed voice told me how bad he felt. "I just couldn't face it. It was too much for me."

Ernie's words came back to me again. We each had our own trip. Jimmie's Buddhism, Ernie's peacock feathers, and my flight of butterflies by the sea.

Chapter Twenty-Eight

兔

We stayed until the last. The long list of credits scrolled across the wide screen. Christopher Isherwood, the author of the novel on which the movie was based, came long after the director, Tom Ford. There were just a few like us, who waited till the very end. Then the house lights came on.

"What do you think?" I was interested in Adele and her sister's reactions, partly because I was the one who suggested the film. Her sister said she liked Isherwood's writing when I mentioned it. I wasn't sure what they felt about the subject matter, but I was determined to see it myself.

"I liked it. But the ending..." Adele didn't quite finish what was on her mind. I could easily guess because both of them were glued to their seats when the character George dropped to the floor from what appeared to be a heart attack. They were not prepared when that was the final event of the film as George's life and the credits started rolling off the screen.

"You read the book?" Her sister asked.

"Long time ago," I said, eyes blinking a bit from the bright hallway lights of the Kabuki Theatre as we were walking out, "I have the book somewhere on my book shelves."

Later that night when Adele was already fast asleep, I got up for my pee break. On my way back, I found the book under the "I" section on the wall of gay authors in my study. Its jacket was distinctive, the outline of an unclothed figure standing starkly in the middle of a mass of ghostly faces in gray black. The red letters, A Single Man, stood out like a tattoo across the middle of his body.

Naked, I sat in the armchair and turned on the reading light. The inscription on the title page popped out when I opened the book. The script was distinctive, clear, and deceptively simple as his writing, "To Tsun Yuan, with memories of my visit to China – Christopher Isherwood," put me back into that weekend he was in San Francisco with Don Bacardy, over a quarter of a century ago.

Isherwood sat in an armchair, toward the back of the Walt Whitman Bookshop, his gray hair and square face with a grand-fatherly smile added to his dignity as he patiently signed the books of the long queue. His presence lent a sense of solidarity to Charles' bookshop, featuring gay authors and gay-related literature and writing from the time it opened. The portrait of the shop's namesake signed by the man himself hung prominently above the books. That afternoon people waiting for Isherwood's signing spilled out onto Market Street, around the corner from the Castro. His partner, Don Bacardy, was by his side, protective like a grown-up son toward an aging father.

Bacardy chatted easily with the people he knew. He was petite, but with delicate good looks, a touch of gray at the temples, and could well be a model for a mature man in the fashion pages today. The occasion was supposed to be for the publication of October, a book of his portraiture drawings in collaboration with words by Isherwood. But Charles had been right in predicting there will be a huge crowd for Isherwood's books for the signing. Bacardy was very good humored, letting his famous older partner be the center of attraction that day.

The night before, I helped Charles set up the table and old armchair for Isherwood after the bookshop was closed for its last customer.

The excitement in Charles at the prospect of Isherwood coming the next day had been palpable. Face flushed and happy as a teenager preparing for his first high school prom, he had me help him carry in the armchair he kept from his first bookshop, Bees Books in Oakland and his favorite Persian prayer rug from his apartment at the Zen Center to put under the signing table. He even forgot to stop for dinner.

This was somehow more important to him than Edmund White's appearance for his breakthrough book, *The Boy's Own Story*, or Ann Rice signing hers from a coffin. Charles felt a kinship in the Isherwood/Bacardy relationship to the one he had with me.

It had been over a year since Charles blustered his way into my life with Ernie.

Ernie and I were very comfortable with each other, both married and divorced and both had teenage children. There seemed to be no need for more commitment.

"Our marriage vows were till death do we part." Ernie's words rang out like a village truth teller, "And see where we are now, both divorced."

I agreed. Nothing was forever.

Charles rushed in when he sensed his chance. He sent me a haiku about finding my dark hair on the yellow tile of his shower, juxtaposing it to seeing the first plum blossom of spring.

He suggested a weekend together from the time he closed the bookshop on Saturday afternoon till Monday morning. He drove down to my home on the Peninsula in his red Beetle. Same as the China Red two-door Beetle Joyce and I had, our first car and bought with our first intern's paychecks as down payment. Joyce chose the bright China Red. I realized later it was emblematic of the passion both she and Charles had in things they pursued, although outwardly Charles seemed to embody the calmness of the Buddhism he espoused.

He brought along a satchel of his favorite books. In the hot tub under the lantern on the deck next to my bedroom, we read aloud Shakespeare's sonnets to each other.

His favorite was Sonnet No.116. Its first line was written for us, he felt: *Let us not to the marriage of true minds admit impediments.*

We talked about our early childhoods without a father, his first job as a junior high teacher in Oakland and mine as a chemical engineer in du Pont's Wilmington, then our mutual interests in zazen and sutras.

On Sunday, he suggested we have a picnic spread of bread and wine and crab salad we bought at the neighborhood grocery. It was our Déjeuner sur l'Herbe in my garden, bordering the County Park, which was my neighbor in the foothills of the Peninsula. Afternoon sunlight scintillated through the tall branches of old California oaks and the first layer of golden autumn leaves rustled under our feet.

A month later, I heard Ernie was seen with another man. I wanted to call him to tell him that I was happy for him. But I didn't move to dial his number.

Charles kept me busy. Introducing me to books I had missed, his friends and authors who came to his bookshop for signings.

One day he was very excited to tell me he found the perfect new location for his bookshop. His first Walt Whitman bookshop was off Fillmore on Sutter, not far from where Ernie had his office. This new shop would be around the corner from Castro, closer to his readers with better exposure for the authors who came for the signings. He wanted it to be an old-fashioned bookshop where people could come and browse and sit in comfortable armchairs to read in a quiet corner. Absolutely no drinks, he decided, although he already had an offer to have a coffee shop on the side where he could double his income. No magazines, except gay journals. It was to be a literary bookshop of his dreams. He wanted to carry all the books with gay authors or gay related subject matter, which he felt were being neglected by the mainstream in the book business.

"You can be a part owner of the bookshop," he offered. It sounded very appealing and coincided with my desire to get more involved with the community of Harvey Milk that blossomed in tandem with the events on Sheridan Square of New York.

He also began to suggest that we should commit ourselves exclusively to each other. Like a married couple, he said. I saw more clearly why the words of Bard's Sonnet No. 116 were his favorite.

Its contrast with what I had with Ernie was not lost on me, whose words came back into my ears. Even when our marriages were sanctified, and we promised till death do we part, he and I both got divorced. To me, it took on a more profound meaning if we declared our love for each other, with each new day we were together.

It was the heady early eighties. HIV was only beginning to rear its Medusa's head. Most of us were basking in finally being out of the closet, casting off the chains and barriers which held us back for so many centuries. I felt Charles' suggestion was taking us backward to the times of drawing rooms of Queen Victoria and Albert, instead of forward toward a more open way of living.

"Look at Isherwood and Bacardy." That was when he first mentioned them as a couple to me. Isherwood had nurtured his lover, sent him to art school in London and allowed him to develop his own artistic talents.

Charles omitted the part about Isherwood's wisdom of letting his much younger partner see other men. The well-established writer had no fear when the young man needed more experience before settling down with him.

Charles' enthusiasm overflowed over at the prospect of the couple coming to his bookshop. He asked me to the dinner set up for them afterwards that evening.

There were a lot of people at the gathering in the Oakland hills. Writers, poets, publishers, book people and the couple's old friends milled around the garden. Charles put me at the same table with Isherwood and Bacardy.

The younger man had changed into something crème colored, bringing out more of his beach boy tan, even with the slight graying of his full head of hair. Isherwood was quiet, but the twinkle in his eyes conveyed a steady cordiality to the guests who came by the table, the feeling of a man whose accomplishments no longer needed trumpets or fanfare.

Charles made a point of telling him that I spent my childhood in Shanghai.

"Were you born in Shanghai?"

"No. I was born in Hankow. It's called Wuhan now."

"I was in Hankow with Auden. When were you born?"

"1937. My father was working with the Railways there."

"Same year I was there," he acknowledged graciously, conveying a sense of egalitarian camaraderie.

"They wrote a book about their China experience," Charles interjected. He already briefed me earlier about the book, Journey to a War.

"You are what my ancestors would call a *Lao Qian Bei,* an eminence gris." The reverence for elders inculcated since my childhood in China came out naturally, then I realized in the U.S. being old had a different connotation.

"No, hardly. Auden and I were just bumming around but calling ourselves journalists, or as they said in those days, War Correspondents."

"I was only in Hankow for a few months. Then my father moved us down to Canton."

"We didn't stay long in Hankow either. As I recall, the Japanese were in hot pursuit."

Then he seemed to have remembered something long forgotten, "Hankow was a lively place in those days. A hotbed of activity, you might say."

I nodded. "I was too young to remember that period in Hankow. But I know it's an important landmark of Sun Yat-sen's revolution."

I was usually tongue tied in front of the writers who came to Charles' bookshop for signings, feeling my own inadequacy in the language. Now in front of the eminence gris of gay authors, I would have only managed to mumble awkwardly about having enjoyed reading his books Charles had introduced to me, feeling like an ill prepared schoolboy in front of the English professor. But Isherwood's kindly demeanor and natural rapport made me feel more relaxed around him.

Charles had given me the first edition of Isherwood's *A Single Man*, which he considered to be one of the author's best. It was already out of print, but he had a copy. I brought it along with me but was hesitant to ask Isherwood to sign it.

Charles took over the initiative, "I'll ask for you. I know you won't open your mouth to ask." He smiled at me and put the book in front of the author.

"I'll be happy to," I heard Isherwood say.

I was still too nervous to read what he wrote, but later that night I was touched that he had put in the reference to China.

"Aren't you cold reading there like that?" Adele got up to go to the bathroom, squinted at me without her glasses and saw me sitting in the study with the book on my bare lap. The two pigtails she braided for the night made her look fifty years younger.

I was just finishing the sentence at the bottom of the first page. "... shambles naked into the bathroom, where its bladder is emptied …" George in the novel was feeling twinges in his arthritic thumbs and left knee.

He was a man of that certain age when every movement of his own body reminded him of the stage of his life. Even breathing took special effort at times.

He was an unmarried man, as I was. Isherwood was articulating the hidden fears I was not yet willing to face.

I realized I could no longer say that I was a single man. Adele was sharing my bed and breakfasts and many dinners. But, I was not married, and I found myself waking up sometimes, having just had a dream of being the man from an earlier life, my life before Adele.

How would that life be different if I had stayed with Charles? It is something that has often given me pause.

"Our lives are like the flights of bumble bees," Charles liked to say, "if we don't seize that rare moment when our paths cross, we might never find it again." He liked the image of the bees. The first bookshop he opened was called Bees Books in Oakland, he told me earlier.

I continued to insist that committing ourselves from day to day was more meaningful than any formal commitment ceremony. Was I too young then to admit there was wisdom in his words or was I not in love with him as much as he was with me? I have asked myself many times afterwards over the years.

He continued trying to convince me to see the paradise of commitment he painted for our lives together. "Love is not love which alters when it alteration finds." The more he pressed for his idea of a permanent union between us, the more I wanted to dig in and hold onto my own. As my mother said, an Ox can be stubborn. The year I was born on the Chinese zodiac cycle.

A good friend of mine comforted me when I told her about the pressure I was feeling from Charles. She lived in Pacific Grove,

In Loving memory of our dear mother

Mrs Theresa Ajai-Ajagbe

2nd August 1932 – 15th September 2012
1st October 2012

From children & grandchildren

a small community in Monterey Bay with early Methodist settlers, where her studies of and meditation on the books of Tibetan Buddhism fit right in.

"I thought he was a student of Zen Buddhism." She reminded me. "The first thing you learn in Buddhism is to let go."

I did not think it would help if I pointed that out to Charles, but I conceded to go see a couples therapist with him.

The office was comfortably furnished in a corner of the building, on Fillmore, the same building where Ernie had his old office. There was an antique shop next door where he had bought things, with Japanese *Imari* in the window framed by a fine bamboo screen. Charles and I sat on the plush beige couch, facing each other and an exquisitely intricate Indonesian carving hung on the wall while the therapist rocked discreetly in his Bentwood chair across.

I couldn't help remembering that ten years earlier I sat next to Joyce, across from another couples counselor in a gray concrete box of a building off of Welch Road next to the Stanford Medical Center. After six months, it was obvious to the therapist the marital cleft could not be repaired.

My wife suggested that we could build a little house at the far end of our deep garden lot where I could bring my male friends on weekends. I did not think that would work.

I thought I would be taking advantage of her because she just wanted us to stay together, at all cost. Our relationship was no longer what it was when we got married. I could no longer bring all of myself into the marriage after I discovered I was also attracted to men.

As Charles sat on the other end of the couch from me, I felt the same kind of clarity, although for quite different reasons. With him, I felt no desire to see other men or women. I believed it made more sense for us to commit to each other with every new dawn, given what had happened to my marriage earlier. Charles was just

28

兔

as convinced as my former wife that we should stay bonded. For him, this needed to be acknowledged in some formalized way.

Our therapist saw the impasse and suggested a six-months cool off period. We could then see how we felt about each other.

The arrangement sounded reasonable. Charles consented to it. We agreed to keep in touch with each other once a month. Looking back now, he could not have been very happy with the outcome.

Six weeks later he told me he found a new friend and wanted to introduce him to me. The three of us had lunch together. The young man was quite good looking, with glistening blue-black skin. Very quiet and did not have much to say about books or anything else.

I realized this was Charles' way of proving his point that once we lose that special moment when our bumblebee flight paths intersected, it would be lost forever.

My own lack of anguish or anger at the loss made me realize I was not or could not be as passionate toward him as he was with me. What I felt was a sense of relief from all that pressure and intensity from him.

A few months later, I got a call from him to have lunch together. I was happy to hear from him. Over soup and salad at the café on Market Street close to his bookshop, he talked enthusiastically about his plans for the bookshop.

He wanted to expand into the mail order business because he was getting lots of calls from men and women living in places without much access to books by gay authors or about gay subjects. He said there was a gay bookstore chain interested in expanding their business into the Bay Area and wanted to be prepared for what he sensed would be his competition.

"How's Otis?" I asked, remembering the name from when we were introduced and wanting to sound as casual as possible.

"I'm trying to convince him to go back to school." I detected an impatience and hint of ennui in his reply. The words, that his new lover was lazy, were on his lips, but he didn't come out with it until some months later.

"There's a certain sweetness to him," I told Charles. "And he's cute," I added, remembering his nicely buffed body.

He insisted on paying the bill. But we agreed to have lunch again in a month, and it would be my turn.

Our lunches together gradually smoothed over the initial uneasiness after we separated. I was happy to see him and hear about his new book adventures, and he seemed just as happy to see me. He began to be more open about being frustrated that Otis did not seem to want to do much other than sit in front of sitcoms, and I was able to feel less responsible for the end of our relationship as a couple.

"You know how young people are." I tried to make light of his complaints. But I also remembered how impatient Charles could be when he thought things were not where they should be.

It was going to be six months from the time we sat on the therapist's couch with cross purposes. The thought occurred to us both at about the same time.

"Let's have lunch at Zuni's next time," he suggested. The restaurant was farther down on Market towards City Center. He had taken me to it during our early days together. He liked it because the people who ran it were from the Zen Center where Charles had taken me to when we were together. The restaurant was becoming very popular around the area, but Charles felt he could always get a good table.

Our table at Zuni's was in a private corner on the second floor. We both ordered a glass of wine, which was unusual for us at lunch. But this was marking a special occasion.

Charles seemed resigned to his relationship with Otis. He said he was going to put him to work in the bookshop. He found another person who was more knowledgeable with books to help while he was training Otis. I was still happy to see him and talk about his books and authors and his plans, which always sounded exciting and interesting to me. I did not feel any pressure from him about changing the way we were seeing each other or allusion to our earlier life together. It was a comfortable camaraderie I felt we were settling into.

"My offer of a partnership in the bookstore still stands, you know," he said looking bright and smiling, as he took a sip of the chardonnay.

"Thanks," I said, "I'm interested. But let me think about it." I was happy that he felt easy enough to make the offer again and for me as well, now that there were no other strings attached between us.

Again, he insisted on paying the bill, even though I had the lobster ravioli, which was a little pricey. He said the people were going to give him a discount because of his long connection to the Zen Center.

We hugged, with easy affection on both sides, as we parted on Market Street outside the restaurant. He was going to walk back to the bookshop, and I got my car and drove home to the Peninsula.

I was annoyed when I picked up the phone at three that morning.

"I'm not on call this weekend," I told the hospital operator on the other end.

"I know, Dr. Chen," the operator replied, "but she said the patient was a personal friend of yours."

The nurse came on the line. "We have a Mr. Gilman here who was transferred from Oakland tonight. He said he is a personal friend and wanted you to know he's in the hospital."

I was trying to understand the words. In back of my mind, I saw Charles walking up Market Street into the afternoon sun.

"What's his diagnosis?" I asked.

"Brain lesion," the nurse continued, "he will be having a biopsy in the morning."

"Is he comfortable?" I asked.

"Reasonably."

"Tell him I'll be right over." I hung up the phone, put on my glasses, pulled on my shirt and stepped into my jeans. Not even time for underwear.

I was used to rushing to hospital emergencies, a few minutes sometimes made a real difference in the outcome of the patient. The routine had become automatic to me. But that night, I knew it was not a matter of life or death if I arrived a few minutes later. I was hurrying because I wanted to be by his side as soon as it took me to get there.

A brain lesion, I kept on thinking. Was it a tumor, a hemorrhage, was it HIV related, could he be positive? We had been to the County Health Clinic together, as soon as the tests first became available, sitting with a roomful of jittery men finding community in commiseration. We were both relieved that we were both negative.

The nurse who spoke to me on the phone said he was reasonably comfortable. I recalled her words as I was driving through the familiar streets toward the hospital. The huge oaks cast dark shadows on the pavement under the streetlights. It did not sound like a hemorrhage, in which case she would not have used the word comfortable to describe him. Most brain tumors were malignant, I went through the list in my mind. A lesion in the brain from a large virus, which attacked HIV positive patients, was being reported.

Which was worse? I couldn't think too much further. I decided the most important thing now was to let him know I would do everything I could to help him.

He looked calm and surreally serene under the white sheets, almost angelic like a monk. The nurse who led me to the doorway of his room on the floor for neurosurgical patients was the one who spoke to me on the phone, and I could sense she understood my anxiety when she gave me a look of reassurance. His head was smoothly shaved, in preparation for his brain biopsy. A distinct contrast to the photo of himself he had given me when we exchanged our baby pictures, after our early days together. A handsome boy of about five or six in his school uniform, a fluffy black bow in front of his white shirt collar.

His words in a poem on rice paper with bamboo and calligraphy in his own hand from those days when we first met came to me.

"Could it be that I am the Zen monk you are seeking? Who, with bottle and begging bowl has come down from the misty mountain..."

I dashed in to hold his hand, not bothering to worry about what the nurse might think.

"I had trouble with my foot after we parted," he was able to articulate clearly, "so, I drove myself to the hospital."

"Don't have to tell me everything now, if you're tired." I looked at him. "I can get everything from your chart."

"I couldn't control the car in the parking garage." He continued in a flat tone as if he were reciting a sutra. "Afraid I banged it up a bit."

"Don't worry about the car, Charles." I found myself sounding like a parent. "We'll take care of it." I meant between Otis and me.

"Does Otis know?"

"Not yet."

"Want me to call him?"

"Let him sleep." He paused for a moment. "Call him in the morning."

"They've got you scheduled for a biopsy."

"I know. They told me."

"Need anything?" I squeezed his palm and looked at him.

"Bring me something to read."

"Paper, magazine? A book?"

He thought for a moment. "How about Isherwood's story?"

"*A Single Man?*"

He nodded and closed his eyes.

28

兔

As I closed Isherwood's book to get back into bed, I was feeling a little chilled with my bare shoulders. Adele liked to set the thermostat low after midnight. She was already purring softly. I thought my life in those days could not have been further from my life with Adele today. It was the life of Isherwood's George as a single man that I thought I was destined to lead after Gene died. Nothing was forever, I felt, and it was all right to live from moment to moment, paraphrasing Sartre in my mind.

There was always the search for a soul mate. Sometimes the intensity verged on a chase. But I also remembered the words of my friend from Pacific Grove, a divorced woman with two married, grown children with their own families. The same friend who was steeped in Tibetan books on Buddhism.

"We came into this world alone, and we'll go alone." She seemed content and accepting of that fate.

When I told her I had parted ways with Charles, she said she always thought he was too intense and possessive to be a Buddhist. She was familiar with the book on Zen Buddhism by Roshi Suzuki. "Did he learn anything from Suzuki? I thought you told me he was a disciple?"

Those words from a friend were reassuring to me then that I made the right decision about Charles, but my feelings of affection and caring for him were still there.

The words of Paul Auster in his book, *The Invention of Solitude*, came to me — Some things will be lost forever. Other things will perhaps be remembered again, and still other things will be lost and found and lost again.

I remembered our moments with Shakespeare's sonnets and Whitman's Catullus poems, our weekends together by the sea in a small village near Point Reyes, or at the Zen retreat in the valley of Tassajara. The closeness of shared interests in books and reading. We were so close that it seemed the only thing we didn't share were our dreams. For Charles, I suspect, he would have wished for that too. There were also our shared histories of strong mothers. Women of a time when men were supposed to be the mainstay of the family.

The visit to Charles' mother in her rest home in Oakland not far from his first bookshop, with the news of his condition, was in some ways more heart wrenching than seeing Charles in the hospital that night. Much more so than the call I had to make to Otis the next morning, who listened quietly and accepted it as a matter of course.

The brain biopsy showed the most malignant form of brain cancer. It was a matter of a few months, at the most, his neurosurgeon told me. A colleague of mine and he didn't ask me about my relationship with Charles although it was unusual for me to show the amount of interest I did in a patient when I was not directly involved in the treatment.

It occurred to me that a positive test for HIV would have been better. Patients with brain lesions from bacterial organisms caused by the immune deficiency as a result of HIV infection were still being treated and survived for a year or even longer. There would have been some small ray of hope for some new medicine offering temporary control. New medicines for HIV were talked about in the Press and among Infectious Disease Specialists at medical meetings I attended.

I knew Charles' mother was a strong woman from what he told me earlier. We had talked about the similarities in our mothers, both raising their only sons single handedly. His during the years of the Great Depression in Kansas and mine a decade later in Occupied Shanghai with Japanese soldiers brandishing bayonets at check points.

I had gone to visit her several times with Charles and got the impression Fannie liked me. A woman of few words, but I felt the strength of her character in those relative silences.

When I stepped into her small apartment in the rest home, she was sitting in her padded Maplewood armchair. The beige and brown afghan Charles had given her was over her lap. I pulled over a chair to be next to her and held her hand. I had the feeling she knew something was up because I showed up alone without Charles. Her thin hand was cold to touch, but she was not trembling after I told her Charles was in the hospital.

"I hope they are doing everything they can for him." She said quietly. "I'm glad he has you." She added.

She knew Charles and I were no longer together. Charles told me he brought Otis to visit her.

I asked her if there was anything I could do for her.

"I'd like to see him."

I promised her I would take her.

When I told Charles, he said he didn't want to let his mother see him like this. It would bother her too much, he said. He was hoping his condition would improve before I brought her over.

I visited her again and told her I was arranging the details and would come and get her as soon as I could.

She held onto my hand a little longer. "You come and see me if you can." She looked up at me. I heard the pleading behind her words.

Charles deteriorated rapidly. His speech was slurring, and he was losing control of his bladder and bowels. The nurse put a diaper on him. Knowing how proudly independent he had always been, I cringed when I heard it. His doctor recommended radiation treatment immediately, and he had to be transferred to a nursing home and then transported to the treatment center. I knew what it meant to be transferred to a nursing home. There was nothing more the hospital could offer him.

Within a week of starting his treatment, I could see he was weaker instead of better. He slept more and didn't want to be aroused.

I decided I couldn't wait any longer for him to consent for his mother's visit.

She was grateful that I was taking her to see Charles when I went over to get her.

"Thank you, thank you!" she said, gripping my hand tighter than usual.

"He's pretty tired out from all the treatment." I thought I'd prepare her for his condition.

The nurse at the rest home told me Charles should be settled back into bed after his treatment by early afternoon. He wasn't eating much anymore by then, but I had the feeling the nurses didn't want to have too many visitors during lunch hour.

We arrived midafternoon. I pushed Fannie into his room in the wheelchair the rest home provided when we got there.

Charles had his face turned to the wall.

"Charles," I called to him, "your mother is here."

He didn't move.

I walked to the side of his bed against the wall to look at him. His eyes were closed.

I put my arm against his shoulder and shook him a lightly. He was breathing soundlessly.

"I think he's just tired out by the treatment today." I tried to comfort Fannie.

I wheeled her closer to his bed. She couldn't reach his head, which was marked with cross hatches in black ink for the radiation treatment. I wished the nurses had put a skullcap on him so his mother wouldn't see his scalp marked up like that. She looked resigned and put her hand on his back for a while. I wasn't sure whether she was stroking him imperceptibly.

"Charles…" she murmured and finally withdrew her hand.

"Stay as long as you like," I said.

"I'm ready to go," she said.

We drove back in silence. I wanted to say something hopeful but couldn't bring myself to say that he was going to be better.

I settled her back into her apartment at her rest home and sat with her for a while.

"Can I get you anything?" I asked.

"No, thank you." She cupped my hand as if in a closing prayer. "You'd better be going. You must have things to do."

"I'll come and see you again." I bent down and gave her a hug in her chair. She hugged me back. That was the closest I felt Fannie came to breaking down.

She released me quickly. "Please do," was all she said.

As I walked toward the door, she called me back.

"There's something I'd like you to have." She pointed to a cabinet on the other side of the room. "It's in the bottom drawer. Would you get it out for me? I can't bend down so low anymore."

Her front room was comfortably furnished. A loveseat and an armchair in maple stood in the center. The backs and arms were covered with crocheted antimacassars. A dining table of the same color seated four.

A cabinet like a lowboy was on the other side of the table. On top was a crystal bowl on an old lace runner, which might have once been white, now the same color as the crocheted antimacassars. Some envelopes stacked neatly and tied with a string were at the bottom of the bowl. I glanced at the handwriting on the top envelope and recognized Charles' left handed script. On the sides of the bowl were several framed pictures of him. A black and white 5x7 of him with Cap and Gown. A colored snapshot in a silver frame of mother and son in front of what looked like some college dormitory. The colors have faded making the figures appear ghostlike. Still, you could not miss the facial resemblance. In front, in a wood frame was Charles in a cardigan, smiling, by the doorway of his bookshop before it moved to the Castro. On the other side, there was a picture of her as a much younger woman taken in a studio. She was wearing a white blouse with a lace collar, looking squarely at the lens, unsmiling.

I knelt on the floor in front of the cabinet and pulled out the drawer she had pointed to.

"There should be a green cardboard box in the bottom." A piece of brown wool yarn held it together as I pulled it out from under some tablecloths and napkins.

She motioned for me to bring it over to her. On the box top was the Singer sewing machine label with its logo below the letters.

She untied the yarn and opened the box.

"This was my grandfather." She pulled out a photograph of a middle-aged man with spectacles and a thick mustache, framed with the name of the studio embossed on the bottom. He was wearing a suit jacket and a vest. A watch chain ran across the front. I looked at his frozen stare but noticed the same high arching brows and firm chin of Charles. There were also pictures of great aunts and uncles dressed in their stiff fineries of the gay nineties. At the bottom of the box of pictorial family history, I noticed a pocket-sized leather picture frame shaped like a locket.

"Who's in this?" I picked it up and held it to her.

"My grandfather's uncle. Go ahead and open it."

The interior was lined with maroon velvet on one side. I could barely make out the ghostly image on the other side. I felt I was looking at someone under the surface of a murky pond at dusk. The first time I saw a daguerreotype was in an exhibit of photographic history at the Museum.

"Charles used to be fascinated by that when he was a child." She paused for a moment, then decided to tell me, "Family history has it that great, great uncle never married."

Charles told me it was a code word for men of a certain persuasion in those days, like Walt Whitman. I wondered why she was telling me all this, then felt comforted that this was probably her way of saying she knew what was going on with Charles' life. It was in the family, and she was all right with it.

I thought of the day I told my mother, after being fortified by years in the therapist's office and practiced encouragement from support groups. My mother waited till I settled down a bit with my nervous fidgeting, then took a sip from her jasmine teacup. Once again, her words came back to me, said without raising the tone of her voice.

"You should ask your father about the male bordellos of old Beijing."

Charles' mother closed the box and handed it to me. "I want you to keep these," she said.

"Nobody would want them after I'm gone," she explained when she saw my hesitation.

"I'll take good care of them." I held her hand in both of mine and realized she understood only too well her son's condition. At that moment, I felt she could have been my own mother. What would my mother have felt if she had to face the reality of having to see me gone before her?

The other day when I was going through a bottom drawer of my desk, which contained my father's medals and documents, I saw that box again, with the Singer sewing machine label on top.

I put Isherwood's book back on the shelf. Outside my window, the few lights on the ocean side of Twin Peaks twinkled like

28

兔

candles floating on the River Ganges in memory of the dead. Adele was continuing with her soft purr under the comforter.

Those were the most tender moments between us now. Proust's words on Albertine could not have felt more true to me. "The pleasure of seeing her sleep, which was as sweet to me as that of feeling her live…"

Adele asleep, I snuggling up against her and remembering the times when she first leaned against my shoulder in the back of the evening bus taking us from San Miguel to Mexico City, instead of the verbal jousts when face to face.

My friend who was with us on that trip, sat in front of the bus because she did not want to miss the sunset of the Mexican hillside. I suspected she sensed something was developing between Adele and me. This friend became very fond of Adele and later had warned her.

"Never get involved with a gay man."

On my way back to bed, I stopped in front of the leather locket on the shelf next to the books, and looked at Charles' picture as a boy. I had put it in place of the daguerreotype of his ancestor. I placed it there on the day after the memorial service for him at the bookshop. On the shelf, next to it was his favorite photograph of Walt Whitman.

I could see on the same shelf the three-volume set of Proust's "*A Remembrance of Things Past*" he gave me as a birthday present when the Moncrieff and Kilmartin translation came out with its distinctive Art Deco cover. He felt it was a better translation than the earlier one.

The sale of his bookshop did not bring as much as we had hoped. It was all Charles had left to pay for the rest of his mother's days at the rest home. The young man who helped run the bookshop when Charles was ill embezzled most of the money in the bank account.

The gay bookstore chain with branches in Los Angeles and New York, which Charles had recognized as his competition already settled on a storefront right in the middle of the Castro. There was no incentive for that chain to pay much for what remained in Charles' inventory.

My worries about his funds were short lived. When I visited her, she always held onto my hand tightly as if that was all she had left. Her caretakers at the home told me she stayed in bed most of the day and usually left her food trays untouched. Fannie did not wake up from her sleep a few months later.

The damaged, still usable, red Beetle, was left to Otis, so he had something to drive to school. Charles hoped this would be some encouragement for him to continue in his studies. The car had been with Charles from the days when he was a hippie junior high teacher, and it was showing battle scars even before now, but Charles held on to it like an old comrade.

On a recent afternoon, I went to a bookshop I have never heard of on the other side of the hill from where I live. For Chinese New Year I was given Murakami's *Kafka on the Shore*, a book I already had. I traced it by the bookmark inside to a store in a neighborhood, which barely had some scattered storefronts when I moved into my home in the City. Now I could see it was alive with new shops, a French bistro on the corner with people waiting to get in and an upscale Japanese sushi bar across the street. But there was still a cozy neighborhood feeling reminding me a little of the Castro of thirty years ago.

The bookshop was next door to a store selling fifties furniture at considerable mark up. Its owner gave me a warm, welcoming look and very amiably took my book back in exchange.

"Look around and see if there's anything you'd like."

On the counter was a pile of poetry journals with the title of the bookshop across the front. Bird and Beckett. People came in and chatted with the owner like old friends.

28

兔

"How long have you been here?" I asked, as I took in the wide range of the inventory, new and used.

"Almost two years. Used to be the neighborhood library." He pointed to the old fashioned wooden bookshelves set into the wall, the kind Charles told me he would have liked for his shop.

On one of the shelves, a new paper back of Isherwood's *A Single Man* caught my eye. Colin Firth, the actor who played George was front cover center, shadowy in the background, Julianne Moore who was in the role of his friend, Charley. They made me think of the night I saw the film.

I wandered toward the back and saw an area off to the side carpeted with an old Persian rug and chairs for reading. Next to it was the section for poetry.

The recently published, *C.P. Cavafy, the Unfinished Poems*, translated by David Mendelsohn, was on the display table. I had read that Mendelsohn was more sensitive to the homosexuality of this Alexandrian Greek poet, something that was often if not completely submerged in some older translations and commentaries, and I was looking forward to reading it.

I picked up the slim book and settled into an armchair over the rug. The signs of wear gave it a feeling of familiarity and coziness, and the chair was as comfortable as the one that used to be in Charles' old bookshop near the Castro. Same kind of armchair Isherwood sat in, that weekend he was there. Charles left it in his bookshop after the Isherwood signing, the same armchair Charles had kept from his first bookshop in the Bay Area.

As I opened Mendelsohn's translation of Cavafy, I thought of the evening of that first weekend Charles and I spent together, reading by the lantern and moonlight. I had not heard of this poet before Charles introduced me to his work.

"I think you'll like him," Charles said as he handed me a copy of Cavafy's poems to read.

As I flipped onto the middle of Mendelsohn's new translations, the title of the poem caught my eye, *Birth of a Poem.*

I read the opening line,

One night when the beautiful light of the moon
poured into my room . . . imagination, taking
something from life.

Charles would have liked it, if he were still around.

I have a small cushion in my study with a bee embroidered in front, which Charles gave me from that time when he compared our lives to bees on the same path of flight.

Chapter Twenty-Nine

龍

Raindrops on a fresh maple outside the window and feathered steps of a crow on the stones in the garden, he began his note.

I was relieved to hear from him. The last time Jon and I had tea together, catching up with our lives of the past year, I was alarmed when I saw him pop in methadone tablets like M&Ms during the few hours of the afternoon. He has been suffering from his injured back from the freak fall over ten years ago, had given up working and been living with persistent back pain.

From where I parked the car he shuffled slowly with a cane toward the teahouse. I had to slow down to be in step alongside him. His black, Brooks Brothers sports coat was as I had remembered, but his white shirt was not up to his usual standards of spiffy ironing. He was someone who was not an open door inviting entry, but entry must wait till invitation was extended.

Jon's note continued, toward its end. "I noticed the shocked expression in your eyes and posture last time."

He has never been one to miss any nuances in words and expressions, and was just as watchful about his own.

Our teas together over time have become a ritual that I looked forward to. Not only in seeing him but also in enabling me to remember the friends we have known separately and together over the same time, for so many years.

His choice of words and affinity for Asian things often brought me into a world I dreamt of finding myself. The world of mid nineteenth century, which did not seem so long ago, yet felt far away and unreachable for me now. Afternoons in the tea house, the only sounds the slow drip from the bamboo spout over a garden pond and an occasional distant temple bell. A book valet with favorite books and tea and sweets. A world that vanished even before I was born but close enough to be in conversations of my parents and their friends.

When we met over three decades ago, Jon was in his twenties, but more mature in many ways than I was, past forty. We both lamented the loss of that world before cell phones and automobiles, not to mention laptops and lunar landings. A world when he was in his ironed, white shirt and shorts, walking safely as a six-year-old, book bag in hand, to the house of his neighbor who showed him hand-colored pictures of gardens and temples of old Kyoto, Japan.

In this lost world, Jon and I found solace, apart from the Men's Group we checked into every week. We wrote each other many paged letters, long in words yet leaving many feelings unsaid because it would be too unseemly. Only occasionally a phrase braved the page to express the emotions we found too hard to articulate when face to face.

We agreed to remain, friends, the way we were, before those words, which edged toward admitting deeper attachment, saw the open page. He seemed more than happy that I took the initiative.

I suggested this teahouse not far from where he had recently moved. A few steps across the street from the old Zen Center where Charles used to live. The area has become gentrified from the time when I used to spend some weekends there with Charles.

A young Asian came up to help us find a table, Japanese or Vietnamese because of his height, but more likely Japanese from his shy body language. We both noticed the sweet, easy smile, flashing bone porcelain teeth behind lips of pale cherry blossoms.

"How about the inside room?" I looked at my friend as he leaned on his walking stick.

He gave quick consent, the way he usually did with things he thought were not worth belaboring.

We settled for a small table at the far end of the room by the window, while admiring the large sunken square in the middle, making it possible for customers to drop down their legs and not be forced to sit with knees bent under torso, but where traditionally the Japanese placed a foot warming hibachi for the winter months. We chose the table away from the larger center seating, to avoid having others around us, making conversation less intimate.

"Very friendly," I commented after the young man took our orders of teas, "easy on the eyes, too."

I guessed the age of the waiter to be about the age of my friend when we first met, cheeks flushed with youth. I caught Jon's eyes for a second and wondered if he might be having that same feeling of distant recognition.

He adjusted himself in the straight-backed chair to accommodate his back, and I reached for a cushion to help.

"Let me try it without." He had become acutely attuned to the amount of stress and pain his injured back could tolerate.

My friend used to be the poster boy for the gym buffed and muscle perfect among our friends. Biceps bulging out of polo sleeves, thighs filling his 501's, and what I could well visualize, washboard for a stomach, even though he shunned tight-fitting shirts. Light gold ringlets framed his well-formed forehead and eyes soft as spring water.

After my teenage daughter met him, close to three decades ago, she always referred to him as Curly Haired Jon, in order to distinguish him from another Jon I knew.

Fifteen years later Adele remembered him as Bamboo Jon, from our trip together to a bamboo farm. A row of tall stippling bamboo outside the window of his new home was what he wanted, he had said.

"This place has over two hundred varieties of them, one of the largest collection this side of the Pacific," he had told us on our drive up north of Sebastopol. His meticulous research into bamboo nurseries did not surprise me.

He pursued his interests and passions with Nabokovian attention to details I have not seen in many others. He was my only non-Chinese friend who was as much in love with bamboo as I was.

For me, it was something close to my soul. A prose poem by Su Che of the Song Dynasty expressed it well:

What I love is the Dao 道 *which I express through bamboo. At first, when I lived in retirement on the south slope of Mount Chong, I made my home in a grove of tall bamboo, looking and listening without awareness so that they did not affect my mind. In the morning, the bamboo were my companions; in the evening, they were my friends. I ate and drank amongst them, and rested in their shade . . . At first, I looked and enjoyed them. Now, I enjoy them without consciousness of doing so. Suddenly, forgetting the brush in my hand and the paper in front of me, I am instantly inspired and forests of bamboo appear."*

Song zhu yan nian was a Chinese saying alluding to the sturdiness and longevity of the special grass and pine on many salutations I had seen since childhood.

In those early days after we met, I had imagined myself leaning on a walking stick when years went by, while he would still be sturdy in his sixties. What I admired more than his youthful appearance was his measured warmth and carefully chosen words, phrasing that reminded me of my father, even though he was two decades younger than myself.

Heretofore, he had conveyed to me his feelings in what he held back.

Thus, I wasn't sure how he would feel if I helped him with a

cushion in the teahouse now, in spite of my natural reaction on seeing someone with evident discomfort. I decided to put the cushion
at the ready in my hand onto the back of my own chair instead.
"I have to be careful with my own back, too," I said, using it as a
cover for the gesture unsolicited.

"How is Willard?" Jon told me once, his close friend, Willard,
used to work in Charles' bookshop.

Our young Asian brought Jon's Oolong from the hills of Taiwan
and my Japanese Genmaicha in the traditional iron teapot.

Last time we got together, he still managed to invite me to his new
flat, pouring tea from the Stickley table in his living room facing the
neighboring church, which had been turned into a Buddhist temple.

"These are from Willard's flat." Jon pointed out, as I settled
into the Stickley chair, which I remembered along with the other
pieces from my chat with Willard in his living room. When he
had to be moved to the Jewish care home from the house they
once shared, he gave some of them to Jon. A pair of Ming chairs
on the side in the hallway, Jon had bought years ago when he
moved in to the flat below Willard's, looked to be in good company with the American classics.

I remembered the house they shared, a Victorian, close to completely gutted and remodeled inside to suit them, with a meticulously maintained façade. It was nestled in a quiet lane just at the
border of the Castro.

The bottom flat where Jon lived was Charles' last home. I had
to box up the large book collection from his library after he died.

A few months after the memorial at Charles' Bookshop, Jon
mentioned in passing, "Willard said I could stay in the flat for as
long as I wanted to."

When invited over to his new home several months later, I
saw the flat had been totally altered from when Charles was there.

The series of small Victorian rooms in the middle were made

into a large, open space. Jon showed me his proud new acquisitions. A large opium bed and a ceiling high Ming wardrobe cabinet were the major pieces. Two Ming chairs with their clean, simple lines flanked the bed. I envied most his four floor length scrolls of ancient calligraphy on a side hall, the way they would have been in the reception room of my mother's ancestral home in Beijing, even though he told me in his understated way they were not originals but stone rubbings purchased on his trip to China along with the antique furniture. It was Jon's appreciation of these Asian things and aversion to ostentation that particularly endeared him to me throughout the years.

I could tell he was happy with his new place and it was Jon's subtle way of telling me about himself and Willard. I did not have any hard feelings. By then I had moved on from our past, although the feelings of mutual affection were always there, and I was happy to see him settled into a place of his liking. Judging from how sensitive Jon was to nuances and feelings, I doubted he would have invited me if he had sensed I might have problems with it.

Charles was already gone. I did not have any feeling that Charles had left any part of himself in this house that Jon was showing to me, unlike the feelings that crept in when I walked into the store which used to be Charles' bookshop on Market Street. I could still see where the old bookshelves used to be, where he had the signed photo of Walt Whitman on the wall, and the backroom where he had his little workspace and chair to write.

I saw the place toward the back of the bookshop where he had a table. The spot where I stood greeting the friends who came to the memorial service for Charles I had arranged. The spot where Gene came up to me to thank me at the end and invited me to have lunch a week later. Gene was one of the earliest of his friends Charles introduced me to, and I felt Charles would be happy that he had something to do with bringing Gene and me together later on.

On one of my visits to Jon's new place, he asked, "Do you want to say hello to Willard?"

He had told me earlier about an exchange between Willard and Charles. When the new translation of Proust's tome he ordered for the Bookshop arrived, Charles told Willard he thought it was better than the earlier Moncrieff editions. Willard replied he had read it in the original French and noted Charles was speechless.

Remembering Charles' pride in his book knowledge, I guessed the relationship between the two was not a cordial one. Charles was very proud of the bookshop he built up single handedly and his Whitman collection for which his shop was named was one of the most complete around. On demand, he was usually able to pull out, even the early obscure gay authors and subject matters from his considerable stock.

Willard came from very different circumstances. His family was listed in the Fortune 500, Jon told me once. Along with many trips to France, he picked up a master's degree in French literature of the nineteenth century. He helped out in the bookshop because he shared Charles' love, if not the passion, for books. He really had no need to work.

Willard had transformed his upper flat from its Victorian past even more drastically than Jon's downstairs. It was a large open space, reminiscent of a Soho loft in New York and the East coast where Willard's family fortune was rooted. The front had a living room library with the Stickley Arts and Crafts armchairs and tables, which were now in Jon's home. At the other end of this long rectangular space, beyond an unadorned wood screen, I could see a large bed of the same style.

As we sat in the space between his bookcases up front, it didn't take long before the cool feelings between them were confirmed, when Charles' name was mentioned. Willard was doubtless also aware of my relationship with Charles given the fairly close circle of people we knew in those early days.

During that afternoon visit between cups of herbal tea, I noticed the tremor when he held his cup, an early sign of the Parkinson's disease. Eventually, it was no longer possible for him to live in his own home, even though Jon was close by in the flat below.

"Not good." I heard the sadness and resignation in Jon's reply to my question about his friend. "He had to be moved into a lock-up unit recently." Willard had wandered out in the neighborhood of his rest home recently and couldn't find his way back.

"I'm the only person visiting daily," Jon added. The family back East was conveniently far away to avoid visiting its black sheep. I imagined with the assets at their disposal, his relatives could easily fly out on their own chartered jets if they chose to. Although Jon said they were never intimate as lovers, he and Willard lived in their separate flats in the same Victorian for over twenty years.

Listening to what Jon was saying now, I thought about their time together and those months when Jon and I wrote our letters to each another. I realized why Jon was the first to notice we were getting too close at the time so long ago. He had the wisdom and foresight to see that it would not have worked between us. I would not have been able to accept the detachment and distance he needed.

But I also realized his life with Willard ended up, nevertheless, with the responsibility now of overseeing the day-to-day needs and care of his disabled friend.

"He looks forward to walking with me every day. But it's not easy lately because he stumbles quite a bit and my back is not in the best condition to catch him." I pictured the two of them, one with a cane and the other with the tremor and the worsening gait of his disease.

The hopelessness and helplessness of those last days with Charles came back to me, even though Willard's illness was a more slowly progressive one.

"And how is the venerable Matriarch?" I thought about Jon's mother who was now also dependent on his care. At our last tea

29
龍

together, I learned his father had died from a fall in inside their plush, old world retirement home uphill from Japan Town.

"She's getting more and more impossible, if you can imagine. Everything is my fault, even if she misplaced something in her own room."

"It was a shame she had children," he added, "She never gave me the feeling she ever wanted us." He had two older sisters. Now the matriarch was in her late nineties. He was committed to seeing her once a week. Both sisters had easy alibis, living far away. The older lived as far away as Finland, the cold ambiance and isolation suited her well, something she had become accustomed to in her upbringing. When he forced himself to offer more frequent visits out of concern, his mother declined. I thought from a mother who did not really want children around, Jon had to overcome quite a lot before he could get close to anyone.

Yet I remembered seeing the exquisitely executed petit point with swans in the foreground she had done for him, in the muted colors of a Song Dynasty Chinese landscape, hanging in the entry vestibule of his old flat. Something he seemed to have cherished as a rare manifestation of her maternal feelings.

"Enough of my groans and woes." He forced a smile and looked at me, the same clear eyes which caught my attention so long ago. "How are your children?"

They were now close to two decades older than he was when we first met. Would my daughter still recognize him, Curly Haired Jon? A rare close friend from that period of my life who was still around. Gone were Ernie and Charles and Gene who had shared my life more intimately back then.

"Oh, they are fine," I said, picking up my cup of Genmaicha next to his mountain Oolong. Then, I wondered, how I was perceived by my own children, now that they have become parents themselves.

Chapter Thirty

"I have decided to let go of my opium bed." It was Jon on the phone from San Francisco.

I had felt more of old China in his room with the antique opium bed than when I had visited the Mainland China of today.

Sasha, his Russian Blue, hid under the bed, when we lingered over a pot of mountain Oolong. His piles of books and cushions sat on the bed. Four floor-to-ceiling scrolls of stone rubbings of the work of the Song Dynasty calligrapher, Mi Fu, hung on the other side of the room. The only thing missing, for me, from this quintessence of a scholar's studio of old China would be a *shu tong* or book valet who brought in the books and tea service with the Oolong.

I could picture his opium bed in front of his living room window, he had placed it there when the bamboos he bought on our trip together shot up to provide a feathered dappling from the southern sun. It was from the Bamboo Sorcery, a nursery specializing in bamboo, he had found and suggested when Adele came along with us. She was new in my life, and I wanted her to meet my circle of friends. With Jon's affinity for Asian things, I thought they would find common ground.

"I am thinking of moving my piano into the living room," Jon said explaining the reason for the sale of his Chinese antique. The internet phone line allowed us to call each other as if we were in the same city, even though I was talking to him from a medieval town in Umbria, where I have been three months of every year since my retirement.

Italy has the most of the world's beauty, it has been said. Adele was the one who had pulled me into this part of the Mediterranean. Her fervor for the land sometimes made me suspect that in another life Adele was an Italian. She seemed to breathe easier and smile more readily as soon as we walked on Italian soil, even though she was born and raised in China and had seen its treasures and tradition first hand.

"So, it will be nice to have strains of sonatas echoing from your tall ceilings," I replied to Jon's plan of making room for his piano.

"I haven't been able to practice for so long." I noticed the touch of melancholy in his voice. "Don't know what it will sound like." My friend alluded to his injury over three years ago.

"When did you decide to let go of the opium bed?" I was also feeling the loss of what was all part of the old world of my childhood that his room brought back to me.

It was a world of gardens and cicada songs, servants and subtle secrets. From *luohan kang* used as opium beds in an old mansion in Shanghai to a summer of old homes hidden in a maze of hutongs of old Beijing.

It was the summer after my eighth birthday, the year after the long eight-year war with the Japanese ended, and my mother was at last able to return to her old home in Beijing. Chewing gum and candy bars and chocolates were flooding the sweet shops on old Avenue Joffre around the corner from where we lived in Shanghai.

The pedicab took us to *Tong Zongbu Hutong*, the section of the old Tartar city full of narrow lanes and alleyways, but also close to where many Foreign Delegations used to be and where my grandfather had his home. It was the house where he stayed when he was on home leave while working in Russia as a diplomat from the last rulers of the Manchu Dynasty of China to the period of the Early Republic.

An old manservant pulled back the tall, creaky gate, revealing a house with deep gardens, both having seen better days, which reminded me of a movie I had just seen in Shanghai before we left, about a haunted house where people died mysteriously from eating watermelon chilled in an ancient well. Overgrown grasses and vines covered the long stone path and trellises along the way. The shade gave me a chill in my short sleeves, even though the cicadas were chirping loudly in the sun-drenched branches above the shade.

"Your uncle has been expecting you." The old man expressed his obvious joy in seeing my mother again by repeatedly bowing along the way. Towering trees and more vines on the second floor spilled over the terrace, looking as if it was barely hanging on.

Half a flight up, stone steps took us to the front door. I was just tall enough to peek through the etched glass panel. The inside hallway was as dark as the wood on the door itself.

"You stayed here when you were young?" I looked up at my mother.

"When I was home from Russia," she answered. She had told me she had spent most of her childhood years with her father in Russia. "He did not want to take your *Waipo* abroad because she had tiny bound lotus feet." It was a very desirable asset when she was married off to my grandfather by her guardian as the orphaned daughter of a prominent magistrate of Shanghai, but she became an embarrassment for a Chinese diplomat in Russia.

My mother's uncle was waiting for us by the door to the living room. I was surprised he did not look much older than my mother. Tall and wearing the same kind of round, horn-rimmed eyeglasses as I had seen on my grandfather and distinguished looking in a dark blue, silk gown with a high mandarin collar. Most of the furniture was Chinese redwood, close to dark mahogany, except for a grand piano at the far end of the room. It was draped in black, but I could still see its intricately carved legs.

The manservant brought in a cold drink in tall glasses on a cinnabar tray that had seen better days. "I had them get your favorite drink." The Great Uncle turned to my mother.

"*Suan Mei Tang*!" My mother held up her drink, deep plum colored in the glass.

"I still remember when we used to play together in the summers, and you always asked for this drink afterwards," he said smiling, "but it's hard to get the real thing after the War."

I took a sip and put it down. It was slightly sweet, but also had a biting tartness.

"And I remember once you crushed my hands when you won't let me eat the peach you had shaken loose from the branches." My mother answered back playfully.

"Did Great Uncle and you live in this same house?" I ventured a question.

"No. He came over to play because there were lots of children in this house."

"May I see the room where you stayed?" I asked my mother.

"Sure. Let me lead the way upstairs." Great Uncle answered for her.

I could hardly wait and rushed ahead up the stairs. There was a door to the right of the top landing that was half open when I got up there. I saw a young man jump down from a large curtained bed and run to shut the door. He was undressed and was clutching a silk sheet for cover.

"Wait for me to lead the way!" I heard Great Uncle's footsteps behind me, followed by my mother's. There was a note of concern and anxiousness in his voice, which I interpreted as disapproval that I had dashed up ahead of them.

My mother's room faced the back, and Great Uncle had to unlock the door. He turned on the light, and I saw the furniture was all covered in dark, dusty shrouds. There was no natural light. He pushed open the shutters, revealing a large garden in the back, taken over by undergrowth. There was a hushed sense of abandon with the thickets of unattended bushes, save for the sighing of cicadas in the branches of a surviving willow.

My mother followed him and looked at the old garden of her memories, trying to see through the overgrowth.

"That was the peach tree!" Her voice raised in excitement and finger pointed toward the deeper part of the garden.

When we were back down to the living room, a large plate of cut watermelon was brought in.

"No peaches." My mother smiled playfully again at her uncle. They must have been great playmates when growing up, I thought, but at the same time remembering the deadly watermelon from the ancient well of the haunted house movie I had seen.

"These are just in season, and I know you like them too."

"So are you living alone in this old house?"

"More or less," he said without elaboration. But I noticed he glanced quickly at me then turned away and added, "lucky they didn't do too much damage during the Occupation."

My mother took a slice of melon with the toothpicks already in it. "I am told a high level Japanese officer lived here for a while." Her uncle continued, recovering his composure.

"It's amazing you were able to get it back so soon."

"There's still a lot of work to be done. As you can see, I have let the garden and the balconies go for the time being."

We didn't stay for dinner as Great Uncle invited us to do. My mother knew he only had the old manservant in the house, and I wanted to get out of there before I was offered the watermelon.

"Come back any time you like and bring Didi." Great Uncle was using a common way of addressing a young boy like me. He saw us to the gate himself and waved at us as we got into the pedicab his manservant had hailed and ready for us.

"What was in that room by the stairway?" I asked as soon as we turned the corner from the hutong.

"That was my grandmother's room with the opium bed. Your Tai Waipo's room."

The image of the young man clutching the sheet over his body lingered in my head. Somehow, I knew better than ask my mother about what I saw.

"I am thinking of asking the Chinese shop where I bought it if they will take it back." Jon's voice echoed the sense of loss that I was feeling.

"I wish I had room in my house for your opium bed," I said over the phone.

I wished I could hold on to some piece of that world, not just memories at Auntie Lu's and my great grandmother's bedroom with the opium beds, but also a world that seemed to continue to tug at me, sometimes when I least expected it.

Chapter Thirty-One

馬

The drive through Willamette Valley from Portland to where he lived had a familiar look although I had never been to that part of the country. Then I realized it reminded me of the old Roman Road in the Upper Tiber River Valley of Umbria in early spring. When I got an apartment in Italy after retirement, Vincent told me he felt the loss of a good friend. I promised him I would visit him wherever I moved and invited him to visit us in Italy when he felt like it. But he had not taken me up on the offer this time, even though he had visited us when Adele and I were in Florence for three months some years ago.

Different shades of green layering on the hillsides were hymnals of Vincent's youth, I imagined, from tender lime bordering on chartreuse to dark evergreens. Names of wineries stopped my eye as the GPS directed me off the Interstate onto the old country road south. I was expecting to find leftover farm towns when I first heard of my friend's move back to where he spent his childhood days.

The sign on the driveway of his retirement home read "The Villa," alluded auspiciously to vacation homes of the rich and famous along the Mediterranean, but was actually a two-story sprawling U-shaped building with well-kept grounds in front.

"Hope I didn't scare your neighbors or frighten the horses on the street," I said, repeating back one of Vincent's favorite bon mots, as he stepped into the living room, closing the door to the balcony behind him.

"Nothing will surprise my neighbors anymore," he said with a twinkle in his eyes, "I'm the only man here with tinted permed hair."

Honey blond ringlets with hints of silvery gray framed his cherubic face. He still had the perennial flushed cheeks, which gave him the look of having just come out of a bar or close to having a baby tantrum. His belly protruded more than I last saw him. But I knew he no longer touched alcohol because of all the pills he was taking.

"Not bad," I said, looking over his large living room with walls covered by his favorite things. "For someone who was attracted to baby Jesus from age three."

I could still see him the first time he walked into the men's group in San Francisco. His partner of twenty-five years died of a heart attack while working on a project in Saudi Arabia and Vincent got the news on a slip of paper handed to him five days later while he was chairing a meeting in front of a large group at the Academy.

Even though the effect of the Stonewall Riots on Sheridan Square had reverberated in the gay community in San Francisco for over a decade, it had not yet reached the corporate world of Bechtel where his partner was employed.

"I was not listed as a member of the family to be notified," Vincent told our men's group.

Lithium finally pulled him back from the black hole he fell into, after settling his partner's affairs. And his therapist referred him to the group to give him some added support.

His gut wrenching story about not being notified till almost a week after his partner of two and a half decades died made me want to reach out to him. I was also amazed by his memory of being turned on by the naked baby Jesus, when he was only three. It could not have been further away from my own retarded realization, past my mid-twenties. But somehow, we became friends.

I envied his quick one-liner repartee while being usually tongue tied myself in front of people I didn't know. I suspect he admired my knowledge in the worlds of science and medicine, which might as well have been outer space for him. In a way, we each envied in the other qualities we lacked in ourselves. We did share a love of books and the world of the arts, even though he was far better read in early English literature and graduated from art school.

Over the years, I had seen him through several more episodes of major depression, falling back again and again into that dark abyss before we first met. Being on opposite ends in temperament, I was afraid he would see me as hopelessly upbeat, but perhaps he realized the singer within might not always be as happy as his tunes. He sensed a deeper bond between us and I told him I would always be there for him.

"You promised to help me," he reminded me, when I refused to give him a prescription to do away with himself. He was seeing a therapist, and I wasn't sure that was just another down turn, something which he would overcome again.

"I'm glad you didn't," he admitted later, wearing long sleeves to cover his cuts, when I picked him up from the hospital several weeks later.

He was there for me, when I stewed and fretted about my dates and dilemmas, his unadorned advice was invaluable even if the truth might not have always been what I wanted to hear.

"I see you have all your pictures and treasures up again," I said, taking in the walls of his new apartment.

He had a shingled English cottage for close to forty years in a small town just north of the Golden Gate, the one he shared with his partner. A stream meandered through the back garden and his living room walls were covered with paintings and artwork they collected over the years of their lives together.

His friends and I had to convince him to give up the cottage when he could no longer keep up the maintenance. He could only afford a small studio in the retirement facility nearby, and he was miserable in the cramped space, having had to put much of what hung on the walls of his old cottage in storage.

"Let me show you around." He sounded happy with his new home.

Its two bedrooms, two baths and the large living room with a balcony, where he could sit outside and have his cigarette, gave him plenty of space for most of his prized paintings and treasures to be back up on the walls.

His favorite nineteenth-century English landscapes still occupied the prominent space they had on his old wall. Scenes of ships and English sea sides on another wall reminded him of where he met his partner. The light filtered through the arts-and-crafts stained glass of a standing lamp showed off his collection with a soft, warm glow. The place had a good measure of the richness of art and culture approximating his old home.

"Let me show you my study." He beckoned mischievously toward the second bedroom. I could tell from the tone of his voice this was not going to be what he showed his sister or niece. "This is where I'm going to put you up."

A whole wall shielded from view by the door was covered with pictures of men in various stages of undress. When he swung the door away from the wall, he pointed out an old photograph of a balding man with spectacles, airs of a respected professor, seated in a wood paneled library. Next to him stood a young man in a crisp shirt and bow tie, with drawers dropped to his ankles. The professor's hand held the youngster's privates, like a prized museum specimen standing up at full attention under the inspection.

"Well, your fourteen-year-old great nephew would have gotten quite an education if you brought him into this room." Vincent had told me every month he hosted his family, which lived within a half hour by car. He marshaled them to play word games with prizes and gifts. No, he said, his study was off limits.

"I don't know if you have room on any wall for what I brought you." I handed him the large brown paper package I put against my overnight bag when I arrived. I watched his reaction as he pulled out the multi-panel photo of a man at various stages of lathering himself in the shower.

"I hope you like it," I said. "I tried to get one with classic Greek or Roman columns in the background, but the artist said he ran out of those when I asked him."

"I like this much better. I have enough of those classic poses. But I don't have anything like this one." He examined each image more closely, and added, "I like it he's at various stages of arousal."

He put the photograph in the middle of his large dining table for twelve. "I'm going to enjoy it close to me for a while before I hang it up on the wall."

Then he ran his fingers over the groin of the nude. The familiar naughty gesture made me realize he had not lost his zest for life. He had been complaining to me when I checked in with him on the phone that all the pills made him unable to even satisfy himself.

To most friends past eighty, I imagined this would not be much of a problem. But for Vincent libido was a major part of his life. He told me once he was accustomed to four times a day, in his adult life before all the pills.

Those were the days before many of our friends were struck down by the new disease. We were clueless, including my colleagues specializing in Infectious Diseases.

Nixon had toasted Mao in Beijing, with *maodai*, the fiery Chinese version of vodka, followed quickly by Watergate and his fall from grace. The war in Southeast Asia ended, and some of us felt our protests had contributed to its ending in some small measure. We thought we had finally overcome and overtaken our past.

Caribbean tours overflowing with gay men were cruising from island to island. Vincent and I shared a room and threw away an old taboo. In those days, we were either "sisters" or lovers. Calling ourselves "sisters," we were sticking up our middle finger at being labeled effeminate.

Sex between "sisters" or buddies were taboo. Neither Vincent nor I had any illusions of becoming lovers, but playing together on that overheated cruise ship when the occasion presented itself came naturally.

This was a unique dimension to our friendship that made us feel more open minded, overcoming another taboo of our past. It even survived Vincent's numerous battles with his demon of depression.

"Would you like to freshen up a bit before we go to lunch?" Vincent asked, looking at the old English grandfather clock, which used to stand in the entry hall of his old home.

"When do they stop serving downstairs?" I had seen a cozy dining room with tablecloth and plate settings on my way up to his apartment. It wasn't crowded, and people were being served at tables set for four, although some only had two or three people.

"I never go down to eat anymore." He curled up his lips in disapproval, the distinct way he was so adept at doing. "The food is terrible."

"I thought you said the food was better than the Redwoods," I remembered he told me when he first moved in the food was an improvement over the old retirement home in Marin County where he stayed for two years and always complained about the food and the people.

"No, I got tired of the same old stuff. I'd rather go into town and choose what I want."

I was happy for Vincent that he could afford to go out for his meals and choose what he wanted, but I made a note to myself he had not made any friends in this new place to share a table in the dining room or found people to talk about books and art and his old world around San Francisco.

"Okay. I'll be ready in five minutes," I said, thinking I did need to use the bathroom.

It was across from the study, and every item in there had his signature touch. Vincent's pictures covered the walls with frames he had retouched, several I recognized from his old home. Forest green hand towels with an appliquéd cowboy on a saddle, next to a small vase filled with flowers, which on closer look were made of paper.

He did not want to be pegged as "piss elegant," he told me once, adding kitsch to good art was his specialty. On a small footlocker covered with a slightly worn tapestry, he laid out a set of matching towels and face cloth for me.

"You drive," he said when we were ready to step out.
"Still have your car?"
"I just use it around town." He once told me he would never give up his car.

As we settled into my rented compact, I remembered our trip together to British Columbia, another turning point in our friendship.

Vancouver was hosting the World Expo, and I booked us into a Bed and Breakfast advertised in *The Advocate*, a gay weekly started by a friend of someone I knew. Our gay hosts seemed like a nice young couple, and we settled into a large, well-appointed room with private bath for the night.

Past midnight, we were suddenly woken from our sleep by one of our hosts crashing through our bedroom door. He was closely followed by his lover, screaming and wielding a cleaver in one hand.

We scrambled out of bed without even time to put on any clothes and dashed toward the balcony. We didn't know whether we should jump or climb up from the balcony, but it seemed safer than staying in bed and waiting to be chopped in the confusion.

It felt like a more violent version of the Bellini opera, *La Sonnambula*, one Vincent had once taken me to see. The sleepwalker in the opera only walked into some man's bedroom, while our host said, by way of apology at breakfast, during the night his lover had forgotten their bedroom was rented out after having had a few drinks.

We decided not to stay another night and drove up to Victoria. I tried to look for another gay run B&B.

"I'm not going to stay at another one of your B&B's." Vincent's already flushed cheeks turned an intense beet red in frustration.

I hadn't realized how frightened he was from the experience of the night before, while I still wanted to support the gay businesses whenever I could. Luckily, the tourist information office had no trouble getting a room for us in a small locally run hotel in town.

That calmed my friend down. He gave me a hug and said he was sorry. I hugged him back, and we held each other tightly for a long while. I think we were both overjoyed our friendship survived, each realizing the limits of the other had been tested.

Years later when I picked him up from the hospital after another one of his serious breakdowns, he looked at me and said, "I knew somehow I could always count on you."

I gave his hand a squeeze. He added, "I guess I figured that out when you didn't blow up at me when I had my little temper tantrum up in Victoria."

But it also showed me for the first time what anxiety could bring out in him.

On our way to my rental car parked in the driveway of his retirement home, I noticed now how slowly he walked and the length of time it took him to get into the car and be buckled up. But he had no problems helping me navigate our way to downtown.

We parked close to Main Street. The buildings were mostly brick. He called my attention to the old hotel with a festive façade on the corner. It dated back to the turn of the last century, he said. "When I got my first bike, I used to peddle fifteen miles from my home to come up here." I thought of the lush verdant hillsides on the drive over.

He led the way to a restaurant tucked in back of a shop selling high-end bed linens and some non-essential gift items. He remembered coming here as a young man. "The food is still good," he added.

The young waitress took our orders and soon came back with a bowl of chowder for him and a toasted veggie sandwich for me.

I noticed his hand shaking badly as he tried bringing a spoonful of the soup to his lips. Not wanting him to feel embarrassed, I tried to look away.

"I eat slowly," he said.

"Have you had the tremors for a while?"

"Seems to be getting worse."

I couldn't think of the appropriate words of comfort without him sensing them to be glib. We knew each other too well, and I just let the subject drop. The silence, which followed didn't seem to bother either one of us. He pointed out at one time that it was a measure of the depth of our friendship.

We walked down Main Street after the meal and by habit, when we found ourselves together, checked out the shop windows. Most were clothing stores selling sportswear, as well as few stores of very tailored women's' fashions and a glittery one for teens or people past that age but still pretending to be. No antique shops, which we would both find hard to resist. A few windows had Out of Business signs.

Finally, a bookstore popped up, spreading across at least two store fronts. I suspected he saved it for the last. One of our favorite past times together.

Vincent used to be the backbone of our book group, especially with nineteenth century and early twentieth-century English writers.

He had to get rid of most of his three roomfuls of books when he moved out of his old home.

"I'm going across the street for a smoke. Meet you back here."

I saw the bench on the other side and was sorry he seemed to have lost some of his old passion for books.

A good selection of recent fiction surprised me inside the store. There were also used books tucked in between, which always sparked my interest. It gave me the feeling of Charles' bookshop in the Castro of years ago. But I told myself I wasn't going to be carrying books back on the plane. I had already bought a scarf at the airport for Adele from a store selling her kind of clothes.

He saw the small clothbound book of the President Obama's speeches in my hand when he came back. It also included two of Lincoln's important addresses, with an essay by Emerson. I was debating whether to buy it.

He saw my hesitation and said, "Let me buy that for you."

I wanted to tell him that I didn't want him to spend any money. But the book was reasonably priced and would be something for me to remember the visit. He told me earlier his finances were in good shape now. He was paying less for a larger place compared to the studio he had in the retirement home in Marin County. He even took his cousin on a cruise last year, and had money to spare, he whispered into my ear.

Leaving the bookshop, I could see he was getting a little tired. On our way back to the retirement home, I noticed the streets were clean, and cherry blossoms brightened neatly tended front yards. There were no flags. A relief for him, I thought. We had talked about our aversion to the flag waving we saw after 9/11, usurping any sense of true patriotism and what this country really stood for.

"I'm going to take a nap," he said, when we got back to his apartment. "But I first want to show you these books I pulled out for you."

He led me to a stack of six or seven coffee table-size books on a side table. They were part of his collection on male nudes. I sat down on the large sofa he draped in chintz with large pink and red flowers. They reminded him of his childhood in the early thirties, he said.

Some of the books had prints from late nineteenth-century and some more recent. He watched me slowly going through the series of black and white studies by George Platt Lynes, and their noticeable effect on the language of my body.

"I'm glad Adele didn't come," he said.

They liked each other when I first introduced them. He took several trips with us when Adele was still a newcomer in my life. Adele and a woman friend of mine shared a room, and Vincent and I took another. She even invited him to stay in her house when he was released from one of his hospitalizations.

She loved his artistic flair when he redecorated part of her house, and she was sympathetic to what he was going through.

But they had a fall out several years afterward, when he came to visit us in Italy. Both were tigers by the Chinese zodiac, strongwilled in their own way. He was twelve years ahead. I felt caught between a tiger and a tigress. They both realized what was happening. Afterwards, they avoided each other like two territorial cats.

Adele did not want to come with me on this visit. I could see Vincent and I would not be having the same conversations now if she came.

"I knew you'd like them," he said mischievously. "You can take them to your room."

"Yes," I said, "Your room with a view."

That evening, Vincent took me to the local Chinese restaurant. He told the owner he wanted her to meet me. The menu was so-so, but it was the best Chinese food the area had to offer, he explained.

31

馬

"This is my friend, the Chinese doctor." He told the woman and her husband at the counter when we walked in. The part of me ingrained with Chinese humility cringed at what I felt was an inflated introduction, even though Vincent was merely stating the fact.

But I also understood what Vincent was trying to do. He was remembering when we travelled together and had Chinese food in small towns, special dishes not on the menu often appeared after I talked to the owners in Chinese.

I hastened to explain to the couple I was retired now. But they seemed impressed nevertheless. They brought out several dishes Vincent had never seen on their menu. The food turned out to be honest home-cooking, although there were no other Chinese customers in sight.

"You can order the same things next time you come," I said when we were getting ready to go.

"I hope she remembers," he said and insisted on paying for the dinner.

"You paid for the plane tickets already." He was determined when I tried to protest further.

Back at his apartment, I said we had better go to bed early because he wanted us to drive to the coast to meet his niece for brunch the next day.

When I used to spend the night with him in his old home before Adele came into my life, we used to talk for hours before deciding to turn off the lights. The next morning, he always laid out a table for a full English breakfast with tea and scones, biscuits and homemade jam, something he always did with his late partner from England, he said.

I showered and got ready for bed with the Lynes' book I was looking at earlier in his living room. He kept the apartment pretty warm, so I barely needed the sheet for cover.

It took me back to the times before Adele came into my life and after Gene died. Although she never made me feel I couldn't look at male nudes and didn't seem to mind the ones in my study, it would be a little awkward and insensitive of me to be looking at a whole book of them with her next to me in bed.

31
馬

I left the door open, remembering the time he dropped in one afternoon when I was taking a nap. He came into my bedroom and slipped his hand under my sheet.

I had just gotten into a few pages of the nudes when he showed up at the doorway. Noticing my arousal, Vincent sat down to be a cheerleader until I scored my goal.

I offered to help him with what he used to always enjoy doing. But he said we'd better call it a night and get an early start for our trip in the morning. Over the years, we got to read each other's needs fairly well, going beyond the usual pretenses and inhibitions.

He told me later he had a hard time getting himself off nowadays, ever since his doctor put him on the pills for his anxiety attacks on top of the depression.

Before I turned off the bedside lamp, I thought of Adele. I wanted to call her, to reassure her I had not forgotten about her. But her bedtime was always much earlier than mine. Being afraid of waking her up gave me a convenient excuse, but to be honest, I also didn't want to break the completely relaxed mood I had just achieved.

I sensed some part of Adele needed the assurance that I was thinking of her. I often wondered whether her need was made more acute because she knew part of me was always attracted to a male body, or whether her own experiences of lost loves and loved ones intensified her needs.

When she said she was not going to come with me on this visit, I was partly relieved, yet I also knew I would be missing her.

As I pulled the sheet to cover myself for the night, my last thought before drifting off was whether she was going to like the silk shawl I bought her at the airport. It was surprising to find a shop there with things she might like, instead of the usual, last minute pick-up items for passengers.

The last time I found something special in an airport was in Rome, en route back from Cairo. It was a keychain in humming-bird colored enamels and silver. I bought two with different color combinations. One for my daughter and the other one, I gave to Adele, when we started seeing each other several years later.

"I want to let you know about Uncle Vinnie," Molly's voice was on the phone message.

The various times he tried to put an end to everything zipped across my eyes, like pages from an old diary.

"They found him the morning after in the bathtub," Molly said when I called her back.

I shuddered. Vincent and I used to talk about the bathtub scene in the film, *Diabolique*. Simone Signoret who starred in the 1955 film was one of our favorite actresses.

"He had cut both his wrists and ankles." Molly's voice was almost breaking into a sob. "It was horrible."

"Maybe I shouldn't have put him in the supervised unit." I could hear she was still trembling. "I thought he'd be safer…" Her voice trailed off again.

"Don't blame yourself, Molly." I tried to console the inconsolable. He was her favorite uncle, and she his favorite in the family—one who never left where he was born.

"She's the only one who understands me." He once told me.

I held on to the phone, even after Molly hung up, as if somehow if I hung on, she would come back to say it was all a mistake. It was not true. Vincent was still there.

I had the same feeling, when I learned that my favorite aunt and her husband died on the same day during the Cultural Revolution.

My mother found out later they couldn't take it any longer, being paraded and pummeled in the streets. Young hoodlums spat and shouted at them.

They both taught at the university. Her husband was head of the Engineering Department. He wired themselves to the electrical outlet and then they swallowed rat poison just to be sure. I thought of their young teenage daughter finding her parents when she got back from school, then forced out onto the streets because their home was censored, locked, and boarded up by the Red Guards. Suicides were counter-revolutionary.

I also thought of Jen's father. She was my childhood playmate. He owned the hospital where we had our tonsils out at the same time, and we stayed in their home on the top floor of the hospital. He jumped from that same floor to his death during the Cultural Revolution, when owning anything was a crime against the people.

These dear people in my life were all trying to end their existence in hell. Vincent must have felt he was in his own private inferno and there was no way out.

I started to question myself, if I had visited him before I left, maybe I could have talked him out of it, one more time. Time and again I had heard my mother say, she wished she had brought her younger sister and Jen out of the Mainland before the Communist takeover, instead of believing that she could not take them away from their family and roots.

"You tried your best." I had managed to tell Vincent's niece on the phone, but wondered whether I had done everything I could.

The Bardo

There came a point along my journey, past the years when I was impatient of the slowness of the hours of the day, as the weeks and months dragged on, and I impatient to leave the constricted feelings of the parental nest, though my mother did not overtly confine me, her covert hovering and words unsaid meant as encouragement were forces enough for me to be ready to grow up and join a world of those who had reached their goals in life.

She used to say she had great confidence in me to always do the right thing because she knew everything about me. "You are my flesh and blood. You came from my body." The words made me shiver, from excitement and fear in equal parts, as I saw she did not really understand me completely, and I came to realize I could not be the person she wanted me to be.

I began to see, once having gotten to that summit as seen from the earlier perspective, my life was more like a many chambered nautilus, with unexpected corridors and byways to choose and negotiate, and there was really no predictable path or set direction as I had once imagined.

My own dilemmas were not the same as my parents. I had to find meaning in my own encounters, changes in myself that my parents had never experienced and could not have really imagined. I remember telling my father in midlife about my affinity for men, how I had separated from my wife. I was hoping for some recognition or even resonance. Not only had my mother told me to ask my father about the male bordellos in old Peking when I confided in her, I also found out there were at least two cousins like me on his side of the family. But my father nodded without any facial expression or comment, only to ask me a year or two later, if I had found another wife!

I then realized I had chosen a path completely alien to my father's temperament, and also unknown to his generation and background. He would have kept his silence. After all, he quoted a proverb when I was barely ten, "One should keep one's mouth shut as tight as the narrow neck of a bottle." If I had continued to follow my father's silence, I would have paid my dues to my therapist in vain.

As I tried to relive the lives of my parents in the writing of these words, I saw much as I have admired and even tried to emulate in them, I needed to find my own footing in another country and at a very different time from that of my parents. When I was afraid of becoming more like my mother, my daughter told me once, "Don't worry, you are so different from Nai Nai." I had been remembering thoughts attributed to Marianne Moore, that we usually exemplify, in some measure, the faults against which we inveigh. My therapist had warned me as much with similar words. It was obvious to my daughter I had chosen stones untread by my mother for my footprints along the path, and I see my children will have to find theirs in their own time. My mother's prediction popped up again, "You will understand when you have your own children." She was only partly correct, though, as I hope I have learned not to wish that my children will take the path I have chosen, but a path they have chosen on their own.

At close to the end of the seventh decade of my life, I was finding myself at the pedestrian crossing of a stoplight in life, where I could see the little man twinkling in red, first moving slowly, then at a faster pace, and finally seeing him rushing ahead to try and reach the other end before it was too late. I wished I could turn back and start over on another cycle, even that would not be quite enough, but three more times, to do everything I still wanted to do before the end of the light.

On this journey of mine, I started with a slow crawl that has now become a relay race where familiar faces began to drop away, one at a time at first, then faster than I was realizing, and I might be alone on the path ahead. My good friend, who comforted me when Charles and I parted ways, reminded me of the common saying, we come into this life alone, and we will go out alone in the end. It seemed harsh when I first heard it from her, but she was really trying to say we should learn to let things go, as the Buddhist teachings say. Another way of seeing it is to live mindfully in the moment, no matter how alien and unexpected the terrain I am facing.

The last time I saw my father, I could tell he was alert, and he acknowledged my arrival at his bedside late in the evening. Early in the ashen morning before any hint of sunrise, I picked up the phone from the hospital. I could feel, even before the nurse came on the line, he was gone. When my mother knew her end was near, I saw the comfort in her eyes after my children flew in from around the country to hold her hand.

I can see my parents' footsteps ahead of me now on the path, albeit a very different one from my own. But I realize in trying to learn about the art of departure and dying, I am really trying to learn how to live in this life.

As I face what my father said was the most important thing he had to leave me, a poem now hanging in my home by Ma Dai of the late Tang Dynasty in the calligraphy of our common ancestor of close to two centuries ago,

> A wild man planting a tree,
> Seeing it age, among the clouds
> Casting for fish by the water, hailing a boy
> To gather mountain herbs
> Shepherding baby calf
> drinking the mountain spring
> Such is my way of well-being—
> No worries of aging

I am hoping these words that I am writing now will be the tree I plant for those who will follow. If not by sitting alongside a mountain spring, perhaps they will have a cup of dragonwell tea in their hands, where the first sip may be bitter to their tongues, but on second pour, it might be refreshing.

PART IV

Chapter Thirty-Two

"Baba!" His words boomed from the phone receiver. I pushed up my eyeshades to look at the clock. Only the hospital operator or the emergency room called me at that hour of the night.

"Sarah delivered an eight pound, three-ounce girl at two thirty a.m." Matt's excited voice and words continued to spill over like champagne about everything at the Birthing Center. A big relief, I felt. Things had gone well. Birthing Centers were something new to me. When his mother and I were in medical training it was not what mothers did, they went to the hospital to have their babies.

"Have you decided on a name?" I pulled the comforter a little higher over my bare shoulders for cover.

Last time we had spoken was a month ago. My son had told me that he was firm in his belief that his children should take their mother's family name.

When he and Sarah started talking about having children several years ago, he told me the tradition of the family name being passed on from son to son was not fair to women. "Why should daughters always be the ones losing their identity after marriage?" he asked rhetorically.

I shivered at his proposition. I could feel the bones of my ancestors rattling in their graves from his unsettling news. For them, to be part of this world was to be a *Lao Bai Xing*, to be one of A Hundred Old Names. Without one's own family name was to be a non-person. Even a bastard son like me was usually given his father's family name.

"But it's precisely this tradition of patriarchal domination that I am trying to stop," my son explained, using the same expert arguments he had practiced and perfected in law school and now used in front of judges and courts to prove his points.

"I can't understand why this would bother you so much." He sounded as frustrated as I was, unable to make him see my point.

"I feel like you're dumping a bucket of night soil at my front door," I blurted, remembering the stench when the night soil man collected the human waste in buckets from house to house when I had lived in Taiwan as a teenager. We had to close our windows every week when he came around.

"I thought you'd be the last person to object, Baba." His disappointment was palpable. "And I love you and respect you, Baba!"

His tone of exasperation I could imagine someday being used in pleading for refugee relief in front of the United Nations.

"We haven't decided whether it would be Tenaya or Mara." I could hear the healthy cry of his daughter on the other side of the line.

He did not mention the subject of the family name, and I was relieved I didn't have to deal with it on this happy occasion. But there was something apparent in the tone of his voice, a tone he used when withholding news that he knew I did not want to hear, such as the time he had crashed the car when a teenager.

"How long will you be at the Birthing Center?"

"They'll probably keep us till tomorrow."

"When are you and Adele coming out for a visit?"

"Well…," I fumbled for an excuse.

"I know how busy your schedule is." I was glad he gave me the way out of a quick decision.

"I'll keep my cell phone on," he added when he realized I was not going to say anything more.

I wanted to say more. Much more. I wanted to celebrate with him, to toast with the bottle of old champagne cognac my father had saved from the coronation of England's last King George.

I wanted to tell him about the joyful moment when I saw him take his first big breath after the obstetrician slapped his bright pink bottom. Or the pride it brought to my father after he heard the news, and the pages from the *Encyclopedia of Chinese Characters* he sent me on the research he did in naming his grandson, *Zhong Tian*: Centerpiece of the Celestial Skies. Such was the hope and importance my father had placed on his grandson.

But my son was separated from my father by a generation, and by even more generations of change from traditional Chinese ways, given the various cultural paths we had tread and the fact that neither my father nor I started our families early. My son was also separated from his grandfather by the vast Pacific Ocean and a new continent; he only saw his grandfather on rare occasions.

I had only myself to blame for not having tried harder for them to bond. It was shortsighted of me in trying to spare my son from his dread of being dragged away from summer vacations in the Bay Area's perennial springtime to the sweaty, humid, near suffocating weather in semi-tropical Taiwan, where my father spent his later years.

Even after the dial tone went dead on the phone receiver, my son's voice still echoed in my head. I felt there was a bone stuck deep in my throat, preventing me from shouting out the good feelings I wanted to have on the occasion of my granddaughter's arrival. I waited for the sun to rise so I could forget my night of tossing and turning from apprehension and foreboding.

Was I becoming just like my mother? I asked myself. The mother I had once held up as a Madonna, that is until she refused to give her blessing when I wanted to marry a woman against her will.

I remembered standing in the payphone booth on a freezing, gray metal February afternoon in Boston, begging and reassuring my mother with my love and respect. I held onto the receiver, hoping for some softening of her voice in the icy silence.

Finally, in words that continue to resurface in front of me, she said in resignation, "Wait till you have your own children!"

My son's words on the phone from a month ago still rang loud and clear in my ears, "I thought you were the most open-minded and progressive member of our family."

"I felt so good about you when we marched together up Broadway on the twenty-fifth Stonewall Anniversary in New York," he added.

Could I ever forget? The mere thought of the time he came down from Cambridge with his roommates made me choke up, and my eyes moisten. I remembered the snapshot of the two of us, he in a simple white T-shirt and I wearing one with the Stonewall March logo on my chest, a large pink triangle with forest green letters—celebrating the uprising and the beginning of gay liberation twenty-five years earlier. The photograph stands next to my daughter's wedding picture, showing her bridal bouquet of lavender and white roses in one hand and my arm in the other as she walked down the pebbled path of the country inn in Point Reyes to meet her future husband at the altar.

"You and Mom taught me always to stand up for what I believed in." My son proceeded to draw the parallel between his belief in ending the patriarchal system of family names and mine in gay liberation.

"When you came out to Nainai," he continued, "you were also going against tradition."

There was a big, basic difference, I thought, when I spoke to my mother.

I was fighting for something where I had no choice. Would I have chosen a life full of uphill battles? From little things, such as hearing someone casually throw out the cuss word *faggot* in locker room conversation. Or having others assume the object of my affection would be a woman? To the pain and humiliation that I would inflict on myself for not having the guts to tell the truth?

My son was choosing to cast off his own link with my family, embodied in my family name. It included all the Chens: my father and myself and the sixteen generations of our ancestors, all on record in the Book of Family Genealogy, dating back to the Ming Dynasty.

He then proceeded to remind me of the story I had read to him from that Genealogy book the year he started college. I had given him a copy, which my father had updated and revised using contemporary Chinese language, but had kept the Ming Dynasty print on its cover, the color of fresh bamboo shoots coming through the good earth.

The family history I wanted to pass down to my son was about the Cantonese branch of our family, which was started by the founding forefather who gave away the money for his return trip to the ancestral home up north in Shaoxing, close to the ancient Song Dynasty capitol of Hangzhou, to save a man and his family from complete financial ruin and disgrace.

"He broke with the tradition of returning home by starting a new branch of the family because he wanted to do what he felt was right, Baba."

"But he did not dishonor the family by throwing away the family name!"

As the words were coming out of my mouth, a Giotto fresco painted shortly after the end of the Song Dynasty in late thirteenth century came before my eyes. The one in the Basilica of Saint Francis of Assisi, not far from where Adele and I spend our time in Umbria every year. In that famous fresco, the saint stripped himself of his family's luxurious garments, to pursue his own calling.

Again, I thought about my own mother discarding her given family name after she was disowned by her father, when she divorced against his will. I knew that divorce in those early days of the First Republic was almost unheard of for women from good families.

I wished I could have told my son to do what he felt was right, as I had hoped I always would. I wished I could have told him it didn't matter. I wished I could have given him my blessings to cast aside my family name.

Instead, I told him I couldn't.

I just could not do it. My feelings ran too deep. Hurt too much.

A package showed up several weeks later. Snapshots of my son beholding his daughter, a steady gaze of unmistakable parental adoration. Pictures of my granddaughter with her eyes opened wide as if she were already capable of a hundred expressions with her little personality. And one in which she was sucking on her father's nose as if a nurturing parental nipple.

Adele drafted a note complimenting the baby's features and had me send it to my son and his wife.

"Hello, Baba," Matt was on the phone several weeks later, his voice a little more subdued.

"We've named her Tenaya Mara."

I held my breath, wondering whether I could endure hearing anything further. There was an edge in my son's voice betraying as much tension in him as there was for me.

"How is she doing?" I managed to say.

"Oh, she's been very easy to take care of. She rarely cries, only when she wants to be fed."

"I hope Sarah's milk is coming along." I thought of asking something neutral and remembered that Joyce did not have enough milk to feed him or his sister.

"Everything is coming along just fine ..." I noticed a pause as if he wanted to say something more, but held back.

"Sarah wants to talk to you," he added a little uneasily.

"Hi, Baba," his wife's high-pitched soprano came on the line, "we wanted to tell you that we decided on a double last name of Chen Lin. Unhyphenated." She waited for a second breath. "We hope that's all right with you."

"That's fine with me." I choked up in my throat, brought by the enormous sense of relief I felt.

"I haven't been able to sleep well for the past weeks worrying about this," she added.

"I'm so sorry, considering you've had enough to deal with during these last days of the pregnancy." I began to feel guilty to have caused her the added distress. "I don't know if Matt has told you," I wanted to explain further, "my mother was the second wife of my father..."

I wanted to tell her the circumstances of my birth that had haunted me and made me feel like a bastard. The story of my parents' clandestine marriage and how I had seen my mother lying in blood after an overdose because she wanted to ensure their marriage was acknowledged so that I had my father's family name.

I wanted to tell her the reasons my reaction was so profound and that I could not even put all of it into words, when my son wanted to throw away our family name, the name which meant so much to me. The name, which made it possible for me to feel I was my father's son, that I belonged to his family of the last sixteen generations in Canton from the time of the Ming Dynasty and before that, those generations in Shaoxing. The family name my son had taken for granted since birth.

"Yes, Baba." My son's voice was soft when he came on again.

I could not articulate clearly because my throat had seized. "Thank you for considering my feelings." My words managed to come out haltingly.

I couldn't continue coherently. The realization that my son had indeed taken my feelings into account was overwhelming. I was glad he asked the next question, "Are you able to rearrange your busy schedule to come out and visit your granddaughter?"

"Yes, I'd like to."

I wished I had recovered my senses fast enough to have said, "Of course, I will come! Of course, I want to come see Tenaya. Of course. I want to hold my granddaughter in my arms!"

Chapter Thirty-Three

猴

Forcing myself to take a deep breath, as if I could inhale some of the dewy morning of San Francisco and let things from the recent past recede into the mist, I padded over to my laptop in my fraying terrycloth bathrobe and clogs.

Was I awakened by a nightmare or a call to the bathroom? Against my better sense to stay with that moment between sleep and awareness, I opened my email. There might be something from him. I have not heard from my son since I sent him the note three days ago. There was not even a call on my birthday yesterday.

Only two new items on the screen. The first from the Daily Astrologer that somehow got into my mailbox and the second from Amazon. I clicked onto the first one to delete it, but couldn't resist from reading the message.

"You've seen the movie where the hero jumps from the bridge onto the top of the speeding train, chases and nabs the bad guy. You may not be doing any train leaping, but don't mess with danger today!"

There it was, right in my face. I did not want to follow that path of anger, I told myself. Little good that did me two years ago, when I had the argument with my son about giving up his family name.

I tried then to ignore the role of anger and frustration as a cause of my heart problems. My coronary artery was almost completely blocked when they had shown me the X-ray scans. Angst and anger alone could not have caused all that blockage in my coronaries, I told myself. The blockage could not have developed over several weeks of frustration.

But why did I suddenly develop those chest-crunching pains? The question lingered and gnawed at me. One New York pathologist told me about his findings in innumerable heart attacks at autopsy. Many did not have enough occlusion to cause the final, fatal blow. Spasm in the coronaries was a major culprit, he pointed out.

I have been trying very hard to let things go these past eighteen months after angioplasties had reopened my coronary arteries. Letting go, I remembered yet again was central to the Buddha's teachings.

Try to be a bodhisattva, an enlightened old Buddhist saint, has been my mantra. A *Laopusa*. A name my son started calling me some years ago, his way of chiding me not to take myself too seriously.

When I tried to go back to sleep, I saw my mother hovering overhead, an angry silver mane like the ghost of an ancestor in the Opera of Amy Tan's *The Bonesetter's Daughter*. Troubled and anxious, my mind had refused to let me rest ever since I discovered that a lock of her hair, the relic I stored in the small box in my bedroom, was missing.

A few weeks earlier around Thanksgiving, my son and his family stayed at my home while I was away. After they had left, things on my shelves, desks, and bureaus, piano and chests looked as if a poltergeist had swept through.

Sparkling pieces of green dust under my bedside table turned out to be from the missing front leg of a Murano glass frog. The lotus root in the hand of a porcelain Kuanyin was decapitated from its stem. The carved cinnabar box containing a small handful of my father's cremated remains wrapped in gold leaf paper sat on a higher book shelf, not where it had been earlier.

The lock of my mother's hair I clipped from her deathbed and placed in the box alongside my father's remains twenty years ago was gone. I had thought to myself, at least in death my parents were reunited in my home. The divorce that parted them for many years had left a knot in my gut.

I looked into every crack and crevice in my bedroom and all of the adjoining study, turned the waste baskets upside down. There was no trace.

Ingrained ancestral teachings and tradition made me feel that our sacred tablets in the Family Temple had been shattered, scattered to the winds and the fierce Temple Guardians were staring me down. Their curse thundered in my head, "May your descendants burn with the fire of the ninth level of hell!"

I trembled when I thought of the frail figure of my toddling grandson in front of me. My son told me the boy was quite underweight for his age.

"He puts down more food than any one of us, and he poops more than anyone I know." My son screwed up his nose, "and the smell! Terrible, terrible!"

The old doctor in me became alarmed. My son was describing the inability of the large intestine to absorb all that food his son was putting down. Malabsorption. One of his wife's sisters had a serious condition of her colon, a condition found to run in the family. Much of her colon was already removed because it showed early changes of cancer.

I shuddered with fear what a curse from the Gods would mean for my little grandson, the last thing I wanted to see happen to the boy with huge inquisitive eyes of an angelic putto painted by Rafaello.

Three days earlier, I sent a short message to my son about my discovery, hoping he or his wife might remember whether they had seen the lock of my mother's hair.

I checked my email for messages every hour as if I were hoping for a sign from the Goddess of Mercy, the Bodhisattva Guanyin.

No messages on my computer screen. I had thought there might be a word yesterday from my son on my seventy-first birthday. The day arrived and passed. No call.

The voices in my head would not let me rest.

I told myself to let it go. My son probably never noticed what was in the box. He must have shoved the gold-leafed packet onto a high bookshelf after his son emptied the box. The lock of my mother's hair was too small for them to even notice. Or he thought it was just a bit of trash and threw it away.

He could not have known it was his grandmother's hair. So what if it was lost? It was only some relic that nobody would even notice after I became a relic myself.

I remembered my daughter telling me that one of her Jewish friends had commented after the reception in my home for her engagement, "Your father's house is like a museum. What are you going to do with all those tchotchkes when he goes someday?"

But another voice in me would not stop. The act was equivalent to ancestral desecration at the Family Temple. "Your son's behavior cannot be forgiven. You have been too tolerant for too long!

"Remember when he tried to change his family name. Even after you told him he was the last male descendant on your side of the family!"

Perceived past slights resurfaced. "He never considered what things meant to you. Remember the time when he was living with you, and there was only one parking spot in front. He had the gall to say he had as much right to it as you. He has become totally Americanized!"

My mother's words of several decades ago rushed back to me once again. "Wait till you have your own children." She was right, again.

The first voice came back again. What does it matter when I am six feet underground? Isn't that the Buddha's teachings are about to avoid suffering in the world? Besides he has considered your feelings, even with the double family name for his children. Don't hold onto these self-inflicted sufferings. Let it go. Let it go.

There was some pressure and tightening on the left side of my chest, but I told myself I must be imagining it. I was just lying back in bed and not exerting myself in any way. All of my latest blood tests came through with flying colors. My heart specialist had said so on my last visit.

My telephone rang, the very next instant. "Take another deep breath. Calm yourself down," I repeated to myself, trying to avoid any further tightening in my chest.

"Hello, BaBa." Before my son said anything more, I could hear the tone of contrition in his voice.

I inhaled deeply and heard the other voice echoing in my ear. Let it go. Let it go. The bodhisattva was repeating. I could imagine how badly my son felt when he found out what happened.

Then I heard his words.

"I'm so sorry."

I hoped my mother heard him, too. She had special niches for her two grandchildren in the chambers of her heart. It meant so much when they flew in from college across the country to be with her when they heard she was succumbing to lung cancer. I could still see the smile on her face when she saw them. She would have forgiven her grandson.

33

猴

Chapter Thirty-Four

雞

My single room had a view of the Bay and my caretakers were cheerful and accommodating beyond anything I had expected. I thought I'd checked into a five-star Sheraton, even though it would have been my last resort if traveling. Adele and I usually preferred the coziness of pensiones and B&Bs, and even better, the tranquil austerity of a Zen temple or an Italian monastery. Now I wouldn't be surprised if asked for my preference of drinks at the bar hidden somewhere behind the heart monitors and suction machines. It was early summertime of my seventieth year, and I had walked into the hospital for what I thought was a rather minor procedure. I had no idea of the surprises ahead, nor that I might not live to see the season's end.

"I'll schedule you for a coronary angiogram," my colleague had told me earlier.

We used to work together at the same hospital, about half an hour by car south of the City where I live now. But he put me in this hospital because it was the center for cardiology and heart procedures in the Health Maintenance Organization where I worked for over twenty years before my retirement.

Having spent over half a lifetime in patient care, an angiogram sounded fairly non-threatening to me, sticking a needle through an artery in the groin and threading a small catheter up to the small arteries of the heart. I had stuck so many needles into patients' veins and arteries from the time I was in medical school, and this was a procedure commonly recommended for people who showed something abnormal in a routine stress test on the treadmill.

When I checked into some details, I noticed my colleague was listed under the title of an Invasive Cardiologist. A small bell for alarm, but I was happy to leave everything in his hands. He had been so helpful from the beginning. Having the procedure done in the City also made it easier and closer to my home.

That first time I experienced the familiar signs of a heart problem, I was racing with my carryon bags in hand to catch our plane connection from Frankfurt to Florence with Adele behind me trying to catch up. The airport in Frankfurt was a sprawling, space-age maze, we hardly had time to make our connecting flight in a different Terminal building. When we finally got there, breathless, we were told the location was changed, and we had to dash back in another direction.

Suddenly there was this heavy pressure against the left side of my chest, making it difficult for me to breathe. A dull ache ran down my left arm to the elbow as if I was heaving a fifty-pound sack of brown rice. In other words, fairly classical symptoms of angina pectoris I had to memorize in medical school.

My initial impulse was to deny what I already logically concluded in my mind. I hedged my bets. It could be a muscle spasm from the packing before our departure or the tension of getting ready for the trip. Having been a physician for over forty years, even the thought of angina was not a source of great alarm to me. My father had it the last fifteen to twenty years of his life, although he stayed in bed for much of the time toward the end. It was not a serious concern in my mind.

My father even continued in his role as Board Chairman of the printing company he founded, holding meetings in his hospital suite of rooms and having his friends and associates visit him there, during those last six years.

My mother actually suspected the real reason for his hospital stay was his way of trying to distance himself from his last lady friend living next door to him, who was the principal cause of my parents' divorce. It was my father's customary way of not making his real purpose too evident, my mother thought. I concluded my father was able to carry on his life much as he wanted, even after the diagnosis of angina pectoris.

But my symptoms did not subside, even a week after we settled down in our place in Umbria. They forced me to slow down, reaching a point where I felt I had to explain the snail pace of my activities to Adele.

"Don't think I didn't notice." She told me later. "You used to walk five steps ahead of me, but now, you're lagging three paces behind." She dragged me to the local hospital that evening.

To my relief and surprise, the facility in the small town where we lived was modern, more modern than the hospital I retired from in the Bay Area. Where I expected to see a bedlam of moaning and pandemonium of patients seeking care in the *Pronto Scorso*, the Emergency Room to us from the U.S., I found it clean, calm and orderly.

I told the triage nurse about my problem and was given a priority number. In less than half an hour I was sitting in front of the Italian doctor. He was very kind, listening patiently with brows knit, while I tried to sound coherent with a limited Italian vocabulary of body parts and malfunctions, hurriedly pulled out from my pocket English-Italian dictionary. He confirmed what I suspected, got lab tests, and kept me overnight. When the tests came back saying that I did not have a heart attack, the floor nurse scheduled me for a treadmill with a heart specialist.

A few days later I sat in front of Dottore Frederico Fedelli. His name was close enough to remind me of the sixties movie, *La Dolce Vita*. He was as good looking as the young Marcello Mastroianni, and tall for an Italian in Umbria, with a well-cut head of dark, curly hair. The gentleness in his gaze told me he was sympathetic toward me. He noted from my history of having been a physician but now on the other side of the medical fence, so soon after retirement, as they say in Italy, *in pensione.*

"What made you retire in Italy?" he asked.

"In another life, la moglie must have been an Italiana." But I had to admit, "My first love was Paris."

Hoping not to offend him, I quickly added, "Now I have come to like Italy as well."

He smiled conspiratorially. "I love Paris, too."

I referred to Adele as la moglie, my wife, in Italian. With the limits of the language at my disposal at that time, it would have been too complicated a mouthful to explain that we were partners committed to each other in life but not married.

The treadmill test and scans I had done before seeing Doctor Fedelli confirmed significant blockage of the major blood supply to my heart. He suggested he could refer me to his friend at the American Hospital in Florence for coronary angiography. Under the Italian healthcare system, for a retiree like myself who was also a resident of Italy, at the equivalent of four hundred fifty dollars per year, I was able to get coverage for everything, including all medications prescribed.

But as sweet as Doctor Fedelli seemed to be, and much as I would have liked for him to hold my hand, I felt the procedure included significant risks. I was also a little hesitant to let a medical care system unfamiliar to me insert a long catheter into a major artery in my groin and thread it up to the arteries around my heart. It was a common procedure nowadays, but from my experience working in hospitals, things could and did go wrong at times, unexpectedly.

"I have decided to wait until I return to California." I tried to explain to my Italian cardiologist on my follow-up visit, all the while watching for a sign of displeasure on his friendly face.

"The cardiologist there is a good friend of mine. I have known him for a long time. He said I could wait till I get back to California."

I added a little uneasily, "But I am very grateful for everything you have done for me." I took out the bottle of Chateauneuf du Pape I found for him. French wines were not readily available in our small town.

"I will be here if you need me. When you're back in Italy." He shook my hand, and held it for a second. "*In bocca al lupo.*" He added an Italian wish of good luck. Literally, 'in the mouth of the wolf.' The Italian way of turning the worst into good.

Back now in San Francisco on my hospital bed with a view of the Bay, I waited to be taken down to the Operating Room. I asked the nurse whether I needed to be shaved in the groin for the procedure.

"They'll do all that downstairs," she answered exuding the full confidence of one who had been asked the same question more than once.

I thought about the comment my good friend made the evening before. "Hope the guy who shaves you is cute."

The technician from the cardiac operating suite who came up to fetch me had an easy way about him. I noticed both of his ears were pierced and he had some tattoos on his biceps.

"How long have you been with Kaiser?" I asked.

"Ten years," he smiled.

"Like it here?"

"Love it. It's a good place to work." He gave me a squeeze on the leg, and added, "I've done this so many times. Don't worry. You'll be fine."

I thanked him and returned his smile. It was as good as getting a congenial and helpful maître d' or waiter in a restaurant who could make the difference between a lovely evening or an experience you'd want to forget. When I was on the other side of caregiving, I tried to remember the extra touch or smile for a patient who was going through something difficult or stressful. But with a harried and overcrowded schedule, sometimes this was hard to keep in mind.

The people working in the cardiac operating suite was quite obviously well accustomed to their routine. Technicians, nurses, X-Ray personnel were all at the ready. The nurse who helped move me onto the operating table was short and stout, reminding me of the Italian grandmothers I saw on the streets of the medieval Umbrian town where I saw Doctor Fedelli.

"I am going to start an I.V. in your arm." She announced with a calming voice. "You think you might need some sedation?" She added when the cold fluid started running into my vein.

"Do you think it's necessary?"

"Up to you." She was as soothing in her tone as a mother hen clucking at her chicks.

"I'll be fine without." I thought I'd rather not be overly sedated and be prevented from going home afterward.

When I was removing skin cancers from patients, many would ask for some sedation prior to the injection of local anesthetics. The groin was a much less sensitive area than the face where most of the skin cancers were found and some of the reconstructive plastic procedures I did after the cancers were removed took many hours. I figured the angioplasty would take less than an hour.

"Now I am going to shave you a little down there." The motherly nurse pointed to my right groin.

"It'll be a little cold," she added as she plunged the surgical sponge filled with ice-cold disinfectant onto my skin.

I felt my buttocks tighten to the shock, which was probably merciful. I hardly felt the razor. Only later did I notice the results of her handiwork. Esthetics was not the strong suit of this maternal hand.

"Felt it less than a phlebotomy!" I told my friend and colleague who was performing my angiogram. He had first injected the area with a small amount of local anesthetic, before introducing the catheter into my groin.

The nurse was very good at distracting me from any discomfort. When she found out I had just returned from Italy, she told me about her elaborate dinner in Rome a month earlier. It was organized by her friend, teaching a class in Italian cooking. She made it sound like a feast in the Villa of Hadrian.

"We got some very good pictures of your coronaries." My attention was pulled away from the Roman banquet by the voice of my cardiologist friend. "There is a 95 to 99% blockage of your LAD," he didn't need to explain he was referring to my left anterior descending coronary artery, the major blood supply to the left side of my heart, "but all the others look fine."

Then he added, "Andrew, I was not able to insert the stent for you because you're allergic to aspirins." I was not too surprised, it was typical for us doctors to first present the good news before slipping in the bad.

"We'll have to look into the possibility of desensitizing you to aspirin." He seemed to have just taken a mental breath.

"Are there no other substitutes for aspirin?" I felt somewhat incredulous that with the vast pharmacopeia of our twenty-first century, there was nothing that could substitute for the common aspirin.

"I checked with the senior member of our invasive cardiology staff, and he agrees with me that it's mandatory for you to be on aspirins for life after the stents are placed, in addition to the other blood thinner you've been taking." Later, when he checked on me in my room, he explained further that all the studies have shown this was the best combination of blood thinners. Other alternatives might work, but he wanted to stick with the best proven.

I took his word for it and was just glad to know the study was successful and there was the possibility of a solution to my allergies.

"Lie perfectly still for five minutes," a basso profundo came from the other side of the table. "I'm putting pressure on you to prevent bleeding."

I saw the voice belonged to a young man with light angelic curls and crystalline blue eyes like Gabriele in a painting of the Annunciation by da Vinci in Florence. He exuded as much sweet assurance as the firm pressure from his palm on my groin.

I had not noticed him when he came into the room earlier. The operating room lights were dimmed during the procedure because my cardiologist was following the progress of the catheter from my groin to my heart on the video screen in front of him.

"I heard you say you have a place near Florence." the angel seemed to be trying to make conversation.

"Yeah, not too far. Little over an hour southeast, in Umbria."

"Did you go to those discount stores?"

"No, I haven't yet. Have you been?"

"I was just there a couple of weeks ago."

"Where are they?"

"There's a bunch of them. Just outside of Florence." He proceeded to rattle off several big-name, luxury Italian stores.

I remembered looking into the windows of the Ferragamo store next to the Ponte Trinita in Florence. Its prices were as imposing as its edifice, which occupied a whole block. Items were displayed like jewels in Tiffany windows across the street. No wonder the store always looked so sedate, without the usual crowds. Who could afford them?

"Must be wonderful to retire in Italy." He shifted his hands on my groin and continued the pressure.

"Our plan is to be there three months and here three months, alternating." Although we were lucky to have a home there, I also remembered the sense of being harried in our comings and goings, wherever we were. Not the feel of serenity I had imagined. But most people would not be sympathetic to my complaint. I just said, "The long flights back and forth are a bit exhausting, when you get to my age."

"I had a great trip though. Champagne soon after take-off and good wines with the meals, I didn't feel a thing after that," he said it with an equal measure of innocence and insouciance that what would have been taken as bragging came off with a certain charm.

"Lucky you. I've only been in first class once in my life for a short trip, New York to San Francisco. And that was by chance." Sofa wide seat and poached salmon with capers, I still remembered. "But that was in the old days. They don't do much upgrading anymore nowadays!"

"My boyfriend is a wine and travel editor for Condé Nast." This explained how someone as young as he could afford it.

"I really shopped to the limits." He continued in his guileless, Alice-in-Wonderland spirit but surprising basso profundo voice. "Maxed out my credit cards in those outlets."

I thought, how wonderful for him to be able to be so open about his life. Times have changed, even for a city known to be at the forefront of things. But still, I was impressed by his straightforwardness. No mincing words about gender when personal matters were brought up.

"What's your name?" I tried to raise my head to read his nametag but found it was flipped over.

"Jason." He too noticed the tag was flipped. "Sorry about that."

Then added, "Remember not to raise your head for six hours." At the same time, he increased the pressure on my groin a little.

When I got back to my room with a view, the upbeat nurse was waiting for me. She reminded me of the jazz cabaret singer, Faye Carol, who livened up the Castro in the eighties.

"Heard they couldn't put the stent in."

"Yes, I feel like the bride who was stood up at the altar." From our earlier exchange, I felt she was someone who could appreciate the comment. "I hope they can find a way to desensitize me to aspirin."

"We just had a patient here last week who was desensitized first."

It was a relief to get that news from her. At that time, the question of why my aspirin allergy had not been considered earlier, did not kick in.

My feelings of gratitude toward my cardiologist friend were overflowing. He made it possible for me to stay in Italy as we had planned and the help of his reassuring voice on the phone calls by long distance were foremost and incalculable to my mind. I was more preoccupied with trying to solve the dilemma, not why he had missed my aspirin allergy.

The nurse's news was a great relief. There was going to be a solution to my problem. She was also good enough to bring Adele back into my room. The relief behind Adele's smile as she walked in made me realize she was just grateful to get me back alive. She had gone through so many near fatal emergencies with her previous partner.

Larry was a junior high schoolmate of mine who eventually succumbed to his cancer after six years of unrelenting struggle. The last few months of his life, when he was essentially bedridden, I was the only friend he wanted to see. Sometimes I suspected he posthumously played Cupid to get Adele and me together. He used to tell me about his experiences roaming in another space before he reentered his body on earth.

Half way out the door with her blood pressure and thermometer machines, the nurse turned to Adele and winked, "Now you help us keep him still for the next six hours. He's not supposed to move his right leg or raise his head!"

Later that day, Steve stopped by after his clinic hours. I had known him for many years from the early HIV conferences I attended assiduously, even when there was little the doctors could offer, but especially after Gene was told that he tested positive and was devastated by the news. I had referred several of my friends in the City to Steve through the years. We also waved to each other at the Christmas cappella concerts of Chanticleer in St. Ignatius Church. Early on with Gene, and later with Adele. I registered the surprise in Steve and his partner the first time they saw me with her.

After I had retired, I asked him if he would be my personal physician. I didn't want to spend over half-an-hour driving down to the hospital on the peninsula where I used to work anymore.

When I was filling out the patient's questionnaire before I saw Steve the first time, I wondered which category I should check. Instinctively I wanted to check "gay." Yet my relationship with Adele was not platonic. To be accurate, I looked for the category "bisexual."

In my mind, I was still troubled by the feeling that this term used to be a shield for closeted men who were not ready to admit they were gay. Yet, I felt this was the most accurate category for myself. If anything, I was clear I was not going back into any closet again.

When I told one of my old friends that my partner was a woman now, he did not communicate with me for several years. He knew I was once married and had two children, then came out over twenty years ago. That was the time he met me. He said he could not deal with the fact, when I told him I was now with a woman again.

Finally, I decided to check the category "gay" on the form. But when Steve walked into the examination room to see me for the first time, I told him that Adele was now my partner. I was very impressed with that first hour-long examination. Thorough and much longer than any I had before, the way I imagined medicine used to be practiced before the modern era.

Stepping into my room at the hospital now, he said, "I'll call the allergy clinic and get you an appointment." He knew that was the most important thing to take care of for me next, having already reviewed what happened in my chart. In five minutes, he was back.

"You can see Doctor Ayran tomorrow morning. Do you feel up to it?" His usual earnest and solicitous tone, as always, delivered with warmth through his eyes. But his speech had the measured cadence of someone who learned English in a foreign country.

He had told me his father was a missionary, on that first visit to his office. He was born in Tianjin, a city known for its lovely carpets we had in our home in Shanghai, and the early Chinese industrialists at the turn of the last century. I felt we shared in the sensibilities of a world known to very few today. Despite my misgivings about missionaries trying to convert the heathens in other lands, many of their children, at least the ones I have met, seemed to express some degree of affection and affinity for the country where they were born.

"Great," I said. "I've seen her before for my rhinitis." I felt I was in good hands with Doctor Ayran.

"Good. Then you're all set. I've written all the discharge medications for you which Adele can pick up on your way out." He had introduced himself to her when he first stepped into the room and included her in the conversation.

His large, sturdy frame hovered protectively over my bed. "Now I won't be checking in on you for the next two weeks. The cardiology team will do that. Feel free to call them."

"Going on a much-needed vacation?"

"Rick and I are going to the Cape."

"That should be nice. One of the things I miss here are the warm sands and beaches on the Cape. Will you be going into P-town?"

"We rented a place near Truro. But will probably visit there sometime."

"I love the sand dunes there. Have a great time and give my regards to Rick and the Cape." I could never forget those dunes where Joyce and I spent that afternoon before medical school, the feeling of their vastness, and a world full of hope and opportunities ahead of us.

Adele drove me to the allergy office the following morning. I inched along from the parking lot, hampered by the bulky bandage still stuck in my groin. In the waiting room, I tried to read the article by Dave Sedaris in *The New Yorker*, but even his humor could not completely distract me. I felt as if I were going in front of a judge who would decide on my sentence.

"Good morning, Doctor Chen." the allergist came out to get me herself. I remembered her from my earlier appointment in her office. A Filipina, looking much younger than what her diplomas indicated on the walls, and could well be my daughter, unfailingly courteous and pleasant but a bit on the formal side.

"I feel I have come to the oracle." I made an attempt to diffuse some of my own anticipation and anxiety. "I hope you will have good news for me."

"I wish your cardiologist, had called me from the Operating Room."

I was surprised by her candor, considering my memories of her reticence from previous visits. Also, doctors generally avoided allusions to any mistakes or oversights made by their colleagues. "I was in the hospital yesterday and could have desensitized you to aspirin at the same time."

The figure of my trusted friend and cardiologist flashed in front of my eyes. Soft spoken and bespectacled, with an Einsteinian laurel of silvery gray. He was the most respected clinician in his field at the hospital where I used to work. He had gone out of his way to call me in Italy, to answer my questions, review my test results and symptoms.

"As long as they don't get worse, you don't need to cut short your vacation." His reassurance enabled us to stay in Italy for the full three months and not disrupt the plans we had made before the problems with my heart put a hole in our bubble.

The trip was to be our first carefree vacation after my retirement, more so for me, than for Adele. I no longer had to worry about the need to return to work within a few weeks. No longer tethered by a leash around my neck. And she could enjoy her beloved Italy without interruption.

It was also going to be the period of healing from the loss of her mother, barely two months earlier. We were just past the *Seven-Sevens*, the traditional Chinese seven-week period of mourning for the dead, when we started off on our trip to Italy. The Buddhist prayers and chants at the funeral *A-mi-tuo-fo, A-mi-tuo-fo* were still ringing in our ears.

I felt enormous gratitude toward and relief from the words of this cardiologist colleague who extended himself to help me.

When I repeated the allergist's comments to my daughter, the first thing she asked was, "Did you tell the cardiologist that you are allergic to aspirins?"

Across the front of my medical records, the sticker for allergies to aspirin was marked on the large red tape from the day I started to see a doctor at Kaiser. It was also common practice to ask the patient about allergies before any important procedure was done. I began to doubt myself when my daughter asked the question. My friend must have asked about my allergies, I thought.

"That's negligence!" My daughter's verdict was quick.

I asked myself had I ever forgotten some fact about a patient? Much as I would like to think that I never knowingly did anything to harm my patients, I could not say I was not guilty of having forgotten some fact about them or unknowingly had done them harm.

Doctors in our culture have been put on a pedestal close to the almighty and were expected to cure everything that has gone wrong with our bodies and until fairly recently have been not only respected but revered. They could do no harm or make a mistake, which in some ways made it harder for them to admit it when one was made. We also know from early childhood, in every culture and country, that if we did something wrong we were going to be punished. A clever person could correct the mistakes made, but it took a superior one to admit and apologize for them.

I remembered hearing about an incident where the surgeon with a good reputation in my hospital had performed surgery on the wrong side of the patient, who was also a fellow physician and a friend of mine. The friend who was the patient had forgiven his surgeon, but the surgeon probably carried the guilt to this day when he sees his colleague. I suspected it was the same for my cardiologist colleague.

When I heard the allergist say that she could desensitize me to aspirin, I was just happy there was help on the horizon. I didn't want to even think about negligence. I wanted to just get on with my treatment and not to worry about what had already happened. I thought my daughter was a bit harsh in her youthful vigor and rush to judgment, although I knew she did it purely out of care and concern for me.

I put things that happened behind me, but every time we come across each other I had the feeling my old colleague was not at ease with me the way he was before. He had probably felt bad enough for having forgotten to check on my allergies prior to the procedure.

"I'll call your cardiologist, and we'll schedule the desensitization for you as soon as possible." Doctor Ayran was very reassuring.

I exhaled a deep sigh of relief. It was the message I so much wanted to hear.

Chapter Thirty-Five

狗

Four days later, the nurse was all set for me in the ICU for my desensitization procedure for aspirin. My room had a direct view from the command center. I began to wonder if they expected something untoward might happen. There must be a reason they put me in such close range to the center of things.

Prior to retirement, I had often stood in front of the squeaking, security-controlled doors into the Intensive Care Unit—those gate-keepers of the bardo. More than once I had found myself taking a deep breath to steel myself for what I was about to encounter. Now I found myself on the other side and teetering on a bed, in that inde-terminate place, where people get stranded between life and death.

I remembered the patient was often comatose, or in a state of semi-consciousness. The steady drone of machines struggled to keep someone's life from ending. A medusa of tubes and lines dangled and crawled out from all sides of the bed, draining out or pushing in fluids for a body no longer capable of performing its customary daily functions.

It was up to me to do my part in this tangled maze of medical intervention. Often, I had the feeling that all attention was going to be focused on what I had to say, hanging onto them like the word from the Delphic oracle.

Facing the dear ones afterward, those waiting for some sliver of good news I might be able to give, I often heard murmured prayers or sutras under their breath. It was wrenching.

There was such a sense of happy relief for me when I was able to deliver good news with a reassuring smile, the words they have been waiting for with drenched palms.

When no such news could be delivered, either because I had failed to help the patient, or the situation was beyond what was medically possible, and I was just hailed by the other caretakers to reinforce their sense of futility, and put more in the role of an undertaker rather than caretaker, I would first have to take several deep breaths and try to carry myself, the expression on my face, and my body language, in such way to convey my compassion for the patient and the dear ones, and yet, not fully express the futility of the situation and the finality of the unfortunate news they would inevitably have to confront.

I had felt the conflicting roles of being someone trained to heal and then finding myself having to say help was no longer medically possible. It was as if I had to put on the garb of condolence, and yet being fully aware this was not just playing the actor's role on stage. I was dealing with the endgame of another fellow human. Words available to a priest or a rabbi who might tell the family their dear one had gone to a better place would sound glib and dishonest from my mouth, a doctor trained in the science of medicine. I realized under the circumstances those words of hope often offered more consolation to the survivors than anything I could say. In the end, the priest, the rabbi, or I were all trying to be healers. The soul for them, the body for me.

In my years of practicing medicine, sometimes also referred to as the art of medicine, if there was anything I learned, it was to listen to the patient and the family, and to try to find out what he or she or the dear ones were prepared to accept, or even wanted to know, before forcing onto them the whole weight of the situation in one slap of a statement, as if it were a Commandment from some cold stone tablet.

"I'm David, and I'll be doing your desensitization." The nurse's booming voice took me out of my reminiscing. I hope he would be as wise as a Solomon if problems occurred, I thought to myself.

He was indeed a bundle of efficiency. The desensitization protocol was on the overbed table, all the medications lined up like on a neat spice rack, and the patient's gown laid out for me, open in the back which always made me think of the toilet-training pants with open bottoms for village kids in China which allowed them to just squat and do their thing.

"We put you by the door and the office because we expect you should be out of here in a few hours," David added cheerfully. "Be right back."

I settled myself into the hospital bed with its guardrails and push-buttons. They often confused me when I used to try to find out which button to push to reposition the patients, depending on what kind of a hospital bed the patients were put into when I came to examine them. They were often barely conscious and could not help with the buttons, much less myself. Sometimes they were even trussed to the bed rails, when they were thought to be too confused and might pull out one of the myriad tubes they were connected to or do something more harmful to themselves.

David whizzed back in and gave me a smile of approval, as if to say, good boy, you got into bed without help. Interesting, I thought, as a patient one was reduced to being treated much like a child, dependent on others for such basic needs and personal comfort. After checking my blood pressure, pulse, and temperature, he pronounced me ready to start the desensitization. "Now," he asked holding up the protocol, "did you get a copy of this?"

"No." I looked over to Adele, making sure she hadn't either. David had offered her a seat on the other side of the bed. "Just told to show up."

"Well," David continued, "let me make sure about a few things for the protocol, since you didn't get one."

35

狗

"Did you take the prednisone last night?"

"Sorry," I shook my head, "nobody told me." The medication was familiar to me, something given to patients to prevent or to slow down any undesired reaction in the body. I sometimes injected it into incisions in my patients who were having excessive amounts of scarring after some plastic surgical procedure I had done. I looked at Adele again because she took the call from the hospital and she shook her head. Nobody had told her anything either.

"Let me check with the doctor." From the way he had everything so well organized, I could tell this was not the first time for David with this procedure. From the smile on his face when he came back, I knew he had found a solution. "We can just give you some Solu Medrol in the vein."

"Great," I said, happy that we could proceed as planned. Although I rarely used it that way, intravenous steroids were often given in the emergency room or in the operating room when we wanted immediate results in reducing or preventing whatever untoward reaction the patient was having.

"And," David proceeded onto the next item on his protocol, "did you stop the beta blocker this morning?" He looked at both of us this time as if to make sure.

Again, I had to tell him no. No instructions to stop any of my regular meds. "I was just told to show up this morning without food after midnight."

"Oh-oh." I thought I detected some real concern, but he recovered quickly and said, "Let me check again with the doctor."

I could tell he was annoyed that someone had not done the job in informing me, and he was trying hard not to appear too alarmed.

Five minutes later, David returned. I was quite familiar with the expression on his face. An expression when I didn't want to put the bad news into words and tried to say something to soften the blow.

He told me the doctor felt it was essential for me to have stopped the beta blocker which was meant to reduce my blood pressure and heart rate. If I should get any reaction to the test dose of aspirin they were about to give me, my blood pressure could suddenly drop, and I would be in a dangerous position with an already lowered blood pressure. It was really for my safety that they did not want to proceed.

"I feel like I've been turned down a second time at the altar."

David had done his job well as the nurse. He had been meticulous in making sure everything was in order. It made no sense to be angry at him. If it were not for him, I might have really been put in a potentially dangerous position.

"Well," I said, forcing a smile on my face, "Where do we go from here?"

"Let me check and see what we can do to reschedule. I know this is your second time here for the angioplasty." His tone was very apologetic and sympathetic.

In fifteen minutes, he was back with the resident doctor from the ICU in tow. The young resident, who could have well been my son, explained to me again why we should not proceed. I knew it was not his fault either that I had not been given the proper instructions and the protocol. There was no use getting aggravated at him. He had already tried to save the day by ordering the intravenous steroid. Unfortunately, that was not the only instruction I didn't receive.

"Usually the cardiology nurse coordinator Angie is very good about these things." I could tell he was trying his best to find a reason for the oversight. "But I think someone said this is the week she's on vacation."

"We got you in for the day after tomorrow," David chimed in as if to save the day again, letting the resident beat a rapid retreat from an uneasy situation. I felt sorry for the young doctor. I had been there before when something unexpected happened, or someone simply forgot a crucial detail. I knew only too well that doctors and nurses are human and can make human errors.

I did a mental check. July Fourth. "You mean you guys are open for this on the Fourth?"

"I'll be here." David said, meaning, "I'll be here for you."

"How did you get so lucky to work on the Fourth?"

David was someone about late fortyish or early fifties and obviously experienced in the ICU I was surprised he had to be on duty on a holiday.

"I asked for it." Then he added, "this way I get time and a half plus overtime for a twelve-hour shift. I can pay off my roommate and get him out of my house," he said it with the gusto of Mitzi Gaynor singing how to get a guy out of her hair in *South Pacific*.

"Wow. That's quite a deal. An expensive roommate to get rid of."

"No, I don't mind. Getting him out of my life is worth two thousand bucks!"

"I hope I'll get you again next time." David's professionalism and frank, good humor was endearing. It would be great to have his company if I had to endure the ICU again.

"I'll make sure of that." Then he added, "That's what seniority gives you. You can choose your patients. The desensitization should be pretty easy, and I get out of here in time for the fireworks!"

David was right. The desensitization went well as planned on the Fourth. I did not have any untoward reaction. But I missed the fireworks. They didn't want to let me go home that night. One of the nurses told me I could see the fireworks from the top floor of the hospital. But I was tired enough from the days' rigmarole of the desensitization protocol and didn't want to bother with asking for a favor. They were probably extra careful with me anyway because of what happened earlier.

Early next morning, I was taken down to the Operating Room. Someone ahead of me had canceled. An angel for my day, I thought.

Adele noticed the happy look on my face. She asked, "Should I get you a lunch?" Not being someone who has worked in hospitals, she didn't think much of the hospital food, while I was accustomed to the Economy Class airline feed from the hospital food service. It was a time when airlines still fed economy passengers. I was just happy I got to something to eat and didn't have to wait around too long with an empty stomach while attending the noontime hospital conferences or meetings. Adele liked to tease me when traveling that the most important thing for me was to get my three meals on time, regardless of whether we found ourselves in a remote hill town in Umbria or on a main thoroughfare in bustling Shanghai. For her, it was the changing color of rooftop tiles after an afternoon shower or the architecture of some ancient wall that grabbed her attention.

"Anything would be fine with me," I told her as she buzzed me on the cheek. "As long as it's vegetarian," I added teasingly. She was blaming my vegetarian diet for my heart problems. She firmly believed my body was reacting to the lack of animal proteins. She didn't say anything further but squeezed my hand as I was wheeled out of my room.

"Third time around is going to be a charm," I said to the nurse at the desk, raising my right thumb. I was a familiar face to them by now.

The morning crew in the operating suite was still buzzing like bees getting everything ready. I looked around me but didn't see Jason, the young angel Gabriele who kept the pressure on my groin the last time around. I told myself at least this time I'll have the stent in and be out of there by the next morning, at the latest.

Many days later my daughter asked me whether I had any apprehension going in for the procedure. I told her, frankly no.

35

狗

When the unexpected happened, I was more concerned about the effect on Adele, who unlike me had not spent half of her waking hours around the hospital.

I had no inkling whatsoever that something untoward might happen. But I was used to warning patients something unexpected could happen, even death. When the possibilities were minuscule, I brought up the comparison of being struck by a car in the street or the chances their house collapsing from an earthquake. For someone living in California, I told my patients, the chances of those events would probably be higher.

.

When my mother faced a serious illness, and she saw I was worried, she always reassured me she would be fine.

"I'm wearing this jacket your grandmother Wai Po made for me, when I was thirteen and was told I had a very serious heart problem." Every time she mentioned her own mother I heard the tenderness in her voice with tears one step behind. "I recovered, and every time I wear this jacket, I feel she is still protecting me."

The moss green brocade bed jacket had delicate, silvery vines tracing around its tiny pink blossoms, but the embroidered ribbons edging the mandarin collar were fraying from use over the years.

My mother planned for every detail of her own afterlife, including the nine layers of funerary clothing, three for every season, spring and autumn were the same, summer and winter, and the chanting of the Diamond Sutra at her burial.

"No medical intervention," she said when told she had inoperable lung cancer. "Unless the doctors could cure me, no reason to prolong my death."

I thought about her brocaded bed jacket when her doctors had nothing more to offer. "It was too worn. I threw it away," she told me when I asked. She probably thought she had overcome so many medical problems, she didn't need it any longer.

For the first three of her four remaining months with us, she acted as if nothing much changed in her life. The round the clock caretaker got her everything she needed. Her hairdresser even consented to come to her home several times.

She was touched my children flew back several times from the East Coast to see her. It was only during the last two weeks that she needed heavy doses of morphine before she slid into a coma.

I remembered reading about Turgenev writing to Tolstoy about how to die. I was learning about that from my mother. I felt in a way it helped me learn how to live.

She was somehow also able to transfer her oversized confidence to me, giving me the feeling of being invincible.

My own talisman was my mother. Two or three years after she succumbed to lung cancer, I dosed off for a few seconds on my way home in the fast lane of rush hour freeway near San Francisco.

Startled, I found myself on the shoulders, having drifted across six lanes of fast moving traffic. At that very instant, I had the warm fuzzy sensation all around me, the way my mother used to wrap me in a blanket when I was ill. That was close to two decades ago, but it also gave me the added reassurance I needed when I came close to facing the ghosts of my ancestors.

Facing the pearly gates was not unfamiliar to me. I had accompanied friends and patients on this walk, and seen their lights dim then fade into darkness.

I particularly remembered my friend Lenny who took his pills and gave me a long embrace, then closed his eyes and listened to his favorite symphony as his breathing gradually became more and more shallow. I sat by his bedside until finally, I could detect it no more. He had chosen his own way and wanted me beside him on this last journey.

There was also Mel, ramrod straight, always impeccably dressed and accompanied by a beautiful woman who was his companion for many years. They were transplants from New Orleans, and he loved to smoke his sweet tobacco pipe. He was one of my first patients when I started my practice as a young man, fresh out of training. Some of the patients asked the nurse whether the doctor I joined had hired an intern.

Mel trusted me to remove the cancerous growth from his jaw, and he underwent irradiation to prevent further spread of the tumor.

But his tumor had a mind of its own. Two years later, it returned like a cauliflower gone wild. The chemicals he was treated with made him lose his hair. His *café au lait* skin turned pasty white. His shirt and jacket began to hang loose like on a coat rack, but he still stood shoulders unbent. As his tumor continued to spread despite the chemicals, he became weaker and weaker, until finally, he could no longer make his way to my office.

Several times I went to see him at his modest home, and he continued to tell me how grateful he was for what I had done for him earlier. He knew he was coming to the end of his road. Yet he never lost the way he carried his dignity, even when he could no longer get out of bed to shake my hand.

My procedure proceeded as painlessly as the first time. The cardiologist this third time around was tall and distinguished looking, snowy mane tinted with gray and a voice as kindly as a St. Nicholas at yuletide. He could easily be taken for a professor of philosophy at the nearby University. His reputation of being the most experienced man in his field at the hospital preceded our first meeting. I was put into his lap, I suspect, because of all the earlier mishaps around my care.

At the termination of the procedure, he leaned over toward the head of the operating table to which I was securely strapped, and held me with his reassuring eyes.

"I was able to put in two stents without any problems. Could see the increased blood flow into your coronaries." He pointed to the video screen of the fluoroscopy machine he pulled over in front of me so I could see the robust blood flow into the rescued coronary blood vessels.

A slight pause, then he lowered his voice, "there was a small complication. A minute perforation was made accidentally." He pointed at the dark screen to an area where there seemed to be a tiny, branching black coral reaching out from the small artery he had perforated. It was just above the major one he reopened.

"The bleeding should stop by itself." His calming voice carried the authority of his years of experience. "To be careful," he added, "I will order an echocardiogram." Gently he patted me on my shoulder.

"Thanks," I said, being much relieved that the whole thing was over and grateful that he explained everything to me with such great confidence.

It was the gift of good healers who were able to convey the feeling that everything will be all right in their hands.

He next appeared like a shadow over the shoulder of the technician in the darkened chamber of echocardiography. The image of my heart pounded like a nebula in a galaxy of white clouds. There was a dark circle around it. The technician pointed out that was the blood leaking into the sac surrounding my heart.

Over forty years earlier, my feared anatomy professor, a big woman with a shrill voice reminiscent of Julia Child on PBS some years later, came over to our table of four medical students dissecting a cadaver and held up the sac and asked me to name it. I did not come up with the right answer for the pericardium.

"That blood will most likely be reabsorbed." My professorial cardiologist told me what I wanted to hear. "But we better move you to the ICU."

By the time the nurses in the ICU settled me down, I was exhausted. I felt I could well fall asleep if weren't for the beginning of some pressure over my chest. I noticed they had let Adele into my room and I saw her standing in a far corner. I wanted to tell her about the cardiologist's soothing words, and there was nothing to worry about.

A few moments later, the nurse checked my blood pressure again.

What followed was like a video clip of the Emergency Room scenes in the nineties television serial ER, based on the LA County General. Doctors, nurses, technicians from the laboratory and the blood bank, the cardiogram machine, the echocardiogram machine, the cardiologist assigned to the ICU, the cardiologist who was taking medical students, interns and residents around the unit, and finally, my cardiologist, all crowded into the small space of my room.

I saw one of the nurses shepherding Adele out of the room. I caught the nurse's eye and asked her to please explain things to Adele. I was afraid for someone not too familiar with real medical emergencies, this sudden pandemonium would be too frightening to witness. I wanted to tell her I was not suffering, had no pain, but she was already whisked out of the room.

Later I found out my blood pressure had dropped to a dangerously low-level doctors call "in shock." Another echocardiogram showed the dark circle of blood around the heart expanding rapidly. This, in effect, was an impending chokehold on the heart muscle, preventing it from pumping out blood to the rest of the body, called pericardial tamponade in medical texts.

As a medical student, I learned it was one of the truly dangerous, heart emergencies. It required immediate intervention. Half of the patients did not make it.

Lucky for me, the memory of these details was not that sharp while everything was whizzing by in front of me. I heard the three cardiologists debating whether there would be enough time to get me back into the operating room. They told the nurses to get ready for bedside tapping into my heart sac to draw out the accumulated blood.

"Hang up some Dopamine!" Someone called out. I remembered having to use it to raise patients' blood pressure when they were dangerously close to dying from blood loss or drop in blood pressure, and there was not enough time for blood transfusions. The chemical would severely constrict the blood vessels around the whole body so that the demand for blood would be lessened, but often, a side effect was the kidneys could shut down, or some other organ would fail from lack of blood supply and oxygen.

These worries did not come into my mind. I merely felt an extreme exhaustion and an increasing pressure on my chest making it harder for me to breathe. I kept on hoping someone would be thoughtful enough to reassure Adele that I would be all right. It was a foolish thought on my part because at that moment the doctors did not really know if I was going to make it. Fifty percent of patients in my condition didn't.

At that time, the nurses were actually asking Adele to contact my next of kin and she was trying to call my daughter who wanted to be with me that morning. But I had reassured her it was my third time around, nothing out of the ordinary would happen to me, and she should not cancel her own patients that morning.

I thought about not having actually seen a case of pericardial tamponade in all my years as a medical student and then as a surgeon. Now I was experiencing one first hand. Strangely I was not anxious or fearful.

Although there were no angels or lyres to welcome me at a distance, I thought if I had to check out this way, it wasn't too bad at all. I was also conscious of the fact that I was in a hospital known for its experience and expertise in cardiac procedures and heart surgery and I had the most experienced cardiologist taking care of me.

My blood pressure responded to Dope, short for dopamine.

"We can get him to the O. R." I heard one of the cardiologists say.

From the speed that the nurses and technicians were rushing me through the hallways to the Operating Room, I knew we were fighting for time.

This time there was no delay in the waiting area. I was wheeled directly into the Room. Nurses, technicians, radiology technicians to monitor the procedure were all dashing about into their positions.

Many weeks later, friends who visited were surprised to see me shake my head when asked if I was frightened. Not even a little anxious? I saw their look of disbelief.

Even when I was active in my surgical practice, I tended to let go of the professional medical problems when I left my office and the hospital. Joyce, who had her own allergy office, used to come home and fret about what she had forgotten to do, or what to do when a particularly difficult patient was being referred to her, or if her nurse or staff were having domestic problems and whether they would show up for work. She told me how annoyed she used to get when I didn't seem to let these things bother me.

I tried to explain to her I was able to close that drawer of medical problems when I walked out of the hospital. It was my way of keeping my own sanity and the reason I felt no particular urgency to retire from my surgical practice.

I was now dealing with my own medical emergency similarly. It would not be helpful for me to fret about all the possible mishaps that could occur in the Operating Room when there was a true life and death situation at hand. I was not going to let it bother me. I knew they were all trying to do their best. For me to be worrying about what was happening was not going to help the situation. There wasn't anything I could do about it anyway.

I saw my father when he was within a few hours from the end of his life. He was pale from years of choosing to live his life in a hospital room in Taipei and undoubtedly uncomfortable from the new feeding tube stuck into his nose. He had choked on his food before the tube was put in. He was calmly waiting for my plane to land and see me one last time.

I saw no evidence of any change in his imperturbability for which he was known throughout his life. As I write now, I can see he and Obama were men of the same mold in that way. The number of years we were together, I could easily count on one hand. His words were few, and he chose them carefully. My mother's words in Beijing dialect, *even if a truck were to run over him, he would not let out any gas*, always came back to me.

The few words he said to me still rang in my ears. Once he heard me raising my voice at the chef because he did not make the dish I requested. After dinner, my father pulled me into his study and told me to put myself in the position of the man who worked for us, someone in his forties who had to leave his wife and kids behind to support his family, seeing them only a few times every year.

My father looked at me steadily and continued in a soft voice, "To someone who is less fortunate, one must be extra kind, because that person is already having a hard time." My father went on to say, "Stand up to those others fear, not those who were defenseless against us." I began to notice how kind and generous he always was to the servants and all those who worked for him.

Three men astride, there must be one who could be my teacher, was another way he used to teach me about humility. *Keep one's mouth tight as the neck of a bottle* was the motto for his own life.

Many years later, when I was sitting in front of my therapist who encouraged me to express my anger and fear, I realized how much I had really taken my father's words to heart and, at times, even carried it further than necessary for my own good.

Once on the Operating Table, I could not remember whether the cardiologist even used any anesthetics. Everything happened so quickly. He was able to get a long needle into the sac surrounding my heart and drew out two pints of accumulated blood.

I felt no pain. There was almost instantaneous relief from the pressure on my chest, and I could breathe easy again.

"I was able to get out almost all of the blood," he said. He must have been happy and relieved that he succeeded in bringing me back from such a precarious moment. Later on, settled into the ICU, they had to quickly transfuse two packs of blood back into me to make up for what I lost.

As I was being wheeled out of the Operating Room, Jason, the guy who had held pressure on my groin the first time was just coming into work. He waved at me with a big smile. My angel Gabriele arrived at the right time.

Adele was waiting outside of the doors to the operating area. She dashed over to grasp my hand this time. Hers were sweaty and icy cold. I saw her eyes moistening as she looked at me, to make sure I was still there for real.

"I feel better." I smiled back.

My story should have ended right here. But in my case, my hard days in the ICU were just beginning.

That same evening, cocooned into my room in the ICU and after the blood transfusions, I thought they had put bedbugs between my sheets. The nurse checked my chest and trunk where they had placed numerous pads for the EKG machine to monitor my heart. The itching was erupting from under all of my skin.

I knew it was best that I was being closely monitored, despite the cardiologist's reassurance he had gotten all the blood out around the heart. My blood was still thinned and will continue to be thin, and I wondered whether the accidental puncture he made through my coronary artery would take longer than twenty-four hours to heal.

I also was aware that I had to take aspirin for the rest of my life now. The process to desensitize me from my aspirin allergy had seemingly gone smoothly, but I had to admit too many things were happening unexpectedly, much as worrying did not come naturally to me.

The intense itching was the last straw for me to fully believe them when they told me everything was going well.

"I don't see anything," my nurse said after checking the skin on my chest, "probably your skin is just extra sensitive to the EKG leads."

She was right about that. I always had extra sensitive skin. Often my skin would start to itch if I stayed too long in someplace too cold or dry. The dermatologist gave it a long fancy name, atopic dermatitis, more commonly known as eczema. I thought I might just have to tolerate all the critters I was feeling under my skin. I knew the EKG leads were necessary to make sure there was no further bleeding from the punctured coronary artery.

"May I have some Benadryl for the itching?"

"Let me check with the doctor."

An hour or so later, she brought me the pill. I must have dozed off after that. I was not certain whether I was dreaming of lying with lice or bedbugs or whether I was just dreaming and thought of my father's saying, *it is easy to have tranquility in a mountaintop temple but takes real enlightenment to find it in pandemonium.*

When Adele showed up early next morning, I asked her to check my back. "I am not sure. But I think you are covered with a rash."

I rang for the nurse because I couldn't see my own back.

When she came in to check, this time there was no question it was a rash. She called the doctor to confirm her findings. He had me take off the hospital gown I was wearing and checked my front and back.

He confirmed I was covered with a rash. In addition, there were areas on my back full of welts.

He couldn't tell whether the skin reaction was caused by the aspirin I was taking, or the blood transfusions, or something else and he listed a slew of other things that came to his mind. I heard him calling in the allergy specialist for help.

Doctor Ayran was the one who wrote the protocol for my desensitization to aspirin, a few days ago. I had to strip naked in front of her to be checked all over again. She found some areas where the doctor in the ICU had not noticed. I wondered whether it really made any difference. I was obviously having an allergic reaction.

I watched for any sign of recognition of my condition. She showed none. She was also unable to tell which one on that long list of possibilities was the real cause. Afterward, she sat down at the command center of the ICU and wrote down her opinion.

To be safe, she decided to start me off on three anti-allergy medications. "It should cover all the possibilities," she said.

The pills also put me to sleep. I didn't wake up till the next day, and the bedbugs receded with the night.

The welts subsided, but the skin rash took longer. They decided to keep me in the ICU. I was too exhausted and drugged to protest. On the fourth day, at last, they decided I was safe enough to leave Intensive Care. I felt I had just won the lottery of the day. I was moved to the section for heart disease patients.

From the window facing the northern part of our city, I could see a stately high-rise with verdigris copper roofing at a distance. "That's where the Clintons stayed when they visited." The nurse offered when she saw my interest in it.

Above all, I was delighted to see a private bathroom with a spacious, tiled shower stall in the corner. I hadn't washed in four days. Everybody had been so preoccupied with more important stuff than to bother with the minutiae of personal hygiene.

The nurse had to get the doctor's permission for me to shower. An hour later, she brought me an armload of towels and sealed off my groin area with a special plastic adhesive.

I stood under the shower and let the warm water splash over me, again and again, feathering my skin, my hair, my face, and every crack and crevice.

Finally, I slowed the water down to a few droplets over my head. It felt like the gentle toll of ancient temple bells, bringing me back to prayers, and to long ago memories such as the time with Ernie, caressed by so many butterflies on the sundeck by the sea, lifting toward a rainbow under the afternoon sun.

Coda

豬

As we drove through the western French country roads, we passed whole fields and hillsides of undulating green carpets and golden wheat. Sudden bursts of sunflowers nodded at us under the mid-summer sun, like bouquets of concurrence for the anticipated occasion. Adele wanted to make sure we arrived at the château near Bordeaux in time for the rehearsal dinner. Otherwise, she would have asked me to stop for photos of this unforgettable palette of color display.

When you come down the aisle again
Daisies and marguerites will be blooming

The beginning stanza of the words I wrote for the wedding was on my lips, quickly followed by the last line of that stanza.

It is summer, a new summer in both of your lives.

I wouldn't be walking down the aisle with her, as I did almost two decades ago. Her twin teenage daughters will be holding her hands this time, while her new husband waits under the arbor of grape vines overlooking the château gardens. A Corot painting come to life.

Mark, the partner of my close friend will be playing an alto flute to the tune of the song from John Phillips of the Mammas and the Papas, *If you're going to San Francisco, Be sure to wear some flowers in your hair,* before I read the words I wrote for my daughter.

Adele's older sister has been a good sport, consenting to nearly every crazy suggestion we made on the trip through the countryside, except when we asked her to try Adele's daily green vegetable and fruit smoothie. She begged off on that potion, "You're trying to poison me," she said with a big grin on her face of hardly a visible wrinkle.

The whole family and our friends from San Francisco will also be coming. My son and his family from Washington, D.C. will be there, too. His daughter, Tenaya, whose tenth birthday will be the week after the wedding and his son, who turned eight a couple of months earlier. I remembered he played the guitar and sang the lyrics of the new Broadway musical *Hamilton*, which he had already learned by heart, when I visited them before his birthday— a few weeks after I had another angioplasty by the same doctor in San Francisco who did my first one ten years ago. This time, thankfully, without the ordeal of the first procedure.

It felt like a new summer in so many of our lives. Young people were marrying again, even same sex men and women. I thought of Charles, who had longed for a formal commitment from me and would have wished we could be in the same dream together three decades ago. I wondered whether he was somehow prescient of times to come. Adele and I still have not taken any formal vows. Could it be because we were both children from the flowery sixties, or was it because we have both been married and divorced and have come through with a jaundiced view of such formal commitments?

Or is it as James Russell Lowell put it, "love . . .is a thing to walk with, hand in hand, through the everydayness of this workday world, blaring its tender feet to every roughness, yet letting not one heartbeat go astray"?

We have been together now for over twenty years. Our grandson, biologically hers but under my same astrological sign with sixty years between us, will be going to college this autumn. He and his younger sisters grew up in the house I built with Joyce close to five decades ago, where my own children had been raised.

My friend, Teng, whose partner will play the flute at the wedding, met my eyes when we arrived at the same time by the main entrance to the château. He squinted at the sun, still bright over our heads, and I sensed we both realized at the same time, that we had been interwoven into the tapestry of each other's lives for the past three-and-a-half decades.

He and Mark, Adele and I, we have been couples over the same number of years. Every year we shared dinners together for Chinese New Year and moon cakes for the Autumn Harvest Festival. When we could not be in the same place, Teng would save the moon cakes for us till we could share them together. Every year, he carefully folded bags full of paper money to be offered at my mother's grave on Chinese Memorial Day. He was virtually her second son.

Teng and I were introduced by mutual friends, trying to be matchmakers for two Chinese men, but we became best friends instead. He was more devoted to my mother than I could have ever been, and he has since become a treasured member of my family. We have shared not only the Chinese festivals and memorial days together, but also the stories of the losses and loves of our lives over these decades gone by.

He had met Jimmie and Ernie, then Charles and Gene, and I was introduced to the men in his life before Mark. He knows Adele so well now that he is one of very few friends who can say something provocative without her getting upset. And she gets just as concerned as I when we don't hear from him for a few days. He had met Adele's partner Larry who was my family friend for many years before he succumbed to cancer. I suspected Larry might have been pulling the proverbial Chinese red strings of matchmaking to get Adele and me together when he knew his time had come. He asked me to look after her when he was in the hospital bed for one of his last stays, the way my mother had asked him to look after me when she had come to the end.

"Let's show you to your rooms!" We were greeted by Anna, one of my daughter's twins, rushing over to us from inside the château. "We have checked them all out." She was trailing her sister and cousins from my son, but was assuming the role of spokesperson as the oldest by three minutes to her twin. The four cousins had arrived separately by noon but have been exploring all the halls and rooms of the château together. To them, the place was the realization of what they have been reading about knights and castles and filled them with a sense of wonderment, adventure, and mystery. "There are secret rooms which are blocked off, and we are not allowed to explore," my grandson said enthusiastically. "And there is a knight's armor in the hallway outside of our room."

Their exuberance nearly lifted us off our feet, as they looked for our rooms in different corners of the château. I tried to keep up with them and thought of all the different byways and chambers I had come along over the decades.

And now, in one more of life's turns, I was following the steps of my grandchildren.

Our room was closer, on the floor above the entrance, because they knew Adele's sister was elderly and could not manage climbing the twists and turns of the countless old stone steps. Teng and Mark's room was at a higher level and at the other end of the medieval edifice. They had a large soaking tub overlooking the towering lindens and sycamores, across a dried-up moat toward the extensive fields in the back. The owner told us later apologetically, he had devoted most of his time restoring the château proper and neglected the garden. But I discerned its fine bones in the fountains and meandering pathways into the trees.

"Are there keys to lock our doors at night?" Teng was mocking fear to the kids while looking up at the ancient beams of the tall ceiling where each beam could stir up the hidden history of what it had seen, and back toward the shadowy hallways we had passed with sudden turns, which seemed to lead nowhere.

"There may be ghosts in this castle!" Justine, the other twin, said in trying to scare her Great Uncle Teng.

After the rehearsal dinner of huge pots of escargot, fresh baguettes, local charcuterie, and ratatouille, we went to our rooms to get ready for the full day of the wedding.

When Adele and her sister were already in bed, I heard a knock on our door.

"Come over and take a look!" Teng stood at the doorway looking excited and a little alarmed.

"I don't know what's flying around in our room." He continued as I followed him out.

"What do you think it is?"

"I don't know." He seemed more than a little anxious.

As we passed a large, tall chamber in the center of the château where the owners had left the high ceiling windows open for fresh air in the summer evening, a dark thing flew overhead, almost brushing the top of our heads and the large chandelier.

When it made another pass over us, I could see it more clearly.

"It's a bat!" I said.

My friend shivered as if facing a real vampire.

"You're not afraid of bats, are you?" I asked, poking him a little in the arm.

He has been a master of martial arts and other practices of the East for many years, including yoga and meditation, marathons, and distance bike rides benefitting AIDS.

"I don't like them!" he answered. "Gives me the feeling the place may be haunted."

"Come on," I said, close to rolling my eyes at him. "They bring good fortune! You know that, don't you? *Bian Fu* in Chinese has the same sound as good fortune. Don't you remember seeing them in embroidery of the Eight Auspicious Things?"

Teng was my friend who most remembered the traditional Chinese customs, many of which I have forgotten. He used to celebrate the various Chinese festival days with my mother, and they would have to remind me when to show up. My father provided the counterbalance to the innumerable ancient customs and beliefs. Although he was better versed than my mother in the ancient texts, he also used to tease my mother that many of the traditional customs were mere superstitions, such as scrubbing the stove and sweeping the kitchen for the kitchen god before the year's end and not cutting one's hair too close to the holidays. His influence was so subtly rendered, much as I have often felt, in his teachings on patience and calligraphy, that only now am I humbled once more to realize the extent I had taken them in throughout the years.

I was surprised that my friend, so steeped in Chinese folklore and tradition, was frightened by bats.

"I don't like them," he repeated. "They remind me of the movie Dracula."

"Now you are the one who's become too Americanized." I kidded him because he was the one who usually chastened me when I let a Chinese festival slip by without observing it.

"The bat is an auspicious sign for my daughter's wedding tomorrow. Have a good night's rest with your beloved," I said, giving him a wink.

"Maybe I'll surprise your daughter tomorrow by wearing a red Chinese dress." He waved as he went into a sashay on his way back to his bedroom and Mark.

I lingered in the huge room with its grand fireplace covering most of the center wall, and tall windows open to the sky and full moon outside. I thought of my mother and her deep affection for Teng, and my childhood friend Larry, with his winning dimpled smile, which made him irresistible to so many in his shortened life. On a night such as this, with bats circling overhead, the memory of him was particularly vivid. He once told me he used to be able to float out of his body and roam around the skies until he got a little scared that he might not be able to get back into his body.

My mother would be past her hundred and eighth birthday if she were with us. How happy she would be to see her grand-daughter's marriage to a Frenchman and with the blessings of so many of the family around. My mother's closest friend as a young woman in Beijing was the daughter of the old French doctor who treated the Imperial family and the Court. How different this oc-casion was from my mother's own marriage when she had to be whisked away right after the ceremony on a night train.

My daughter had told me how much she admired her grand-mother, a woman who started life in a China when there was still the tradition for a woman to refer to herself as *nu*, the word for a slave, then coming to this country at forty-six with three words of English but ending up as a public school teacher in New York and campaigning for Shirley Chisholm, the first African-American woman elected to Congress. My cousin on my mother's side in Beijing said to me when she first met my daughter. "She has the looks of her grandmother."

I had the feeling while looking out the tall windows into the dark-blue sky, seeing the clear ring around the full moon, and the Milky Way not far beyond, that these dear people could be hovering very close by, even a whiff of the high note florals of my mother's French perfume seemed to be floating in the midnight air.

Historical and Personal Time Lines

Dynasty Ming	1368–1644
Dynasty Qing [Manchu]	1644–1912
Opium Wars with England	1838, 1854
Dowager Empress Cixi reign	1861–1908
Sino Japanese War	1894–1895
[Taiwan seceded as colony to Japan, Manchurian control seceded to Japan]	
Father born in Canton	1894
"Boxer Rebellion"	1900
Eight Nations Allied Invasion	1901
[sacking of Peking and burning of Yuan Ming Yuan]	
Last Emperor PuYi	1906–1967
Mother born in Suzhou	1907
First Republic of China	1911–1949
[established by Sun Yat-sen and KMT-Kuomintang]	
Death of Sun Yat-sen	1925
Manchukoku established	1932
[by Japan with PuYi as First Emperor]	
Xian Incident	1936
[Young Marshall Chang forces Chiang Kai-shek to unite with Chinese communists]	
Parents' marriage in Nanking	1936
Marco Polo Bridge Incident	1937
[outside Peking. Start of Japanese invasion of China and eight-year war with Japan]	
Author born in Hankow	1937
Nanking Massacre	1937
Japanese occupy Shanghai	1937
Chungking made war capitol	1938
[by Chiang Kai-shek of KMT]	
Pearl Harbor, start of WWII	1941
Japanese occupy Hong Kong	1941
End of WWII	1945

Peoples' Republic of China   1949
[established by Chinese Communist Party and Mao Zedong]
Author moves to Taiwan   1949
Author moves to Tokyo   1950
Peace Treaty with Japan   1951–1952
Author arrives in U.S.   1954
Author's Italian residency   2007

Map of Chinese Places in Text

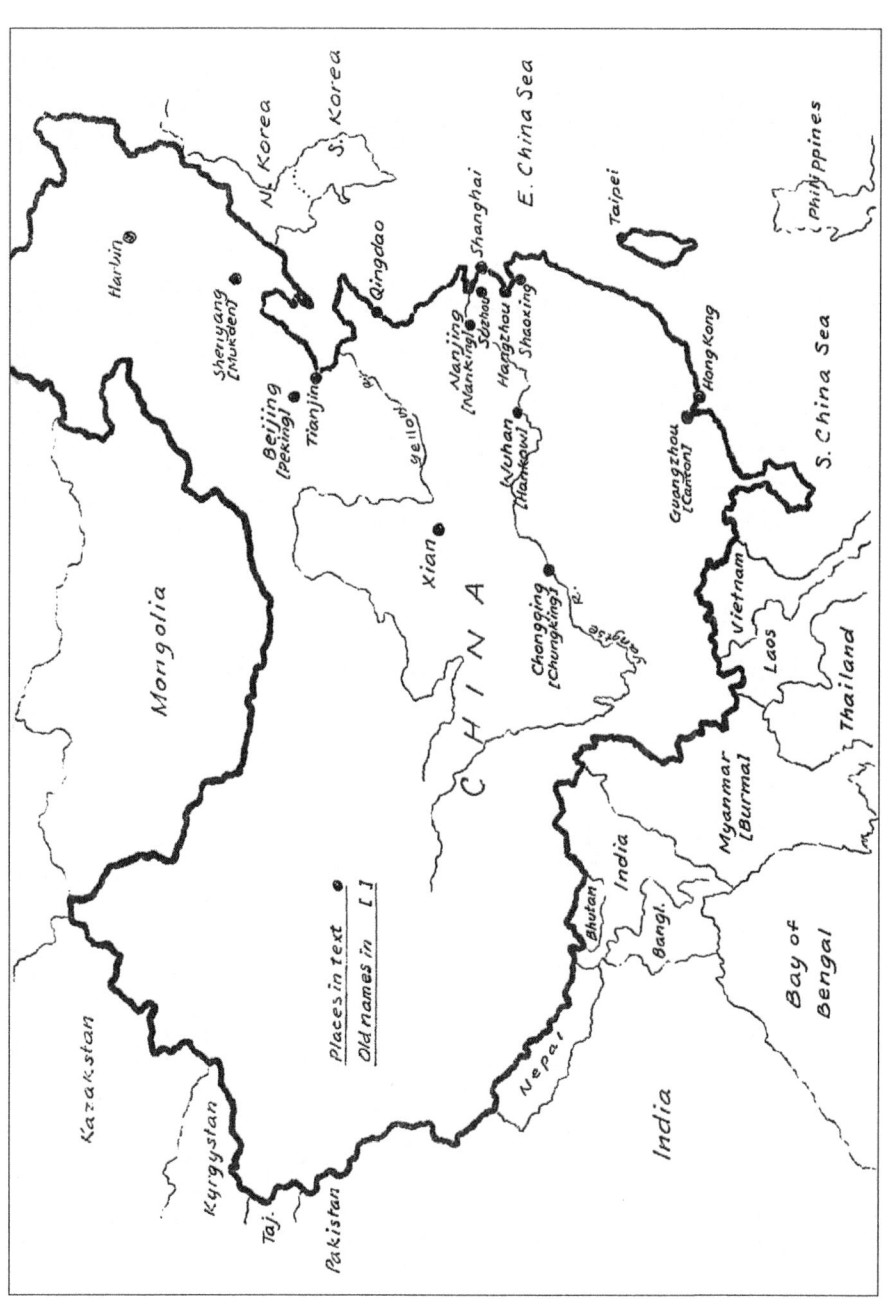

Acknowledgements

It is hard trying to thank everyone who lent me a hand in the long birthing process of this book. It would take a whole chapter in itself. In the beginning, I thought I was writing my mother's book because she was my story. I would thank her if she were still here, but she is probably still watching out for me somewhere and would feel slighted if I didn't convey my deepest gratitude for giving me life, as she would have said, and the life to tell her story, and from there my own.

I would not have been able to complete this story if it were not for all the writing groups and classes which have encouraged me, tolerated my untrained voice patiently until I found my tune. In particular, I would like to first thank Aaron Shurin who was so kind and didn't shred my seedling pieces but allowed them to grow on their own, and finally Michael Allen, for inviting me into his writing circle, without which I would never have completed this manuscript. His insightful comments and recommendations, not to say his encouragement and friendship have been invaluable and more than my words can express.

Then above all, my gentle editor, Katia Noyes, who knew when to use the carrot and when the nudge, to make the delivery of this book possible. She was the ideal editor that I could have wished for, but was blessed to have. And of course, my friend, Mark Lapin, for helping me realize the book cover which I saw in my mind, and he was able to bring to life. And for accomplishing the close to impossible task of locating my scattered photographs through my daughter, then the countless hours of arranging to get them ready for the printer, when I was far away in Provence.

Last, but not least, I cannot begin to say how much I appreciated the patience and understanding of the person closest to me in life, my dearest Helen, during the decades-long gestation of my work, all the late night hours I could have been keeping you warm by your side, or the quiet evenings when I could have been listening to the mellow strains from your cello. It has been heaven's greatest gift to have you in my life for the past two decades and more. It is what my ancestors would have called karma, better expressed in the Chinese word, yuan, 緣.

Printed in Great Britain
by Amazon

43601167R00255